OTTOMAN RULE IN DAMASCUS, 1708-1758

Princeton Studies
on the Near East

OTTOMAN RULE IN DAMASCUS, 1708-1758

KARL K. BARBIR

PRINCETON UNIVERSITY PRESS
PRINCETON, NEW JERSEY

Published by Princeton University Press, Princeton, New Jersey
In the United Kingdom: Princeton University Press,
Guildford, Surrey

Library of Congress Cataloging in Publication Data will be
found on the last printed page of this book

Publication of this book has been aided by a grant from
The Andrew W. Mellon Foundation

This book has been composed in VIP Bembo

Clothbound editions of Princeton University Press books
are printed on acid-free paper, and binding materials are
chosen for strength and durability

Printed in the United States of America by Princeton
University Press, Princeton, New Jersey

For Leila

CONTENTS

	LIST OF TABLES	ix
	NOTE ON TRANSCRIPTION AND DATES	xi
	ABBREVIATIONS	xiii
	GOVERNORS OF DAMASCUS, 1708-1758	xv
	PREFACE	xvii
	INTRODUCTION	3
	MAPS	11,12
One	CHANGING PATTERNS IN THE GOVERNORSHIP OF DAMASCUS	13
	The Ottoman Provincial Governorship	14
	First Set of Patterns: Limits on the Governor's Functions and Mobility	33
	Second Set of Patterns: Provincial Centralization	44
	Retrospect: the 'Azms and the Governorship of Damascus	56
Two	CONTAINMENT OF PROVINCIAL GROUPS: NOTABLES, JANISSARIES, AND TRIBESMEN	65
	The Notables: Provincial Patricians	67
	The Janissaries	89
	The Tribes	97
Three	THE PILGRIMAGE: CENTERPIECE OF OTTOMAN RULE IN DAMASCUS	108
	Financial Base	110
	The *Sürre*	126
	The Pilgrimage Fortress Network	133
	Organization of the Pilgrimage Caravan	151
	The *Cerde* and Pilgrimage Security	167
	CONCLUSION	178

APPENDICES 181
I. Rank and Position at Start of Damascus Governors' Careers, 1516-1757 181
II. Top Posts Attained by Damascus Governors, 1516-1757 182
III. Sources of Local Damascus Janissaries' Pay, 1706 183
IV. Projected Income and Expense of the Pilgrimage (*Tertib Defterleri*) 184
V. Summary of Damascus Provincial Accounts, 1741-1742, 1759-1760 191
VI. Register of *Dawra* Revenues, 1771-1772 193
VII. The Pilgrimage Fortress Network between Damascus and Medina 196
VIII. Pilgrimage Retinue Expenses, 1742-1743 198
IX. Attacks on the Pilgrimage Caravan, 1517-1757 200
BIBLIOGRAPHY 203
Archives. Note on the Ottoman Archives 203
Manuscripts, Printed Sources, Secondary Works, Reference Works 205
INDEX 213

LIST OF TABLES

1. Damascus' Contribution to Imperial Campaigns, 1683-1780 35
2. Complements of Damascus Janissary Corps, 1693-1746 95
3. Formal Divisions of the Province of Damascus, 1527-1641 102
4. The Pilgrimage Timetable 153
5. Goods Sold to Pilgrims along the Pilgrimage Route 165

NOTE ON TRANSCRIPTION AND DATES

BECAUSE two Near Eastern languages are used in this study, complete consistency in transcription has not always been possible. Unless otherwise indicated, the names of Ottomans, and Turkish technical terms and phrases, have been transcribed according to the system followed in the *New Redhouse Turkish-English Dictionary* (Istanbul, 1968). Well-known Arabic place-names are transcribed as they are commonly recognized. Names of Damascene notables, Arabic phrases and expressions, and citations from Arabic sources are transcribed as in the *International Journal of Middle East Studies*, except that long vowels are noted by a dash instead of a circumflex.

Dates in the Islamic calendar have been converted in accordance with the tables provided by Faik Reşit Unat, *Hicrî tarihleri Milâdî tarihe çevirme kılavuzu* (4th expd. ed. Ankara, 1974). The terms "beginning," "middle," and "end" refer to the three decades of each month.

ABBREVIATIONS

BA	Başbakanlık Arşivi (archives of the prime minister's office, Istanbul)
BA-Cevdet	Cevdet classification (collection of loose documents)
BA-Cevdet/Askeri	Military affairs subdivision of Cevdet
BA-Cevdet/Dahiliye	Interior affairs subdivision of Cevdet
BA-Emiri	Ali Emiri classification (collection of loose documents)
BA-Emiri/III Ahmed, etc.	Subdivision of Emiri by sultan's reign
BA-Ibnülemin	Ibnülemin classification (collection of loose documents)
BA-Ibnülemin/Dahiliye	Interior affairs subdivison of Ibnülemin
BA-Ibnülemin/Tevcihat	Appointments subdivision of Ibnülemin
BA-Kepeci	Kâmil Kepeci classification (collection of assorted registers)
BA-Maliye	Maliyeden müdevver defterleri (assorted financial registers)
BA-Mühimme	Mühimme defterleri (registers of selected outgoing orders)
BA-Nâme	Nâme-i hümayun defterleri (registers of imperial letters)

EI[1] and *EI*[2]	*Encyclopedia of Islam*, first and second editions respectively
IA	*Islam Ansiklopedisi*, Turkish translation of *EI*[1], with many articles revised and expanded
SO	Mehmed Süreyya, *Sicill-i Osmanî*
TDS	Mehmet Zeki Pakalın, *Osmanlı tarih deyimleri ve terimleri sözlüğü*
TKS	Topkapı Saray Arşivi (archives of the Topkapı Palace, Istanbul)
TKS-D.	Defterler (registers) designation in TKS
TKS-E.	Evrak (loose documents) designation in TKS

GOVERNORS OF DAMASCUS, 1708-1758

1708	Nasuh Paşa
1714	Topal Yusuf Paşa
1716	Kapudan Ibrahim Paşa
1717	Köprülü Abdullah Paşa
1718	Receb Paşa
1719	Çerkes Osman Paşa (Abū Ṭawq)
1721	Ali Paşa Maktuloğlu
1723	Çerkes Osman Paşa (Abū Ṭawq)
1725	Ismail Paşa (al-'Aẓm)
1730, November-December	Muhsinzâde Abdullah Paşa
1730, December	Aydınlı Abdullah Paşa
1734	Süleyman Paşa (al-'Aẓm)
1738	Hüseyin Paşa Bostancı
1739	Muhassil Osman Paşa
1740	Abdî Paşazâde Ali Paşa
1741	Süleyman Paşa (al-'Azm)
1743	Esat Paşa (al-'Aẓm)
1757	Mehmed Rağıb Paşa (9 days)
	Mekkizâde Hüseyin Paşa
1758	Çeteci Abdullah Paşa

PREFACE

THIS BOOK began as a doctoral dissertation, with all the advantages and disadvantages normally associated with that genre. I wish to acknowledge here the debts I owe to persons and institutions whose support or criticism have contributed to the writing of this book and have brought it to publication. Any errors or faults, however, are mine alone.

I began five years of graduate study at Princeton University with an interest in the modern Arab world but, within a short time, decided to concentrate on Ottoman history as a perspective from which to view modern Arab history. From this simple recognition of an obvious political fact—that most of the Arab lands were, until fairly recently, a part of the Ottoman Empire—I came to realize that far more was involved. Much as each of the Arab provinces of the Ottoman Empire may have retained and developed its own local traditions and culture, each was subjected in some degree to the influence of one of the last great Islamic states. Much of the evidence for this influence—and not simply the political—may be found in the Ottoman archives, that vast storehouse of information upon which this work is primarily based. An appreciation of the Ottoman environment from which modern Arab history, and in particular that of Damascus, developed made me dissatisfied at first with previous interpretations. Then, in my research, I tried to offer an alternative perspective. Furthermore, one of the pleasures of producing this study has been to emphasize and bring out many issues that remain to be explored. It is my hope that those interested in both Ottoman and modern Arab history will find here some questions to pursue in future research.

That this book has resulted from the process of graduate study is due primarily to the guidance of Professor Norman Itzkowitz of Princeton, whose searching criticism, wit, concern, and persistent encouragement are qualities that all of his students over the years have come to appreciate. To him I owe my introduction to Ottoman history and most of my training. L. Carl Brown, Charles Issawi, and Martin Dickson, all of Princeton, also offered criticism and suggestions.

A year of research in Istanbul (1973-1974) was made possible through a Fulbright-Hays Doctoral Dissertation Research Grant from the U.S. Department of Health, Education, and Welfare. National Defense Foreign Language Fellowships from H.E.W. supported my study at Princeton University both before and after research in Turkey. Permission to use the archives and to photograph material was kindly granted by the cultural affairs section of the Turkish prime minister's office and by the Turkish foreign ministry. I would like to thank Mr. Hüsnü Ersoy of the Fulbright Commission office in Ankara for his efforts to obtain that research permission. The staffs of the Topkapı Saray Müzesi Arşivi, and especially Turgust Işıksal and Rauf Tuncay at the Başbakanlık Arşivi, were most generous with their assistance. Professor Halil Sahillioğlu of Istanbul University, generously offered his vast knowledge of the Ottoman archives and Ottoman history. To all these institutions and individuals, my thanks.

Several portions of this book were read as papers at meetings of the Middle East Studies Association of North America and the American Oriental Society. I would like to thank those who commented on the papers, particularly Albert Hourani, Thomas Naff, Stanford Shaw, and William Ochsenwald. Two readers provided valuable comments on the manuscript of this book for the Princeton University Press: Herbert Bodman and Abdul-Karim Rafeq. My special thanks to them.

To the Department of Near Eastern Studies of Princeton University, my thanks for including this work in the series Princeton Studies on the Near East. I owe a special debt of gratitude to Margaret Case of Princeton University Press for her patience, courtesy, and efficiency. Margaret Riccardi provided invaluable advice and assistance in preparing the manuscript for composition at the Press. Financial assistance to the

Press for publication of this book has been provided by The Andrew W. Mellon Foundation.

Finally, I would like to express my appreciation to family and friends whose encouragement and support over the years have been such an important stimulus to my work.

KARL K. BARBIR
Siena College
Loudonville, New York

May, 1979

OTTOMAN RULE IN DAMASCUS, 1708-1758

INTRODUCTION

At the close of the seventeenth century, the Ottoman Empire suffered a series of disastrous defeats in war with Europe, which ended with the Treaty of Karlowitz of 1699. A succession of comparatively strong Ottoman grand vezirs in the first half of the eighteenth century sought to restore the state along the lines dictated by the traditional wisdom of the "Mirror for Princes" literature. The best-known contemporary representatives of that tradition were the historian Naima (d. 1716) and the chief treasurer Sarı Mehmed Paşa (d. 1717). They called for the empire's restoration to the order represented by the centralizing reign of Sultan Süleyman the Magnificent (1520-1566).[1] During the first half of the eighteenth century, the Ottomans were relatively successful in meeting the external challenge of Europe's military power. Apparently vindicated by the strictures of the "Mirror for Princes" literature, the Ottomans, with the exception of their setback in 1718 with the Treaty of Passarowitz, won back the Morea (1709), defeated Peter the Great (1711), then the Venetians (1715), and won concessions—including recovery of Belgrade—from the Austrians and Russians (1739). On the front with Persia, they enjoyed mixed success.

Although this brief half century of relative recovery—embedded in centuries of what is regarded as steady decline—has not been the object of extensive research, its striking features cannot be denied. Yet, students of Ottoman history have tended to concentrate on the disastrous wars (particularly with Russia) and internal upheavals of roughly the second half of the eighteenth century. As the last period before the beginnings of modernization in which the Otto-

[1] The idea of eighteenth-century recovery is of recent vintage. See Itzkowitz, *Ottoman Empire*, pp. 103ff. For the intellectual foundations of this recovery, see the analysis of the late seventeenth-century historian Naima by Lewis Thomas, *A Study of Naima*, pp. 86-89; and the ideas of Sarı Mehmed Paşa, *Ottoman Statecraft*.

mans had the opportunity to revitalize their state along traditional lines—albeit with ultimate failure—the first half of the eighteenth century deserves greater consideration.

It is also necessary to examine internal challenges to which the state responded during this period, particularly in the provinces. Research in this area has tended to focus on the central government and Istanbul or has treated the provinces as self-contained units to be studied from the perspective of local history. In fact, of course, Ottoman history was a single process, in which diverse groups, individuals, and regions interacted. To think in such terms is not to reduce a complex society to a uniform pattern that may be labeled "Ottoman," or to assume that all is known about it. Rather, it is to recognize that the Ottoman Empire possessed a certain unity in all its diversity and that change in one part might have an impact on the whole system. To overemphasize, for example, what happened either at court—what the sultan and those around him wanted or did—or what happened in the provinces—what local groups and individuals wanted or did—may distort what, in fact, occurred. Recognizing interrelationships between capital and provinces helps to direct attention away from an oversimplified model that opposes "state" to "society." In this light, although rebellion and assertions of local power had long been a familiar feature of Ottoman history, the state could and did assert its authority in the provinces when it so chose. The central government's elastic response to conditions in the provinces depended to a great extent, but by no means exclusively, on the personality and vigor of the sultan and his grand vezir. It was possible for one sultan or one grand vezir to restore governmental institutions to a degree not normally conceivable for so vast and diverse an empire. Reassertion and revival of central control were assisted by the fact that, until the late eighteenth century, the empire's provinces—with such notable exceptions as Egypt, those of Iraq to some degree, and those in North Africa—lacked autonomous local groups that could challenge, for any meaningful length of time, the central government's resources and continuity. As M. A. Cook has written, but of the sixteenth century: "We are dealing with a highly centralized political system which was not embedded in any stable and autonomous structure of local interest. In other words, the imposition of order depended to an unusual extent on the toughness and ability of the empire's rulers."[2] This is not to say that the initiative for change lay solely with the central administration; other forces were at work to transform Ottoman society. It is important to remember, however, that the provinces were still linked to the center.

The history of four hundred years of Ottoman rule in the Arab lands has, until recently, received rough and uneven treatment from historians. Ottomanists, on the one hand, have tended to disregard the Arab lands in favor of the Balkans or, for that matter, Anatolia. Most interpreters of the Arab provinces, on the other hand, have primarily sought to explain the sharp transformation of Middle Eastern society in the nineteenth century. For many of the latter, what preceded that transformation has been of secondary importance—a period of decline or stagnation. Students of modern Arab history have, then, tended to regard the Ottoman period as the murky backdrop from which the Arabs emerged only in the nineteenth century and, then, under the impact of the West. In the 1930s, George Antonius put forward a popular and influential version of this view:

> With varying fortunes, frequently accompanied by wars, revolts and massacres, the Ottoman dominion maintained itself in those frontiers [of the Arab lands] until the close of the eighteenth century. Its authority was generally loose and insecure and was sometimes openly flouted, whenever a rebellious vassal would successively defy the ruling Sultan. Sensational figures stalk across the stage of those three centuries, now martial and heroic like Fakhruddin and Daher al-'Umar, now merely brutal and sanguinary like Ahmad al-Jazzar and the Mamelukes of Cairo; but always solitary and self-seeking. They appear and disappear in tedious succession, with the clatter of operatic tyrants,

[2] Cook, *Population Pressure*, p. 44.

> blowing the trumpets of their local triumphs, but never overthrowing or seriously threatening the hold which Soliman the Magnificent had fastened upon the Arab World.[3]

Antonius was by no means alone in advancing this interpretation, although his was not strictly scholarly. Other examples may be cited. At the conclusion of a scholarly essay, the late G. E. von Grunebaum likewise glossed over the Ottoman era: "The Arab countries, especially those that had been the centers of Muslim civilization, submitted apathetically to the twin domination of [Muslim] orthodoxy and the Turks. It was only with Napoleon's expedition to Egypt (in 1798) that, through the impact of Europe and the rise of local nationalisms in its wake, Muslim civilization regained the willingness to change. . . ."[4] In its essence, this approach to the history of the Arab lands under the Ottomans rests on two fundamental assumptions. The first is the unquestioned theme of Ottoman decline, which is brought forth as a master cause of a multitude of events. It is almost as if "decline" must be read into every act of the Ottoman state and every aspect of provincial affairs. It is thus convenient to ascribe any perceived irregularity in provincial government—whether the rise of a so-called "dynasty" of governors, factional warfare, or tribal incursions into settled areas—to the "decline" of the empire. Such an explanation is especially attractive when the actual causes of the events are not known. What is in dispute here is not the empire's decline, but, rather, the assumption that decline is everywhere and why bother to look closer. Similarly, the second assumption unfavorably compares the allegedly static, inert quality of the sixteenth, seventeenth, and eighteenth centuries with the ferment of modernization in the nineteenth century. In conformity with this interpretation, the preceding centuries of Ottoman rule are expected to show an undifferentiated pattern of decay. Thus, there is no reason to investigate continuities or changes in that pattern.[5]

[3] Antonius, *The Arab Awakening*, p. 20.

[4] Von Grunebaum, "Islam in a Humanistic Education," p. 68.

[5] This lack of interest in the seventeenth and eighteenth centuries is well

The quality and pace of change in the nineteenth century were indeed dramatic and are subjects that have been intensively studied in their own right, but it is wrong to assume that change before that period was negligible or unimportant by comparison. The artificially sharp historical divide between "traditional" and "modern," between the earlier Ottoman era and the nineteenth and twentieth centuries, has yet to be bridged.

Implicitly or explicitly, the limited, but growing, scholarly literature on eighteenth-century Damascus accepts the twin themes of decline and lack of dynamism. The works of Abdul-Karim Rafeq and Shimon Shamir are, despite this limitation, however, pioneering in their own right. They piece together invaluable narratives and descriptions of local institutions from local Arabic chronicles and biographical dictionaries (Shamir also uses Hebrew materials), as well as from European consular and travel reports. Both include comparatively brief chapters on the province's political and social structure.[6] These descriptive chapters do not compare favorably with the narrative chapters, however, because they are not based on Ottoman and local archival materials, which are the best evidence for this purpose. Due to the limited focus of both authors—clearly justified by the state of the field—their efforts are largely confined to well-documented local history. They devote less attention to the Ottoman framework in which that history developed. It is regarded as a "facade."[7] More recently, Amnon Cohen has published an important study of the political-fiscal history of Palestine during the eighteenth century, coupled with analyses of the careers of two important local political figures, Ẓāhir al-'Umar (d. 1775) and Cezzar Ahmed Paşa (d. 1804). Although Cohen exploits large amounts of Ottoman archival material, his emphasis remains on local history, particularly that of the second

illustrated by the nine-page survey, good as it is, of Syria by Holt, *Egypt and the Fertile Crescent, 1516-1922*, pp. 102-111. The title of the chapter is "Ottoman Decline and the Syrian Provinces."

[6] Rafeq, *Province*, pp. 1-76; Shamir, " 'Aẓm, Wālīs," pp. 217-256.

[7] Rafeq, *Province*, p. vii.

half of the eighteenth century, with the Ottoman state largely seen as an inert and helpless observer.[8]

The present study of Ottoman rule in Damascus attempts to resolve some of the interpretive difficulties arising from the history of the province during the first half of the eighteenth century. It does not attempt to recast events into new narrative form, to present a purely descriptive survey of administration, or to cover in detail all aspects of the period. Rather, the emphasis is on change in provincial organization at the same time that the Ottoman state was making its recovery from the Karlowitz debacle of 1699. Setting aside the theme of decline, and written from the point of view of the central government, this study puts forward a new interpretation based on previously unconsulted material in the Ottoman archives of Istanbul. The principal argument is that between 1708 and 1758, most probably in partial response to the disaster represented by the Treaty of Karlowitz, the Ottoman state tried to revitalize its administration in the province of Damascus in three distinct but interrelated areas: the governorship of the province; the containment of local groups; and the reorganization of the annual pilgrimage to the Holy Cities of Arabia sponsored by the Ottoman state and directed by the governor of Damascus. After 1758, as this study will argue, that program no longer worked and no new approaches were tried.

Chapter One discusses changes in the provincial governorship of Damascus. First, the governor's duty to serve in the empire's wars was abolished, which resulted in a loss of opportunity for promotion through service to the sultan. On the other hand, the governor was seemingly compensated by being appointed commander of the pilgrimage, the equivalent of a military campaign. Professor Holt has rightly emphasized the importance of this change.[9] But there was another equally important and related change that has escaped notice. The governor's powers were increased when he be-

[8] For an analysis of Cohen, *Palestine*, see Karl Barbir's review in *International Journal of Middle East Studies* IX (August 1978):416–418.

[9] Holt, *Egypt and the Fertile Crescent*, pp. 106–107.

came directly responsible, through his subordinates, for nearly half of the province's subunits (*sancaks*) in addition to the customary *paşa sancağı*, the subunit in which the governor resided. These two patterns of change were related in the sense that command of the pilgrimage replaced military service outside the province and that lack of opportunity for promotion within the Ottoman system was seemingly balanced by the expansion of the governor's direct authority over the province and the immense prestige associated with command of the pilgrimage.

Chapter Two describes the manner in which the Ottoman state was compelled to come to terms with three substantial regional forces: the notables of the provincial capital, the janissaries of that city, and the beduin, Turkman, and Kurdish tribes of the countryside. By offering inducements of patronage and state employment, the central government was able, with mixed success, to keep these three groups within the Ottoman system. The notables derived their power as much from state recognition as from local support, whereas the janissaries were controlled through frequent checks of muster rolls and assignment to duty outside the provincial capital. As for the tribes, the Ottoman state attempted to use the *Şam urbanı şeyhliği*, or chieftainship of the Arab tribes of Damascus, to contain increased tribal pressure on settled areas. It patronized selected tribes to provision and escort the pilgrimage. Governors of neighboring provinces tried to contain the Kurdish and Turkman tribes (about which very little is known) and to induce them to settle on agricultural lands.

In the third and final chapter, a detailed analysis of the pilgrimage serves to illustrate the themes developed in the preceding chapters. Because the Ottoman sultan was considered to be servant of the two holy places (Mecca and Medina), it was of vital importance that the pilgrimage be conducted safely and efficiently. The province of Damascus, because of its geographic proximity to Arabia, received special attention from the central government during the eighteenth century, when local officials were dislodged from pilgrimage administration. Taking the initiative, probably in response to the consequences of defeat at Karlowitz and a reappraisal of the government's mission and function, the Ottoman state began to exercise greater control over the pilgrimage, reinforcing its image as the paramount Islamic state. From 1708 onward, the governor of Damascus took charge of that task, but received considerable direction from Istanbul. A well-planned budget, a tax-collecting tour of the more troublesome *sancaks* to raise additional funds, expansion of the network of forts along the pilgrimage route, reorganization of the relief force that escorted the caravan on its return to Damascus (the *cerde*), and partly successful efforts to assure security were the elements of Ottoman pilgrimage administration during this period.

Taking root with the governorship of Nasuh Paşa (1708-1714), the Ottoman program of provincial reorganization in Damascus appears to have run its course by 1758, following a disastrous beduin attack on the pilgrimage caravan on its return from Mecca to Damascus in late 1757. After 1758, although the state continued to try to make its program work, it had lost the initiative. It attempted no innovations and, in the face of external threats, left the initiative to the governor without the careful control of the earlier period. By the 1780s, only local proxies like Cezzar Ahmed Paşa, with his well-equipped retinue and private military force, could maintain the semblance of an Ottoman presence, but on his terms, not Istanbul's. A new phase in the relationship between center and periphery had begun.

Map 1. Divisions of the Province of Damascus (by Sancak)

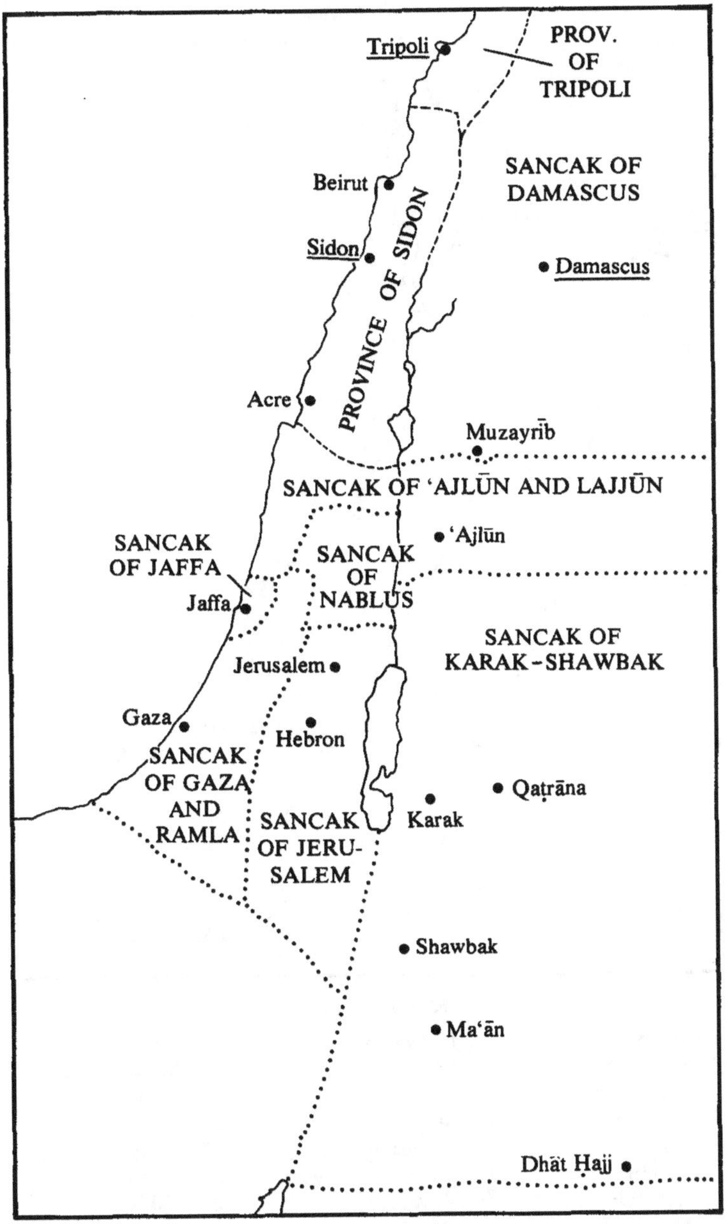

Note: Boundaries are approximate

Map 2. The Pilgrimage Fortress Network between Damascus and Medina

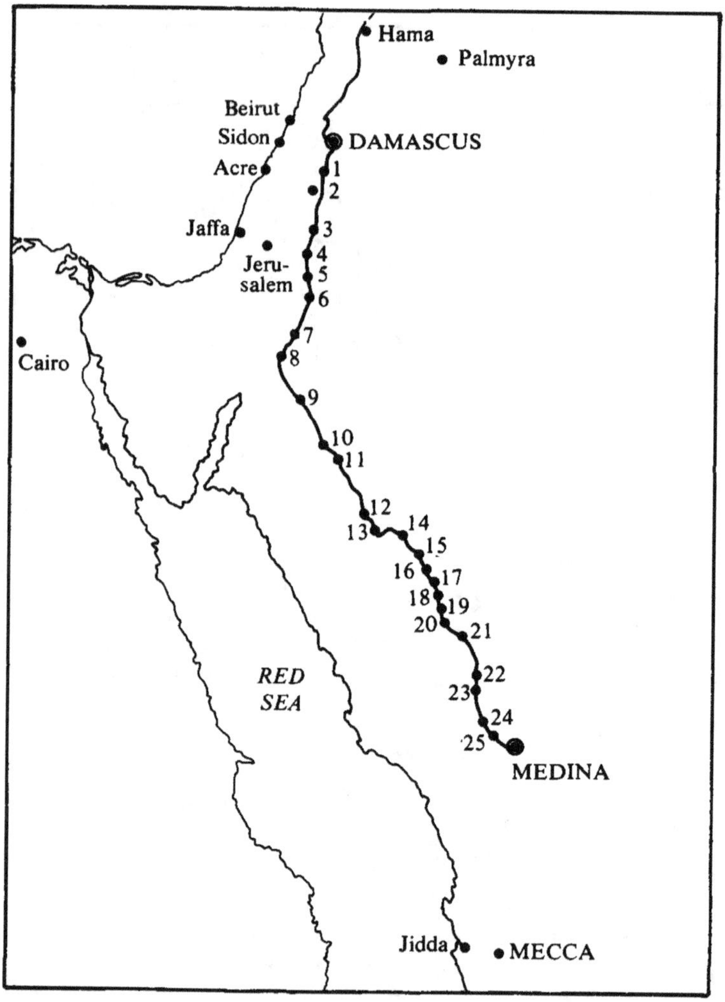

Numbered Forts

1. Sanamayn
2. Muzayrīb
3. Tall Far'ūn
4. 'Ayn Zarqā
5. Balqā
6. Qatrāna
7. Zahr 'Unayza
8. Ma'ān
9. Zahr al-'Aqaba
10. Jughaymān
11. Dhāt Hajj
12. Tabūk
13. Maghāyır al-Qalandarıyya
14. Ukhayḍır (Haydar)
15. al-Mu'azzam
16. Dār al-Hamrā'
17. Madā'ın Ṣāliḥ
18. 'Ulā
19. Abyār Ghanam
20. Zumurrud
21. Valide Kuyusu
22. Hadıyya
23. 'Antar
24. Nakhlatayn
25. Wādī al-Qurā

ONE

CHANGING PATTERNS IN THE GOVERNORSHIP OF DAMASCUS

IN THE FIRST HALF of the eighteenth century, during the brief revival that took place at the imperial center, the Ottomans reorganized the administrative structure of the province of Damascus. Two related sets of patterns of change occurred in the governorship of that province. We have called them, respectively, "limits on the governor's functions" and "provincial centralization." They began roughly at the turn of the century and continued for approximately fifty years. Whoever was the sovereign or chief minister regarded them as precedents for provincial administration in Damascus.

"Limits on the governor's functions" involved two related departures from the classical system of Ottoman provincial organization. In that system, governors of Damascus had military obligations to the sultan outside the province and could thereby hope to achieve promotions to other provinces or to the grand vezirate. After 1708, the governor no longer left Damascus to participate in the wars of the empire. At the same time, no governnor of Damascus—with two minor exceptions—attained the grand vezirate in the first half of the eighteenth century.

"Provincial centralization" evolved when, after 1708, the governor of Damascus was regularly assigned supreme command of the annual pilgrimage to Arabia as well as direct administration of a varying number of the province's subordinate units (*sancaks*). Both of these changes represented an attempt by Istanbul to centralize affairs in the provincial capital.

The two patterns of change were related in the sense that the pilgrimage was the equivalent of a military campaign, and that the governor's lack of mobility outside the province was balanced by the expansion of his direct authority within the province as well as by the prestige he derived from being commander of the pilgrimage. Whether similar changes developed in other provinces is a question to be posed in future research. The purpose of this part of our study is to analyze the patterns as they developed in Damascus. To set them in context, a brief review of relevant aspects of the Ottoman provincial governorship precedes the analysis.

The Ottoman Provincial Governorship

"At the beginning, in the Ottoman dynasty, it was Osman Gazi who distributed offices of rank."[1] So begins a sixteenth-century administrative ordinance (*kanunname*) that sought to codify accepted past practices in the structure of Ottoman government. As the eponymous founder of the empire, Osman Gazi began the process of extending sovereign control over all state appointments, whether in the bureaucratic, religious, or military careers.[2] Until the time of Sultan Mehmed II (d. 1481) the first minister, or vezir, was drawn almost exclusively from the ranks of the great ulema families who, alone in the fledgling Ottoman state, possessed the education to be administrators. As the absolute deputy of the sultan, the first vezir (later known as the grand vezir) was, at least in theory, the sole means of access to the sovereign in all matters of state. He alone could propose candidates for state posts and obtain the sultan's approval of those appointments. In certain cases, if he were on campaign or far away from the sultan, he could make appointments by proxy.[3] During the reign of Mehmed II, the number of vezirs rose to seven, in-

[1] "Osmanlı Kanunnameleri," *Millî Tetebbüler Mecmuası* I, no. 2, p. 325. The anonymous editor of the *kanunnames* informs us that this passage appears in an ordinance compiled by the famous seal-keeper (*nişancı*) Celalzâde Koca Mustafa Çelebi, who was responsible for the codes that gave Sultan Süleyman the Magnificent (1520-1566) his reputation as the "Law-Giver" (*Kanunî*). For Celalzâde, see Danişmend, *Osmanlı Devlet Erkanı*, pp. 319-320, 322.

[2] For this evolution and transformation, see Inalcık, *The Ottoman Empire*, pp. 55-57.

[3] "Osmanlı Kanunnameleri: Tevkii Abdurrahman Paşa Kanunnamesi,"

cluding the grand vezir, and the vezirate was no longer the pinnacle of attainment for members of the ulema. Mehmed II systematically appointed vezirs from the ranks of thousands of Balkan and Anatolian Christian peasants who were recruited, converted to Islam, and trained for service as honored "slaves" of the sultan.[4] In later centuries, freeborn Muslims were allowed entry into the "military" (*askeri*) ranks, at the top of which was the vezirate.[5] The number of vezirs increased to nine during the reign of Süleyman the Magnificent (1520-1566). Members of the official council of state (*divan-ı hümayun*), which met in a domed chamber, the nine were known as vezirs of the dome (*kübbe vezirleri*). As the number of qualified recruits rose, more vezirates were created. There were sixteen in 1596: nine as members of the council, seven as governors of major provinces. The total rose to twenty-three in 1599. During the seventeenth century, a number of minor officials of the central government and the provinces gained the vezirate, and, after 1640, most provincial governors were vezirs.[6] During the reign of Sultan Ahmed III (1703-1730) the vezirate of the dome was abolished.

The trend of sending out vezirs as provincial governors was one important element of change in the provincial system. In the classical scheme of provincial administration, the basic unit was a *sancak*, whose governor (*sancakbeyi*) commanded the local military forces (*timarlıs*), who enjoyed usufruct from agricultural lands. The basis of the system was the maintenance of a fighting cavalry force that at any time could be called upon to participate in the empire's wars. A combina-

---

Millî Tetebbüler Mecmuası, I, no. 3, p. 498. Abdurrahman Paşa's code is dated 1087/1676-1677. Short reference: "Tevkii Kanunnamesi."

[4] For the slave recruitment system, see the masterful article by Halil Inalcik, "Ghulâm," *EI*², II, 1085-1091. There is evidence that the system had begun under earlier Ottoman sultans and was gradually expanded until it was reorganized by Mehmed II.

[5] For a discussion of the implications of this practice, see Itzkowitz, "Eighteenth Century Ottoman Realities."

[6] This account has been drawn from Uzunçarşılı, *Merkez ve bahriye*, pp. 195-213; *TDS*, III, 590ff; Gibb and Bowen, *Islamic Society*, I, 1, pp. 113ff; and Franz Babinger, "Wazīr," *EI*¹, IV, 1135-1136.

tion of *sancaks* made up a larger unit of administration known earlier as a *beylerbeyilik* and later as an *eyalet*, or province.[7]

Aside from natural geography, the limits separating provinces from one another were arbitrary and subject to many changes. They were fixed for military, fiscal, and administrative convenience and were altered at will. There is a hint of this in the standard letter of appointment of provincial governors, in which the sultan is referred to as having the power to divide his realm just as God has made divisions in the human race.[8] It might be added that, no matter how the realm was divided for administrative purposes, the local populations had their own notions of local boundaries, often determined by agricultural patterns or ancient divisions.[9] The problem of provincial boundaries in the Ottoman Empire has been taken too seriously by modern observers.[10] They tend to assume that boundaries were literally fixed and provinces clearly defined. This often reflects a desire to project the limits of modern states back into the past. Difficulties arise with many cases, however: the temporary separation of Sidon province for a few years from the larger province of Damascus in 1614, a separation made permanent after 1660; the attachment of the *sancak* of Nablus to Sidon for a brief period in the early eighteenth century, although the two were not even contiguous;[11] and the fact that the *sancak* of Ḥimṣ, though theoretically a part of the province of Tripoli, was assigned to several governors of Damascus.

Such displacements and rearrangements of *sancaks* marked crucial changes in the military structure of the empire after the last part of the sixteenth century. Inflation and the rise of an expanding janissary army in Istanbul threatened the livelihood and effectiveness of the military forces scattered

[7] Halil Inalcık, "Eyālet," *EI*², II, 721-724.

[8] For a sample appointment letter, see Uzunçarşılı, *Merkez ve bahriye*, p. 198; an almost identical document nominating Esat Paşa (al-'Azm) to Damascus is BA-Cevdet/Dahiliye 5468, dated 25 Receb 1156 (14 September 1743).

[9] For example, see Cohen, *Palestine*, p. 164.

[10] For example, see Gibb and Bowen, *Islamic Society*, I, 1, pp. 142-144.

[11] Cohen, *Palestine*, p. 164.

throughout the provinces. It became necessary to strengthen provincial governors to maintain local order.[12] Recent research has shown that, as a consequence, the administrative importance of the *sancaks* diminished during the seventeenth century, whereas that of the larger units—the *eyalets*—increased.[13] At the same time, the state resettled thousands of janissaries in the provinces in order to keep them from making trouble in Istanbul. These forces came to play powerful roles in provincial life. They penetrated the economic structure—particularly the urban craft corporations—and acted as a check to ambitious governors, of whose control they were relatively independent. As if to balance the social and economic power of these new forces, the state allowed displaced and underpaid *timarlıs* to join the retinues of governors. A retinue's size in the classical system was "in proportion to the income received from [a governor's] fiefs."[14] It afterward rose above the earlier average of roughly two hundred armed retainers ready for service in imperial campaigns. Whereas the state, during the seventeenth century, appears to have acceded to this transformation of the provincial system, particularly to the diminished importance of the *sancaks*, it nevertheless attempted to retain control over the size of each governor's retinue. After 1707—this date being significant for our analysis—the *timarlıs* attached to governors' retinues, and called *paşa defterlisi*, could no longer draw income from their original *timars*. Their support was now the problem of individual governors.[15] Thus, all provincial military forces—with the exception of the relatively few *timarlıs*—were either janissaries, or mercenaries and their descendants.[16]

[12] Inalcık, *The Ottoman Empire*, p. 105.

[13] The precise manner in which this transformation took place has only recently been explored and documented. See Kunt, *Sancaktan eyalete*.

[14] Inalcik, *The Ottoman Empire*, p. 87; Uzunçarşılı, *Merkez ve bahriye*, p. 207.

[15] *TDS*, II, 757; Uzunçarşılı, *Merkez ve bahriye*, pp. 207-208; and Mehmed Râşıd, *Tarih-i Râşid*, III, 138 (dismissal of Cretan *timarlıs* and their replacement by 1,561 salaried local militiamen, or *yerli ulufeli*).

[16] See, for example, Rafeq's research on Damascus in particular and on the rest of Syria in general, in "The Local Forces in Syria."

Changes also took place in the ranks and titles held by provincial governors. Here some distinctions are in order. In the Ottoman system, all officials held *rütbes*, or posts of rank, but some persons enjoyed as well *payes*, or state salaries graded by rank and granted as favors. Hence, a teacher in a mosque might hold an Istanbul *paye* or Mecca *paye* without living in Istanbul or Mecca, yet have the right to an income equal to that of an official in the religious career actually holding such a post.[17] Similarly, a governor might be granted the Rumeli *paye*—the rank and income of the empire's senior governor, the governor of Rumeli—while holding some other governorship. As a rule, however, there were three ranks of governors distributed over two provincial units, the *sancaks*, and the larger entities known earlier as *beylerbeyiliks* and later as *eyalets*. A *sancak*, formerly the basic administrative unit, was headed by a *sancakbeyi*. The latter possessed the symbolic single horse tail (*tuğ*) and the title of *bey*. In later periods, a *sancak* might also be assigned to a *beylerbeyi* (*bey* of *beys*), of two horse tails, and with the title of *paşa*.[18] Those holding the highest rank, the vezirate—*paşas* of three horse tails—might govern *sancaks* or *eyalets*. By 1760, the increase in numbers in the two top ranks led to the following pattern of relationships between ranks and administrative units:[19]

Units	*Sancaks*	Number	*Eyalets*	Number
Ranks	*Vezir*	6	*Vezir*	21
	Beylerbeyi	29	*Beylerbeyi*	9
	Sancakbeyi	13		
Titles	*Bey, Paşa*	48	*Paşa*	30

It has long been maintained and generally accepted that, by the end of the seventeenth century, the typical Ottoman gov-

[17] *TDS*, II, 764.

[18] In earlier periods, the *beylerbeyi* had been commander in chief of the sultan's army. Later, with the empire's expansion, he governed a group of *sancaks* known first as a *beylerbeyilik* and later as an *eyalet*. See Inalcık, "Eyālet," *EI*², II, 721-724.

[19] BA-Cevdet/Dahiliye 13472, dated 1174 (1760-1761); see also Gibb and Bowen, *Islamic Society*, I, 1, p. 140.

ernor was a mere figurehead who, in the face of growing provincial "autonomy," had few powers aside from the collection of taxes.[20] The "reality" of political life is said to have stood in sharp contrast to the prescribed modes of provincial governance. In the classical system, the central government imposed four duties on all governors: to be the sultan's deputy in the provinces in all matters within their competence (*umur-u siyaset*); to enforce the sultan's orders and all decisions by officials of the religious-judicial system (*kadis*); to preside over provincial councils' deliberations pertaining to members of the military class; and to maintain public security.[21] Governors, however, had to defer to the provincial *kadis*, treasurers (*defterdars*), and janissaries in their spheres of competence, for which they had direct access to Istanbul.[22]

What is usually implied by the thesis of the governors' limited effectiveness is the assertive nature of local groups—fluid in composition and varying in immediate goals—and the limited tenure of most governors. This theme has not been extensively tested, but, instead, has been accepted as a working proposition by historians. A great deal of research is needed to clarify the changes in provincial governorship during the sixteenth and seventeenth centuries and the composition and goals of local groups. In this and other parts of the present study, we will show that, in the first half of the eighteenth century, governors of Damascus continued to exercise considerable power to regulate communications, to encourage economic activity, and to maintain stable patterns of settlement in the face of encroachment by tribes in the countryside. Governors, in other words, were still expected to apply—and continued to attempt to apply—the political theory of the "circle of equity." In brief, this theory—whose origins go far back into Near Eastern history—held that strong and conscientious royal authority was the foundation of justice and prosperity. The *Kutadgu Bilig*, an eleventh-century Turkish

[20] See the ambivalent remarks of Gibb and Bowen, *Islamic Society*, I, 1, pp. 200ff.

[21] Inalcik, "Eyâlet," *EI*², II, 721-724.

[22] Ibid. and "Tevkii Kanunnamesi," p. 528.

manual of administration, summarizes the theory as follows: "To control the state requires a large army. To support the troops requires great wealth. To obtain this wealth the people must be prosperous. For the people to be prosperous the laws must be just. If any one of these is neglected the state will collapse."[23] In a related conception, Ottoman society was regarded as consisting of four "estates": the ruling elite (*askeri*, "men of the sword"), the businessmen ("men of negotiation"), bureaucrats ("men of the pen"), and the peasantry (*reaya*, "men of husbandry").[24] Artificial as these propositions may seem, they were very much at the heart of government practice. At the beginning of the eighteenth century, the historian Naima's recommendations for implementing justice for the four "estates" were taken seriously and contributed in part to the Ottoman state's relative revival. A significant example of this policy is the grand vezir Damad Ibrahim Paşa's 1727 letter of warning to the governor of Damascus, Ismail Paşa (al-'Aẓm). It gives important evidence of early eighteenth-century provincial policy and shows that the ideals were expected to become reality. According to Damad Ibrahim, the just ruler (*hâkim-i âdil*, apparently equated with the men of the sword)—in this case the provincial governor—is the originator or first cause of justice for the other three estates: the elite (*rical*, including the ulema, *eşraf* and *ayan*), the businessmen (*tüccar*), and the peasantry (*reaya*). Note that, in this conception of provincial society, the elite is substituted for the bureaucracy, "men of the pen," of the four-estate theory. If the ruler does not follow the precepts of the "circle of equity" theory, the other three estates are corrupted: "In the first place, if the ruler is not just and inclines to tyranny, the elite, men of negotiation, and the peasantry will become savages."[25] Damad Ibrahim catalogues the abuses of Ismail Paşa and blames him for being the cause of local disturbances and the flight of the population. He concludes his

[23] Quoted in Inalcık, *The Ottoman Empire*, p. 66.

[24] See Itzkowitz, *Ottoman Empire*, p. 102.

[25] TKS-E. 12109, letter dated 3 Rebıyulâhır 1140 (18 November 1727).

letter with a severe warning and an Arabic aphorism: "Be alert and ponder your fate."

The functions of Ottoman provincial governors thus extended far beyond the collection of taxes. They covered security of life and property, the prevention of mass disturbances, the maintenance of residential patterns, as well as a whole range of matters whose extent and significance have yet to be explored. By the eighteenth century, when the classical social and economic organization had largely been transformed from its sixteenth-century basis, the Ottoman sultan nevertheless continued to regard his subjects as being under his absolute domination and protection. The provincial governors were expected to perform accordingly. Indeed, as Professor Inalcik maintains, the "circle of equity" theory was the cornerstone of Ottoman political philosophy until 1839 and the *Tanzimat* reforms.[26]

The aspect of Ottoman provincial administration that is, perhaps, the most difficult to understand is the basis for the appointment of governors. Intimate, personal records shedding light on Ottoman officials of that rank have so far not been available in satisfactory numbers. Instead, scholars have had to contend with the hearsay and gossip of local chroniclers and foreign observers. Two generalizations have been made on this point: (1) that governors gained appointments through the influence—political and financial—of their agents and protectors in Istanbul[27] and (2) that the central government made appointments with the purpose of flattering powerful local groups in a province—primarily the notables, ulema, and the janissaries.[28] These points may seem plausible against the background of Ottoman history in general. But, based as they are on the records of local chroniclers and foreign observers, they still require careful testing, case by case, against the records of the central government. Because a shroud of secrecy and anonymity covered the actions of the central government with regard to provincial appointments

[26] Inalcık, "Traditional Society," p. 43.
[27] Rafeq, *Province*, p. 7. [28] Ibid., p. 11.

(as well as most other affairs of state), the truth may never be satisfactorily known. It is possible, however, to gain some insight into the mechanics of appointments through a discussion of four points: the formal, bureaucratic machinations; the "sale" of office; the governors' representation in Istanbul; and the procedures regarding the dismissal of governors.

The customary practice was to give one-year terms to appointees. Once a year, usually in the month of Cemaziyelevvel, the grand vezir would review all provincial appointments. He would keep in office those named in recent months and either confirm or dismiss those who had been in office the full year.[29] In principle, no province could be left without a governor, even for a short time. Replacements were appointed with great dispatch and arrangements made for surrogates to assume governmental functions and to await the arrival of new governors. Through such arrangements, the Ottoman state attempted to overcome problems of distance and logistics and to maintain formal provincial authority. For example, one imperial order appointing Aydınlı Abdullah Paşa, the governor of Niş (in the Balkans), to proceed to Damascus at once in time to prepare for the pilgrimage, stated: "At this juncture, it is not suitable for the province of Damascus' governor to be distant from his province."[30] This statement was made because Abdullah Paşa was slow in leaving Niş for Syria. The state had already made arrangements for Abdullah's deputy *(kethüda)* to govern Niş with the concurrence of the new governor's deputy, a janissary officer. Abdullah Paşa's deputy could leave Niş only when the new governor arrived.[31]

Once the decision was made to appoint a governor—whether the decision itself was the grand vezir's or his archri-

[29] Examples of this practice are plentiful in the 1760 list of all appointees: BA-Cevdet/Dahiliye 13472, cited in Note 19 above.

[30] BA-Mühimme 136, p. 290, dated middle Cemaziyelâhir 1143 (21-30 December 1730).

[31] BA-Cevdet/Dahiliye 7267, dated middle Rebiyülâhir 1143 (23 October-1 November 1730), some two months before the order to Abdullah Paşa cited above.

val for the sultan's favor, the chief black eunuch of the harem—the grand vezir's formal approval had to be obtained, then the sultan's. This usually took the form of a brief, two or three-line memorandum, drawn up by the deputy of the grand vezir. The memorandum stated that a certain person was appointed to govern a certain province.[32] After the grand vezir scrawled "so ordered" and "verified" (*buyuruldu* and *sahh*) on the document, it was redrafted in more elaborate form for the sultan, who approved it with the formula, "My imperial favor is granted [*Ihsan-ı hümayun'um olmuştur*]." Sometimes the more elaborate memorandum would include more than one appointment, particularly when govenors "exchanged" provinces.[33] Then, yet another copy was drawn up and the imperial seal (*tuğra*) affixed at the top. It was this copy that was sent to the appointee. Other copies were entered in the registers of the *Tahvil Kalemi* and *Ruüs Kalemi*, the chancery bureaus that recorded the names of those who had specified incomes respectively from land or from state monopolies.[34]

To win these rights cost an appointee very large sums in cash and gifts. This aspect of provincial appointments is surprisingly well documented, the gifts, in particular, being authorized by administrative ordinance (*kanunname*).[35] From available evidence, it appears that gifts were presented to the sultan on days when the imperial council met. Examples of the gifts recorded as received respectively from the *sancakbeyi*

[32] Examples of such appointment memoranda for Damascus are: BA-Ibnülemin/Tevcıhat 2170 and 2381, dated respectıvely 1 Rebıyülâhır 1127 and 22 Rebiyülevvel 1133 (6 April 1715 and 21 January 1721); and BA-Emiri/ııı Ahmed 15096, dated 1 Cemaziyelâhır 1116 (1 October 1704).

[33] For such a memorandum, see BA-Cevdet/Dahilıye 5344, dated 1 Safer 1165 (20 December 1751), which includes seven appointments: Aleppo, Sıdon, Bosnıa, Ağrıboz, Damascus, Morea, and the chief debt collectorshıp of the financıal bureau (*başbakikulu*). In thıs case, the governors of Aleppo and Sıdon, and Bosnia and Ağrıboz, respectıvely, switched posts. The new *başbakikulu* was formerly the chıef poll-tax collector for Istanbul (*Istanbul cizyedarı*).

[34] Shınder, "Ottoman Bureaucracy," pp. 29-30.

[35] *TDS*, ııı, 590ff; ı, 794-795.

of Jerusalem and the *kadi* of Damascus in 1720 are as follows:[36]

5	bolts of varied *Rumi* brocade
4	more bolts of *Rumi* brocade
10	bolts of "Cathay" [*Hatâyı*] silk brocade
10	bolts of pure "Cathay" silk
5	bolts of European [*Frengi*] satin with notched pattern
2	bolts of Indian silk brocade
2	Istanbul-type jackets
2	bolts of *Rumi* gold brocade with flower pattern
2	bolts of "Venetian" brocade
4	bolts of European satin
4	packs of muslin cloth for turbans
4	bolts of Indian cotton
4	bolts of striped cloth for cloaks
4	cashmere belts
2	bolts of cashmere

Another authorized appointment fee was the *caize*, literally an award, but actually a series of payments to the sultan, grand vezir, and other top officials of the central government. In the 1760s, these are said to have amounted to 22,500 *kuruş*,[37] but, in fact, they varied widely according to the relative importance of each appointment. A governor of Sidon in the 1730s, for example, paid a *caize* of 15,500 *kuruş* to the following officials:[38]

The sultan (*rikâb-ı hümayun*)	5,000
The grand vezir (*sadr-ı azam*)	5,000

[36] TKS-E. 3317/1, 2. The first document is undated, but its script is identical to the second, dated 26 Rebıyülevvel 1132 (6 February 1720). The meeting days of the imperial council on which these gifts were presented were Tuesday and Sunday.

[37] *TDS*, I, 255, citing BA-Cevdet/Dahiliye 1121, dated end 1180 (1767).

[38] BA-Cevdet/Dahiliye 11975, dated 1 Rebıyülâhır 1144 (3 October 1731). The document is badly damaged and the appointee's name is illegible.

The deputy of the grand vezir (*kethüda-ı sadr-ı azam*)	2,500
The chancery chief (*reis efendi*)	500
The chief pursuivants (*serçavuşân*)	500
The grand vezir's [?] (*mülükânî-i sadr-ı âli*)	250
First clerk (*tezkire-i evvel*)	250
Second clerk (*tezkire-i sâni*)	250
Clerk of the grand vezir's deputy (*katip-i kethüda-ı sadr-ı âli*)	250
Treasurer of the grand vezir (*hazinedar-ı sadr-ı âli*)	500
Clerk of the grand vezir's treasury (*katip-i hazine-i sadr-ı âli*)	250
Guard of the grand vezir's chamber (*ağa-ı miftah-ı sadr-ı âli*)	250

It is noteworthy that the last three officials were members of the grand vezir's private retinue[39] and were not entitled to these payments according to the *kanun*.

A third type of payment for both the appointment and renewal of provincial governors—not legally permitted but openly acknowledged—was an outright gift to the sultan known as the *rikâbiye-i hümayun*.[40] Funds so collected were unrestricted, that is, not tied to any set expenditures (such as the military). They were dispensed either by the grand vezir in accordance with the sultan's orders or transferred directly to the inner treasury, the sultan's private "account." In April and May 1762, for example, the fees collected from the governors of Damascus and Tripoli (25,000 and 7,500 *kuruş* respectively) were transferred to the inner treasury, whereas those paid by the governors of the Morea (Greece), Bağdad-Basra, Rumeli, and Sidon (10,000, 12,500, 10,000, and 5,000 *kuruş* respectively) were entered in the books of the grand vezir's personal treasury.[41] Here is possible indication of the

[39] Gibb and Bowen, *Islamic Society*, I, 1, pp. 363-364.

[40] *TDS*, III, 46.

[41] TKS-D. 4480, dated Şevval 1175 (April-May 1762). The distribution

grand vezir's opportunity to profit from the sale of office. It appears, however, that, in this case, he simply provided his treasury as a depository for the appointment fees. He had to maintain records of this "trust fund" (*ber vech-i emanet*) as did the inner treasury, which received the funds intended for the sultan's own use.

One other fee related to provincial administration was the *ücret-i kadem*, which covered the expenses incurred by state couriers who traveled to the provinces to collect money due the central government. During the sixteenth century, couriers were compensated according to the distance they traveled and the following scale:[42]

Within Istanbul	5 *akçes* per thousand collected
Medium distances from Istanbul (such as Konya and Akşehir)	15 *akçes* per thousand
Long distances (such as Aleppo and Damascus)	20 *akçes* per thousand
Very long distances	25 *akçes* per thousand
Maximum allowed (for Basra and Yemen)	30 *akçes* per thousand

During the eighteenth century, a similar, if not identical, fee, called the *mübaşiriye* (after the word for courier, *mübaşir*), was collected from the local population of each province to which a courier was sent and entered as income into special local registers (*tevzi defterleri*). Transported to Istanbul and inspected twice a year, the registers also recorded the expenditures of this income, theoretically for the upkeep of local bridges and government buildings but subject to many abuses and extortion.[43] Later in the eighteenth century, this income was col-

---

and allocation of these appointment fees are described at the top of the document.

[42] "Osmanlı Kanunnameleri," p. 325.

[43] *TDS*, IV, 485-486. For the *mübaşiriye*, see *TDS*, II, 592.

lected and sent to Istanbul for the purpose of funding pensions for retired officials.[44]

Each governor had an agent in Istanbul to handle his affairs—mainly financial—with the grand vezir's offices. Known as the *kapıkethüda*, this agent was appointed and dismissed along with his master in the provinces. If the latter was unable to be in Istanbul to receive the ceremonial robes of office from the grand vezir, the *kapıkethüda* performed that function.[45] This agent by no means lived exclusively on his services to a governor. On the contrary, for governors who had large debts to pay (whether taxes due from their provinces or the *rikâbiye* fee), it was essential to have representatives in Istanbul who possessed the capital and hard cash to settle these debts with the central government on their employers' behalf. Hence, a deputy to the commissioner of mines (*madenbaşı halifesi*) was the agent of Nasuh Paşa, governor of Damascus, 1708-1714; a chief customs officer (*gümrük emini*) represented Gürcü Osman Paşa, governor of Damascus, 1760-1771; and Yağlıkçı Yusuf Ağa, wealthy chief of the Istanbul linen-makers' guild, represented Süleyman Paşa (al-'Aẓm), governor of Damascus, 1734-1738, 1741-1743.[46] At the request of Osman Paşa's agent, a debt of 333,207 *kuruş*, on which Osman had paid a first installment of 25,000 *kuruş*, was postponed. This debt size seems to have been the norm for governors of large provinces. Mehmed Rağıb Paşa, as governor of Egypt twenty years earlier, accumulated a debt of

[44] For example, see BA-Cevdet/Dahiliye 6246, dated by the archivist as from the reign of Sultan Selim III (1789-1807).

[45] Uzunçarşılı, *Merkez ve bahriye*, pp. 209-210; *TDS*, II, 172-173. It should be noted that representatives of foreign governments also maintained *kapıkethüdas* to receive and transmit correspondence with the Ottoman state. See Sami, Şakir, and Subhi, *Tarih*, folio 44a, for the agent of Austria (Nemçe).

[46] *SO*, IV, 210, for Nasuh Paşa's *kapıkethüda*; TKS-E. 9557, undated, but from internal evidence belonging to the period of Gürcü Osman's governorship of Damascus (1760-1771); for Yağlıkçı Yusuf Ağa, see *SO*, IV, 664 and TKS-D. 5864, in Arabic, dated 15 Cemaziyelevvel 1155 (18 July 1742).

340,000 *kuruş*, over half of which was forgiven.[47] Süleyman Paşa, on one occasion, paid a debt of 23,860.5 *kuruş* by bill of exchange through Aleppo merchants and their correspondents in Istanbul. The latter advanced cash to the *kapıkethüda*, Yağlıkçı Yusuf Ağa, who in turn handed it over to the central government. Süleyman Paşa, through this paper transaction, avoided the dangers of transferring large sums of cash all the way from Damascus to Istanbul. It is significant that four of the fifteen merchants named in this transfer—as well as their correspondents—were Europeans.[48] Here is evidence of growing European involvement not only in the internal trade of the Ottoman Empire, but also in aspects of provincial administration long kept from the knowledge, much less the participation, of Europeans.[49]

Of possibly greater significance is the career of Yağlıkçı Yusuf Ağa, Süleyman Paşa's agent. In addition to heading the linen-makers' guild, he conducted a brisk trade with India and resided there for five to six years in company with the Ottoman ambassador. Through the influence of his patrons, Yusuf Ağa probably obtained the scribal post in which his son, Mehmed Emin, pursued a career in government. Mehmed Emin finally attained the grand vezirate (1768-1769), after marrying into the imperial family and serving as keeper of the seal (*nisançı*).[50] Such connections with agents in Istanbul enhanced the positions of governors in their dealings with the central government. Although there were more important persons in Istanbul—the chief of the sultan's harem in

[47] TKS-E. 9557; the data on Mehmed Rağıb Paşa are contained in TKS-E. 11595, undated, but covering debts of the years 1157-1160 (1744/45-1747). A copy of the latter document was kindly provided by Prof. Norman Itzkowitz.

[48] They were, respectively, Strachey, Currie (?), Burke, and Cantran in Aleppo; and Barker, Lyle, Hobbes, and Jean-Baptiste in Galata, the foreigners' quarter of Istanbul. The names have been rendered from the Arabic text of TKS-D. 5864, cited in note 46 above. Cf. Rafeq, *Province*, p. 93.

[49] For Ottoman methods of keeping secret the details of state administration, see Porter, *Observations*, I, 204. The author was the British ambassador to the Ottoman Empire between 1747 and 1761.

[50] Danişmend, *Osmanlı Devlet Erkanı*, p. 63; *SO*, IV, 664.

particular—who could press a governor's claim to his post or to a better post, the *kapıkethüda* handled the finances and routine correspondence of his master, and his contact with the central government was of great importance. The central government, on the other hand, had a wealthy hostage at hand should a governor prove recalcitrant or not pay his debts. When Süleyman Paşa (al-'Aẓm) was dismissed from Damascus in 1738, Istanbul applied pressure on his *kapıkethüda* in order to compel Süleyman to step down, pay his debt of 12,500 *kuruş*, and surrender his movable and immovable property to a special agent, in accordance with customary practice.[51]

Grounds for dismissal of governors are often more difficult to determine than those for appointments. Even a straightforward transfer to another province had overtones of loss or gain of status, personal considerations, and so on. For instance, perhaps the most celebrated dismissal in eighteenth-century Damascus was that of Esat Paşa al-'Azm. To this day, we are not sure why he was transferred suddenly to Aleppo in 1756. We only know that Mehmed Rağıb Paşa, the former governor of Aleppo, was promoted to Damascus for only a few days before being called to the grand vezirate. He never left Aleppo for Damascus.[52] The result was that Esat Paşa remained in Aleppo while Mekkizâde Hüseyin Paşa became governor of Damascus. Were these maneuvers designed to dislodge Esat Paşa from Damascus? There is no solid evidence to prove it, but there were two important consequences: the sack of the pilgrimage caravan in 1757 because of Hüseyin Paşa's incompetence, and the execution of Esat Paşa in 1758, probably prompted by suspicion that Esat Paşa had instigated the attack on the pilgrimage caravan.

Dismissal of governors took several forms. The general term for dismissal, *azıl*, applied to a number of situations. If a

[51] See BA-Cevdet/Dahiliye 8619, letter from the grand vezir to the new governor of Damascus, Osman Paşa Muhassıl, dated 1 Rebıyülevvel 1152 (8 June 1739).

[52] Itzkowitz, "Mehmed Rāghıb Pasha," pp. 135-138; Rafeq, *Province*, p. 204; Shamır, "'Azm Wālīs," pp. 142-143.

governor were given another province, he would, obviously, have to be dismissed from his previous post. If no post was available immediately, a dismissed governor was termed "detached" from duty *(munfasil)* until he was given an appointment. On the other hand, when serious grounds existed to justify revocation of rank *(refi)* as well as dismissal from a governorship, an official so affected might be demoted and given the post of *kapıcıbaşı* (formerly a head doorkeeper; in actual practice, a messenger and agent with special powers who was sent to the provinces).[53] This was sometimes tied to exile to a major fortress and suspension from all duties *(ikamet)*.[54] When Ismail Paşa (al-'Aẓm), for example, was dismissed from Damascus, he was confined to that city's citadel. His relatives in Sidon and Latakia were similarly imprisoned.[55] On rare occasions in the sixteenth century, deposed governors were brought to trial, but no evidence of this practice is available for eighteenth-century Damascus.[56] Even in the case of Mekkizâde Hüseyin's incompetent and disastrous conduct during the Damascus pilgrimage of 1757—when 20,000 pilgrims died of heat, thirst, and beduin attacks—the state at first exiled the dismissed governor to his hometown, Gaza, and merely made note of the fact in his personnel record.[57] Somewhat later, Hüseyin Paşa was given the governorship of Maraş in southeastern Anatolia, and then the *sancak* of Gaza, where he died in battle against the beduin at the end of 1765.[58]

Connected with the dismissal, execution, or death of governors was the important practice of confiscation of all assets

[53] Gibb and Bowen, *Islamic Society*, I, 1, p. 347.

[54] Uzunçarşılı, *Merkez ve bahriye*, pp. 204-205. The fortress of Resmo on the island of Crete was especially favored for such exiles. See Samı, Şakir, and Subhı, *Tarih*, folio 44b.

[55] Shamır, " 'Aẓm Wālīs," p. 60; and BA-Mühımme 136, p. 264, dated middle Rebıyülâhır 1143 (24 October to 2 November 1730).

[56] For the trial of Hâdım Sınan Paşa, governor of Damascus in 1545-1546, see Heyd, *Studies in Old Ottoman Criminal Law*, pp. 211-212, citing TKS-D. 162, a register of 197 folios containing records of the trial.

[57] *Vezaret kaydına şerh verilip*. BA-Mühimme 160, p. 1, dated 8 Rebıyülevvel 1171 (20 November 1757).

[58] *SO*, II, 211.

by the state. To modern students of the subject, confiscation of the wealth of high Ottoman officials—whether governors or members of the central administration—was merely another method by which the Ottoman state met its perennial need for hard cash.[59] There is no question that the state gained income from these estates (in the case of Esat Paşa al-'Aẓm, fifty million *kuruş*),[60] but several important aspects of this practice have been distorted or ignored. It has been assumed that such confiscations were somehow illegal. For example, witness the outcry of the people of Damascus when, after Süleyman Paşa al-'Aẓm's death, a group of tough agents from Istanbul came to seize the wealth of the deceased. Süleyman's retinue and family were assembled and questioned about secret hiding places where thousands of *kuruş* in cash and jewelry were stored. At first the family and retinue professed ignorance. It required considerable persuasion—of an ugly sort—to break their resistance and to obtain the information. In one spot alone, the agents found 16,000 gold coins.[61] The chronicler who reported these incidents was indignant, not simply because of the methods used, but also because the procedure itself seemed illegal and alien to him. The heart of the estate problem was that governors were, by custom, "slaves" of the sultan. When the Ottomans began the practice of the levy of Christian boys who were converted to Islam and trained in the Ottoman way, confiscation was not ordinarily a legal and social problem. Non-Muslims by birth, and "slaves" by social estate, the recruits who rose in state service and held state posts owed their livelihood and status to their master, the sultan. According to Islamic law, the master inherits the estate of his slaves, regardless of whether they have heirs. However, in later periods, when born Muslims (some of them sons of "slaves") entered the highest ranks of government, they apparently surrendered their rights as free Muslims to pass on their wealth and possessions to their heirs. This was, strictly speaking, contrary to the law, but it did not

[59] For this view, see Rafeq, *Province*, pp. 160, 164.

[60] Shamır, " 'Aẓm Wālīs," p. 148.

[61] Budayrī, *Ḥawādith*, pp. 57-60.

prevent born Muslims from seeking to join the *askeri*, or ruling, military class. In practice, governors and other high officials accepted confiscation as a necessary part of assuming office. Sir James Porter, a penetrating observer of Ottoman practices in the mid-eighteenth century, noted that officials "eagerly solicit, and contentedly accept [office] . . . submitting, or, it may be said, covenanting and agreeing, that he [the sultan] should inherit at their death."[62] But they attempted to avoid confiscation by placing as much of their wealth as possible in irrevocable family trusts, or *vakıfs*, managed by and benefiting themselves and their families. The best example of these "tax shelters" from eighteenth-century Damascus is the *vakıf* created by Esat Paşa (al-'Azm) to keep within his family the famous palace he built in the heart of the city.

To summarize, in the event of a governor's dismissal or death, the central government calculated and adjusted outstanding debts, unpaid tax revenues and appointment fees, as well as debts to the local population.[63] Personal possessions, including documents and cash, were usually confiscated as well, although occasionally a number of items were sold or given to the deceased's heirs. For instance, the stores of wheat belonging to Süleyman Paşa (al-'Aẓm), his armory, and some of his property were sold to his nephew and heir, Esat Paşa, for four hundred purses (200,000 *kuruş*).[64] For eighteenth-century Damascus, at least, confiscation was an instrument of state control, of restraint upon governors who sought to accumulate wealth for themselves and their families. The inevitable arrival of agents from Istanbul did not necessarily prevent such accumulation. In addition to hard cash, however, the state obtained governors' private papers, and, thus, knowledge of its officials' dealings. Through confiscation, the state possessed the means to control and limit the rise of wealthy local groups that could threaten to match

[62] Porter, *Observations*, I, 85.

[63] See, for example, BA-Cevdet/Dahılıye 8619, cited in Note 51 above, concerning Süleyman Paşa al-'Aẓm.

[64] Budayrī, *Ḥawādith*, p. 60.

the state's authority, resources, and continuity.[65] In eighteenth-century Damascus, the Ottomans continued to apply these principles of provincial administration but made two sets of changes.

First Set of Patterns: Limits on the Governor's Functions and Mobility

In addition to his duties within a province, a governor had an obligation to serve the sultan in imperial military campaigns. Through such service, and through competent management of his province, a governor could hope for transfer to another province or to a high post in Istanbul with income, prestige, and proximity to power. In eighteenth-century Damascus, both the governor's mobility and duties outside the province were severely circumscribed. This state of affairs has been recognized by scholars in its general form but has not been studied closely.[66] Instead, the inference has been made that Damascus was steadily being lost to the central government because of the latter's own vicissitudes in war and palace intrigues, and because of the rise of assertive provincial groups.[67] The first contention—loss of control—is exaggerated and misleading, and the present analysis will provide a somewhat different explanation. The second contention—the rise of local groups to political prominence—will be dealt with in the next chapter.

The fact that the functions and mobility of governors of Damascus underwent change does not, in our view, show a loss of control by Istanbul over provincial affairs. Rather, these changes were deliberately intended to strengthen Ottoman rule in the province by freeing governors from military

[65] The writer has treated this practice more fully in his "Confiscation of Ottoman Governors' Wealth: Five Cases from Eighteenth Century Damascus," read at the Eleventh Annual Meeting, Middle East Studies Assocation of North America, November 1977.

[66] Rafeq, *Province*, p. 8.

[67] See especially Hourani, "The Fertile Crescent in the Eighteenth Century," specifically pp. 40 and 47.

service elsewhere and restricting their ambitions to the local scene where their efforts could work to the advantage of the state.

In the classical system of Ottoman provincial administration, it was expected that a governor should respond to the sultan's mobilization orders—normally for the campaign season of March to October—by assembling two sets of forces: his own private troops (*kapı halkı*) and the *sipahis*, or "feudal" cavalry, that is, those who benefited from the income of agricultural land and who organized themselves for war by provincial subunit.[68] Throughout most of the sixteenth century, the *sipahis* formed the bulk of the Ottoman army, but gradually, the number of salaried troops—janissaries and mercenaries among others—increased. The number of *sipahis*, however, particularly in Damascus, seems to have decreased.[69] During the seventeenth century, provincial janissary forces became a factor in local Damascus politics. With the influx of fresh mercenaries, a two-tiered system of local and imperial janissaries caused further complications in the provincial military structure. By the late seventeenth century, when a Damascus governor went on campaign for the sultan, his own private force often outnumbered the janissary troops; the few remaining *sipahis* went along only irregularly.[70] Damascus had ceased altogether to contribute forces toward the empire's wars by the third decade of the eighteenth century (see Table 1).

The gradual diminution and extinction of Damascus' role in the empire's wars is illustrated by a number of significant details related to these campaigns. In the first campaign, the 1682-1683 siege of Vienna, Damascus' 500 troops were part

[68] Inalcik, *The Ottoman Empire*, pp. 113-114.

[69] For sixteenth century Damascus and Aleppo, the taxes raised from peasants on land under the *tımar*-sipahi military system represented 38% of the total revenues from those provinces. See Barkan, " 'Feodal' düzen ve Osmanlı Timarı," p. 2. During the eighteenth century, the numbers seem to have dwindled to less than 2% of the total revenues for Damascus. See Cohen, *Palestine*, pp. 298ff.

[70] Cohen, *Palestine*, pp. 298ff.

TABLE 1
DAMASCUS' CONTRIBUTION TO IMPERIAL CAMPAIGNS, 1683-1780

Front	*Date*	*Governor*	*Numbers, type*
Austrian[a]	1682-1683	Sarı Hüseyin	500 local janissaries
Austrian[b]	1686	Salih	?
Austrian[c]	1689	Salet Ahmed	?
Austrian[d]	1691	Murteza	300 men
Austrian[e]	1694-1696	Kanijeli Osman	104 *sipahis*, governor's retinue, 200 local janissaries, 3 brass cannon
Austrian[f]	1697	Bozoklu Mustafa	300 *sipahis*
Russian[g]	1710	Nasuh	500 men
Iranian[h]	1727	Ismail (al-'Aẓm)	15th *orta* of local janissaries
Iranian[i]	1732	Ḥamâ-Ḥimṣ local governor (Esat al-'Aẓm)	500 men
Russian[j]	1738	Süleyman (al-'Aẓm)	30,000 *kuruş*
Iranian[k]	1745	Esat (al-'Aẓm)	100,000 *kuruş*
Russian[l]	1780	Osman Paşa	55,000 *kuruş*

[a] Ibn Jum'a, "al-Bāshāt," p. 44; Uzunçarşılı, *Osmanlı Tarihi*, III, 1, p. 440.
[b] Ibn Jum'a, "al-Bāshāt," p. 45.
[c] Mehmed Râşid, *Tarih*, II, 113.
[d] BA-Cevdet/Askeri 16055, dated 24 Receb 1102 (23 April 1691).
[e] Silahdâr Fındıklılı Mehmed, *Nusretname*, I, 2, pp. 24, 38, 56, 66, 84, 102, 109, 148, 171, 192-193, 200.
[f] Ibid., 3, pp. 292-293.
[g] Ibid., II, 2, p. 267.
[h] BA-Cevdet/Askeri, 16490, dated 20 Ramazan 1139 (11 May 1727).
[i] Samı, Şakir, Subhi, *Tarih*, folio 49a.
[j] BA-Cevdet/Askeri 29773, dated Rebiyülâhır 1151 (July-August 1738).
[k] BA-Cevdet/Askeri 28092, datd 13 Şaban 1158 (18 September 1745).
[l] BA-Cevdet/Askeri 23302, dated 2 Rebiyülâhır 1194 (7 April 1780).

of an Ottoman force estimated at 350,000.[71] The 1689 campaign had a curious aftermath for the governor of Damascus, Salet Ahmed Paşa. He returned from the front and petitioned the central government for leave to rest in his Istanbul home. In response, the state dismissed him, apparently indicating that it still took the military obligation very seriously.[72] In the 1694-1696 campaigns, 104 Damascus *sipahis* arrived at the front on 18 Zilkade 1106 (30 June 1695). The governor of Damascus, Kanijeli Osman Paşa, and his private troops arrived a month later. They were mustered in the commander of the janissaries' division and performed only rearguard functions. Two hundred local Damascus janissaries arrived on 29 Şevval in the following year (2 June 1696), very late indeed.[73] When the governor presented himself to the sultan during Zilhicce 1107 (July 1696) to receive the customary robes of honor before battle, the sultan made a remarkable statement to him: "You deserved a reprimand for your offense of arriving late. Should you render service in accordance with my hope, your crime will be canceled by pardon."[74] The governor soon had a chance to prove himself. At the defense of Temeşvar (1696), when the Ottoman army won an exceptional victory over the Austrians, the governor protected the imperial baggage train and treasury.[75] In the heat of battle, the Damascus artillery contingent helped keep the

[71] The army was composed as follows: 60,000 janissaries, armorers, artillery; 15,000 *kapı kulu* cavalry; 50,000 Crimean Tatars; 40,000 *sipahıs*; 3,000 Egyptian troops (*Mısır kulu*); 500 Damascus troops (*Şam kulu*); 30,000 troops from the Transylvanian, Wallachian, and Moldavian autonomous governorships; 20,000 men from the King of Middle Hungary (Orta Macar); 8 *vezirs*, 23 *beylerbeyıs*, 11 *sancakbeyis*, and their armed retainers, some 131,500. The rear echelon troops numbered another 150,000, including 6,000 private troops of the grand vezır and 3,000 troops from the retinues of other *vezirs*. Uzunçarşılı, *Osmanlı Tarihi*, vol. III, pt. 1, p. 440, citing Lâleli MS 1608, folio 45b. No author or title of the manuscript is supplied. It appears that the figures are greatly inflated.

[72] Râşid, *Tarih*, II, 113.

[73] Silâhdar Fındıklılı Mehmet, *Nusretname*, I, 2, pp. 24, 38, 56, 66, 84, 102, 109, 148. Short reference: *Nusretname*.

[74] Ibid., pp. 161-162.

[75] Ibid., p. 171.

Austrians at bay. The governor was also called to the sultan's tent to receive an order to kill any deserters.[76] In the following year, another governor of Damascus, Bozoklu Mustafa Paşa (a former grand vezir), arrived for war with 300 *sipahis*, who were assigned to rearguard police functions (*karakol*).[77] After that disastrous campaign, ending with the total defeat of the Ottomans at Zenta, Amcazâde Hüseyin Köprülü became grand vezir. Mustafa Paşa was promoted to *kaymakam*, or chief deputy to the grand vezir, an example of the opportunities for promotion to be gained through military service.[78]

The significance of these events is, first, that Damascus governors had difficulty in meeting their obligations of military service in faraway places. They either showed up late or, like Salet Ahmed, were so exhausted that they could not continue in office. Second, the numbers they contributed were minuscule in proportion to the total size of the army and the effort required. The service rendered was, at best, marginal, except for Kanijeli Osman's. It was the latter's good fortune that the battle he was involved in provided his chance for a pardon. Indeed, for a dozen years after that battle, no indication can be found of the participation of any Damascus governor in imperial campaigns. In 1710, 500 local janissaries were ordered mobilized for the successful war against Peter the Great, but there is no evidence that they ever actually participated.[79] Similarly, there is no proof that the mobilizations ordered for 1727 and 1733 were effected. At the same time, it is significant that, in 1715, the governor of neighboring Aleppo participated in a campaign (the governor of Damascus did not) and was promoted to the rank of vezir (he later became governor of Damascus), another example of the opportunities for promotion through military service.[80] Similarly, in 1745, Aleppo sent troops to the Iranian front but Damascus did not.[81] In later years, there is evidence that the contribution of Damascus to imperial campaigns took the form of

[76] Ibıd., pp. 192-193.

[77] Ibid., I, 3, pp. 282-283.

[78] Ibid., p. 300.

[79] Ibid., II, 2, p. 267.

[80] Râşıd, *Tarıh*, IV, 68.

[81] Izzî, *Tarih*, folios 38b-39a.

either extraordinary taxes or the diversion of regular tax revenues from their customary appropriation.[82] Although there is no direct confirmation of the state's shift in policy toward the military obligations of Damascus governors, the weight of the evidence presented here shows that a decided change did take place around the turn of the eighteenth century. Distance from the front lines may partly explain this change, but the fact that neighboring Aleppo, and even Egypt, provided troops shows that this was not the only reason. We can conclude that some pressing need for Damascus governors to stay in the province was the primary cause for the limits placed on their functions. As we shall see shortly, that pressing need was the protection of the pilgrimage and the stabilization of internal security.

Ottoman governors of Damascus during the first half of the eighteenth century no longer enjoyed the mobility that their predecessors had enjoyed in the Ottoman system. Whether this was a direct consequence of not participating in the empire's wars is not known, but there were other consequences that deserve attention. In the classical pattern of career lines, officials of the palace and trainees in the palace school in Istanbul had eventually "graduated" (through a process known as the *çıkma*) to positions in the army, the "feudal" cavalry (*sipahis*), or the provinces.[83] Upward mobility from such positions tended to follow a pattern of rotation from province to province, attainment of the vezirate, a post in the imperial council, and even the grand vezirate. By the late sixteenth century, non-*devşirme* recruits, that is, freeborn Muslims, many of them sons of *paşas*, could enter the palace school and follow a course of training and study that would give them a start in a career of service to the sultan. During the seventeenth century, officials without palace education or experience were given appointments in the provinces and elsewhere in the state system. These successive processes in-

[82] BA-Cevdet/Askeri 29773, dated Rebıyülâhır 1151 (July-August 1738); and BA-Cevdet/Askerı 23302, dated 2 Rebiyülâhır 1194 (7 April 1780).

[83] For a summary table of the graduation process, see Inalcık, *The Ottoman Empire*, p. 82.

volved thousands of Ottomans and have not received the close attention they deserve.[84] Enough is known about them, however, to demonstrate that new routes to high office were created parallel to the palace school. One such route was through the shift of career lines from the bureaucratic to the military class, by which an *efendi*—a scribe-bureaucrat—rose through the ranks to achieve promotion as a *paşa*.[85] This shift was effected through the accepted practice of *intisap*, or patron-client relationship, by which an official attached himself through loyalty and service to a higher official. The client's promotion was tied to the patron's; conversely, a patron's fall from favor and position had the same effect on his client. Another means of mobility was offered by an official's marriage to a member of the imperial family, although this honor could be achieved in the first place only through outstanding service and good connections with a patron. Yet another route to high office—again through *intisap*—was achieved by local landholders and military men in their own provinces. Some of the members of this group were sons of *paşas* and *beys*; others were low-ranking janissaries or members of a *paşa*'s retinue who advanced when their masters were promoted. The latter route to high office was well established by the beginning of the eighteenth century and appears to cover the case of the 'Azm governors of Damascus. Thus, military service and palace education were no longer the exclusive avenues of mobility that they had been in previous centuries. Loyalty to a patron—as well as overall loyalty to the sultan—and marriage into the imperial family were now of considerable influence and importance. It was these two factors that enabled officials posted to faraway provinces to maintain the contacts and status in Istanbul that could advance—or, in some circumstances, hinder—their careers. Desirable as many prestigious governorships may have been, proximity to the capital—and even actual residence and office there—was the ultimate goal of Ottomans ambitious enough

[84] An exception is Metin Kunt, *Sancaktan eyalete*, cited in Note 13 above.

[85] A detailed description of this shift is contained in Itzkowitz, "Mehmed Rāghib Pasha," pp. 121-122.

to desire promotion to the highest office in the empire, the grand vezirate.

Caught in the workings of these processes and having lost the way to mobility through military service, governors of Damascus during the first half of the eighteenth century depended almost exclusively on their connnections in Istanbul to keep them in office. For the 'Azms, it was certainly vital. For the others, it is significant that virtually all received subsequent assignments that were roughly equivalent to the Damascus post or of only slightly greater prestige. None was able to obtain a post in Istanbul from which to rise to the grand vezirate. In order to document this loss of mobility, we have compiled biographic data on each governor of Damascus from 1516 to 1757, that is, from the Ottoman conquest to the pilgrimage disaster that marked the loss of Istanbul's program of provincial reorganization. Because of the limitations of the field and of the sources—Ibn Jum'a's chronicle; a late nineteenth-century Syrian almanac (*Salname*) for names and dates; and the terse biographies of the *Sicill-i Osmanî*—the discussion here is limited to a group of characteristics that can help to explain why the mobility of Damascus governors was so circumscribed. The broader question, among others, of the role of this group in Ottoman society must, perforce, be set aside for future research.

Our main focus will be on the last fifty to seventy-five years of the period between 1516 and 1757. The variables considered are: (1) ethnic-regional background; (2) palace education and/or career; (3) rank and post at start of career; (4) rise to the grand vezirate; (5) marriage into the imperial family; and (6) relative importance of an appointment to Damascus in an Ottoman governor's career. This sample of Damascus governors should not be expected to reflect patterns that may have obtained in other provinces of the empire or in the central administration. That question, though of interest, cannot be answered here. Nonetheless, the variables themselves can, of course, be applied in other cases.

There were 148 governors of Damascus between 1516 and 1757, with 45 of them governing between 1516 and 1600, 75 governing in the seventeenth century, and 28 governing between 1708 and 1757. No biographic data could be found for 22 members of the sample. Almost all of these were from the earlier period, with 9 from the sixteenth century and 10 from the seventeenth century. The figures given must therefore be judged accordingly. Although the sample is divided by centuries, it is obvious that the Ottomans would not have done so. Good arguments may nevertheless be advanced for such a division if we consider the sixteenth century to cover the period roughly from the Ottoman conquest of Damascus to the start of the Celalî rebellions in 1595, and the seventeenth century to end with the Treaty of Karlowitz of 1699. These were major events in Ottoman history: the first marked the breakdown of the *timar* system of land tenure and the disruption of the social order; the second marked the beginning of the brief Ottoman revival that we have described elsewhere. A more refined periodization, though desirable, can only be developed when more detailed data become available.

The variable of ethnic-regional background is of interest simply to demonstrate its extent during the eighteenth century, when local *beys* like the 'Aẓms came to occupy the governorship of Damascus for extended terms. Although members of the ruling class theoretically owed complete loyalty to the sultan regardless of their background, there is no question that ethnic and regional ties were of considerable importance in forging patron-client relationships and in forming political alliances.[86] The subtleties of these ties—often inexplicit and difficult to demonstrate—must be considered within the context of other loyalties developed during an Ottoman's career, such as education, early service, and marriage.[87] Ethnic-regional background had its clearest influence among those recruited into Ottoman service through the levy of "slave boys," the *devşirme*. Within this group, there seem to have been two broad categories: "the Albanians and the Bosnians on the one hand, the 'westerners,' as it were; and, on the other

[86] We rely here on the preliminary research of Kunt, in "Ethnic-Regional (*Cins*) Solidarity in the Seventeenth Century Ottoman Establishment."
[87] Ibid., pp. 238-239.

hand, those from the Caucasus region, the Abazas (Abkhaz), Circassians, and Georgians, making up the 'eastern' group."[88] Data for governors of Damascus tend to confirm this rough division, with sixteen "easterners" (seven Circassian, four Georgian, four Abaza, and one non-*devşirme* Tatar) and twenty-one "westerners" (eleven Albanians, seven Bosnians, two Herzegovinians, and one Croat). It is noteworthy that the "easterners" came to prominence as governors of Damascus in the seventeenth century, confirming the fact that the Ottomans began to intensify recruitment of manpower from the slave markets of the Caucasus and Black Sea region after 1600.[89] Similarly, governors of Damascus whose known origin was Greater Syria, including Aleppo, were prominent only after the end of the seventeenth century. The high number of governors of unknown origin (seventy-eight), however, makes the data inconclusive on these points.

In contrast, the data on palace education or career service are much clearer. Governors without that experience gradually outnumbered the palace-educated, with thirteen in the sixteenth century, thirty-two in the seventeenth century, and sixteen in the eighteenth century up to 1757; as against twenty-two in the sixteenth century, thirty-four in the seventeenth century, and nine in the eighteenth century up to 1757. (No information is available concerning twenty-two governors.) These figures tend to confirm our contention that a palace education did not figure prominently in the background of Damascus governors after 1708, although it was by no means entirely absent.

The same trend shows in the data on the ranks and posts in which governors of Damascus began their careers (see Appendix 1). Those who had a palace education tended to "graduate," first, to positions in the palace, then, during the sixteenth century, to positions in the provinces; after the sixteenth century, they were most often "graduated" directly to the provinces, particularly as *beylerbeyis*. Very few members of our sample began their careers as simple *sipahis* (as did

[88] Ibid., p. 237.

[89] Ibid., pp. 237-238.

Küçük Ahmed for the seventeenth century, a notable exception). Similarly, even fewer governors began at low rank at the local level or shifted careers from the bureaucratic and religious to the military lines. It would appear, then, that the phenomenon of the "*efendi* turned *paşa*"—an important aspect of mobility in the seventeenth and eighteenth centuries for the empire as a whole—was absent from the careers of nearly all Damascus governors. Another aspect of mobility was promotion to the grand vezirate. Of our sample of 148 Damascus governors, only 19 attained this highest office, 7 in the sixteenth century and 12 in the seventeenth century, and none in the eighteenth century.[90] If we leave aside the number of governors in the earlier centuries who were killed in battle during campaigns, we are still left with the vast majority who did not make it beyond the provincial governorship. The explanation for this is to be found both in the qualities of each governor and in the efficacy of his connections with the power brokers in Istanbul. Governors of Damascus and of other far-flung provinces as a rule did not advance far in the Ottoman system to the prestige posts of the imperial capital. Their mobility was, so to speak, limited "by definition." In contrast, the Ottomans who served as governors of Egypt had far better chances of promotion to the grand vezirate, given Egypt's exceptional position in the Ottoman system as a challenging, rebellious, but wealthy province that, if properly governed, would give its governor great prestige. Even the tie of loyalty and favor created by marriage into the imperial family did not assist governors of Damascus in upward mobility, although such marriage increased sharply from the sixteenth to the seventeenth century, from three to ten governors. During the eighteenth century (to 1757), nine governors were so favored at some point in their careers.

[90] There were two exceptions for the eighteenth century: in 1730 and 1757 respectively, Muhsinzâde Abdullah Paşa and Rağıb Mehmed Paşa, without coming to Damascus, were given the post of governor for a few days. Abdullah Paşa received another post within a month and was promoted to the grand vezirate seven years later; Rağıb Paşa was named grand vezir within a few days of his appointment to Damascus.

The last variable—the top post attained in a Damascus governor's career—confirms this limitation of mobility, showing its effect by the eighteenth century. The data fall into three categories: Damascus as the top post attained; positions in Istanbul; and other comparable, or slightly more prestigious, appointments (see Appendix II). A comment about the last category is required. There were over thirty provinces in the Ottoman Empire and the prestigious ones were few: Rumeli (for senior govenors), Anadolu (western Asia Minor), and Mısır (Egypt). Damascus ranked after these three in prestige. Our figures in this category depend, therefore, on this ranking, which may appear arbitrary, but which is derived in part by the relative importance of each province in the careers of successful Ottomans and by the patterns of their promotion. In the Damascus sample, the top post attained was either Damascus itself (especially in the eighteenth century) or the grand vezirate (prior to the eighteenth century).

The preceding analysis—preliminary as it is—demonstrates that a relative decline in mobility during the early eighteenth century affected the careers of governors of Damascus. The decline was the product of trends in the empire as a whole, reorganization of the state after the 1699 debacle and the increase in the number of governors trained outside the palace system. At the same time, it was affected by the suspension of military service for Damascus governors and by the security situation in the province. In short, governors were both freed from outside obligations and restricted in mobility to face problems within the province. The Ottoman state initiated direct measures to reorganize and centralize provincial affairs. These measures constituted the second pattern of change in the governorship of Damascus.

Second Set of Patterns: Provincial Centralization

Like those of the first pattern, the elements of the second were intimately related to one another. In order to achieve internal security and adequate tax revenues to support the pilgrimage, the Ottoman state centralized virtually all provincial affairs in the hands of the governor of Damascus. Such an awesome concentration of power, as we shall see in the next chapter, was also designed to check the influence of three local groups: the notables, janissaries, and tribes. Through a process designed largely to achieve stronger control of the pilgrimage, the Ottomans attempted at the same time to limit the growth of autonomous structures in the province. The violence in Damascus during the first half of the eighteenth century may thus be regarded, in part, as the reaction of these local groups to serious threats to their power and attempts to achieve autonomy.

Beginning in the late seventeenth century, the process of provincial centralization advanced haltingly as the state sought the right combination of powers with which the governor of Damascus could assure the security of the province, the pilgrimage, and control over local groups. By 1708, that process was virtually completed. Thereafter, all governors of Damascus were commanders of the pilgrimage and direct administrators of most of the province's important subunits (*sancaks*). Indeed, these subunits came to be regarded as "appendages" or annexed entities (*mülhakat*) to the governorship of Damascus.[91] In 1734, they were referred to as "old subordinate units" (*mülhakat-ı kadime*) and were so regarded thereafter.[92]

The process of centralization was achieved through considerable experimentation on the part of the central government. For many decades, initiative in all matters relating to the pilgrimage had been left to individual pilgrimage commanders, almost all of whom had been residents of the province of Damascus.[93] Some were tribesmen, such as Qansūh al-

[91] For *mülhakat*, see *TDS*, II, 612.

[92] Sami, Şakir, Subhı, *Tarih*, folio 61a. In 1753, these terms were used in the reappointment of Esat Paşa (al-'Azm). See Hâkim, *Hâkim Tarihi*, folio 50b. Prof. Norman Itzkowitz kindly provided a microfilm copy of this manuscript. In 1760, the same terms were used in BA-Cevdet/Dahıliye 13472, the list of appointments to all provinces cited in Note 19 above.

[93] Bakhıt, "Ottoman Province," pp. 117-118.

Ghazzāwī of 'Ajlūn (1571-1587) and Manṣūr ibn Furaykh (1589-1590). Others were *sançakbeyis* of Nablus or Gaza, such as Aḥmad ibn Riḍwān ibn Ḳara Muṣṭafā (d. 1606) and Farrūkh ibn 'Abd Allāh (d. 1620). In 1692, the state appointed the future semiautonomous ruler of Mecca, Şerif Yahya ibn Barakât, as commander of the pilgrimage, but with disastrous results.[94] Toward the end of the seventeenth century, then, local officials failed to perform their duties to the satisfaction of the state. There were several reasons for this: the ever-increasing costs of the pilgrimage; the greed and embezzlement practiced by some pilgrimage commanders; and the sharp increase in beduin attacks on the caravan. Of all these factors, the last was taken the most seriously by the Ottomans, in the sense that attacks on the pilgrimage threatened both the state's prestige and its sovereignty in the province of Damascus. It could afford, under these circumstances, to overrule the protests of local notables who saw centralization of pilgrimage affairs as a direct threat to their own authority, in the sense that the governor's increased powers could be exercised only at their expense and that the increased costs of the pilgrimage would fall on the whole province rather than only on some of the provincial *sancaks*. One of the loudest protests against centralization came from Sayyid Murād al-Murādī (d. 1720), a Damascene scholar and mystic, whose influence extended to the imperial court at Istanbul.[95]

A critical turning point appears to have occurred in 1693 when 'Assāf, the pilgrimage commander, committed two errors that resulted in disaster. First, he wrongfully extorted money from some Persian pilgrims. Second, he did not prevent the beduin from surrounding the pilgrimage caravan at Hadiyya (about halfway from Mecca to Damascus) and extorting protection money, which was fortunately provided by a Crimean Tatar former prince who happened to be a pilgrim that year.[96] In the following year, Ibşir Ismail Paşa, the

[94] Ibid.; for Şerif Yahya, see Uzunçarşılı, *Mekke-i mükerreme emirleri*, p. 99.

[95] Murādī, *Maṭmaḥ*, folio 26b. The Siena College Arts Division defrayed the costs of microfilming this manuscript.

[96] For the charge of extortion, see Râşid, *Tarih*, II, 113. For protection

governor of Damascus, replaced 'Assāf as commander of the pilgrimage.[97] Also, apparently for the first time, the state was compelled to come to terms with the beduin in a manner that would avoid the appearance of extortion and to enlist beduin assistance and support for the pilgrimage on a regular basis.

The joint appointment of Ibşir Ismail Paşa was not to last, however. In 1695, Kanijeli Osman Paşa became governor of Damascus, only to depart shortly afterward to participate in an imperial campaign. He was replaced by Bozoklu Mustafa Paşa, who later became grand vezir (the last governor of long tenure in Damascus to be so promoted). At the same time, reverting to the practice of appointing a minor official to the pilgrimage command, the state named Hekimbaşı Hayri Mustafa Paşa, the *sancakbeyi* of Gaza.[98] In the two years that followed, Bozoklu Mustafa Paşa remained governor of Damascus, and the pilgrimage command was given, successively, to Mehmed Paşa, the governor of Jidda and Habash (Habeş), and to Arslan Mehmed Paşa, the governor of Tripoli.[99] It was significant that the state should call upon the governor of Jidda, a province remote from Damascus, yet involved in the affairs of the Holy Cities (Jidda was the Red Sea access port for Mecca). It demonstrates that the state experimented by appointing pilgrimage commanders not directly involved in the affairs of Damascus and its neighboring provinces. Also significant is the fact that Mehmed Paşa was allotted the tax revenues of Jerusalem and Gaza with which to finance the pilgrimage. These revenues were called *arpalıks*; that is, they were designated as income credited to a governor outside the province or *sancak* from which they were raised.[100] Arslan Mehmed, on the other hand, was asked to

---

money, *Nusretname*, II, 1, p. 21. The Crimea was at this time a semiindependent state whose ruler, the Tatar *han*, was a vassal of the Ottoman sultan.

[97] Râşid, *Tarih*, II, 250.

[98] *Nusretname*, I, 2, p. 24; Râşıd, *Tarih*, II, 313.

[99] Râşıd, *Tarih*, II, 360, 392.

[100] *TDS*, I, 85. The more commonly recognized beneficiaries of *arpalıks* were retired men of religion and bureaucrats, who received these monies as pensions. See Gibb and Bowen, *Islamic Society*, I, 1, p. 188n; 2, pp. 12, 126.

finance the pilgrimage as best he could in his capacity as governor of Tripoli, because no tax revenues were available in 1696-1697 due to the heavy costs of the disastrous wars then being fought in the Balkans.[101]

For the pilgrimage of 1697-1698, the Ottomans reversed their policy once again, uniting the governorship of Damascus with command of the pilgrimage. This time, Ahmed Paşa Salıh Paşazâde (son of Arap Salıh, a former governor of Damascus) was assigned direct administration and the revenues of four *sancaks* within the province of Damascus: Jerusalem, Gaza, Nablus, and 'Ajlūn. With these revenues, he was expected to finance the pilgrimage.[102] All apparently went well on that year's trip, but Ahmed Paşa is said to have shown concern for financing the next year's caravan.[103] He wrote an unclear letter to the grand vezir in which he complained that the income from the four *sancaks* would prove insufficient for the task. Then, abruptly in the month of Şaban (two months before the scheduled departure of the pilgrimage), Ahmed Paşa, with a retinue of eight men, arrived in Edirne, making an extremely fast, ten-day trip from Damascus. The sultan, upon learning of Ahmed Paşa's arrival, was horrified that the governor of Damascus and commander of the pilgrimage had left his post when he should have been making preparations for the upcoming caravan departure. Infuriated, the sultan ordered Ahmed Paşa's execution on the spot.[104] At a stroke of the sword, Damascus was without a governor and pilgrimage commander. It was not till 14 Şevval (some two months later) that Çerkes Hasan Paşa was named governor of Damascus. In the interim, the governor of Sidon, Kaplan Paşa, was immediately appointed commander of the pilgrimage. His physical proximity to Damas-

[101] Râşıd, *Tarih*, II, 392. [102] Ibid., II, 424

[103] The following account is based on a long passage in *Nusretname*, II, 1, p. 10.

[104] For Ahmed Paşa's execution, see also Râşıd, *Tarih*, II, 478-479. In *Nusretname*, II, 1, p. 10, Ahmed Paşa's name is incorrectly given as "Mehmed"; in a later passage, which repeats the story of the execution (II, 1, p. 18), he is referred to as Ahmed Paşa.

cus is cited by a chronicler as the principal reason for the appointment.[105] Once again, the governorship and pilgrimage command were separated, but not for long.

Three years later (in 1700-1701) Çerkes Hasan was given the joint appointment, only to be the victim of a beduin attack whose consequences were not to be matched until the 1757 disaster. Thirty thousand pilgrims are said to have died in the 1701 attack.[106] Çerkes Hasan was arrested, brought to Edirne, then exiled with a suspended death sentence. Arslan Mehmed of Tripoli was recalled to take both posts and was given a grant of 300,000 *kuruş* toward the expenses of the 1702 pilgrimage.[107]

In the following year, arrangements seem to have become confused, some sources informing us that Mehmed Paşa Kurd-Bayram (also known as Çerkes Mehmed) was appointed as governor and Arslan Mehmed as commander of the pilgrimage.[108] Other sources claim that Kurd-Bayram held both posts, taking command of the pilgrimage shortly after becoming governor of Damascus. In that year, he succeeded in holding off a beduin attack on the caravan.[109] In 1703, Kurd-Bayram was sent to govern Rakka and was replaced by Arnavud Osman, a former Ağa of the janissaries, who was dismissed in mid-year. Once again, the veteran Arslan Mehmed returned to power.[110] Shortly before the pilgrimage caravan departed, however, Arslan Mehmed suddenly died and the state abandoned the joint appointment pattern, giving command of the pilgrimage to Defterdar Mustafa Paşa, governor of Tripoli, and of Damascus to Firari Hüseyin Paşa.[111] Kurd-Bayram returned to the province to command the pilgrimage of 1704-1705. He was also given the tax reve-

[105] Râşid, *Tarih,* II, 478-479; see also *Nusretname*, II, 1, p. 18.

[106] *Nusretname,* II, 1, pp. 83-84.

[107] Ibid., pp. 86-87; Râşıd, *Tarih,* II, 523.

[108] Râşıd, *Tarih,* II, 532.

[109] *Nusretname,* II, 1, pp. 117, 137; Râşid, *Tarih,* II, 536; Ibn Jum'a, "al-Bāshāt," p. 50.

[110] *Nusretname,* II, 2, pp. 201, 206; Râşıd, *Tarih,* III, 91, 109.

[111] *Nusretname,* II, 2, p. 211; Râşıd, *Tarih,* III, 124-125.

nues and direct administration of several *sancaks* (instead of a cash grant from the central government). Once again, it seemed that the state had found the right combination of powers and funds to control Damascus (through Firari Hüseyin) and the pilgrimage (through Kurd-Bayram).[112] Yet, this was not to last. On his journey back from the Holy Cities, Kurd-Bayram was defied by Hüseyin Paşa and some of his military aides in a dispute over marching orders. The result of this petty disagreement was a rout at the hands of the beduin in a sudden attack in which Hüseyin Paşa was killed. The people of Damascus, upon hearing the news, sent, on their own initiative, a complaint to the grand vezir. When the sultan heard what had happened, he ordered Kurd-Bayram's execution. A large force was gathered from provinces near Damascus, but, for some unknown reason, the force hesitated to carry out the sultan's order.[113] Kurd-Bayram held on through the next year's pilgrimage, but, finally seeing that his position was hopeless, he fled to the Crimea.[114]

In the face of a succession of failures, disasters, and unexpected mishaps (such as the death of Arslan Mehmed, who was probably the most effective pilgrimage commander the Ottomans appointed during this period of transformation in provincial affairs), the Ottoman state made two more efforts to bring Damascus and the pilgrimage under control. In 1706, Teberdar Süleyman Paşa, a formidable governor of Jidda and Egypt, was transferred to Damascus with a joint appointment. He was dismissed within a year—not for incompetence, but for abuse of power. Süleyman was accused of wrongfully closing the Damascus bazaars and of instigating a disturbance in Mecca during the pilgrimage in which the escort forces of the Egyptian and Damascene caravans engaged in an unruly brawl over protocol.[115] Reverting briefly in the

[112] *Nusretname*, II, 2, p. 214.

[113] Ibid., II, 2, p. 222; Râşid, *Tarih*, III, 140.

[114] Râşid, *Tarih*, III, 208. Kurd-Bayram presumably enjoyed the Crimean *han*'s protection.

[115] Râşid, *Tarih*, III, 225-226; *Nusretname*, II, 2, p. 236. For the biography of Teberdar Süleyman, see *SO*, III, 72.

next year to the older practice of keeping the governorship separate from the pilgrimage command, the state appointed a veteran local military officer, Kavasoğlu Şamlı Hasan Paşa, a Turkman chieftain, as commander of the pilgrimage, while giving Damascus to Helvacı Yusuf Paşa, a distinguished and experienced Ottoman governor and former grand admiral.[116] This was the last split appointment that the state made.

In 1708, a fateful year for Ottoman rule in Damascus, Nasuh Paşa Osmanoğlu was sent to govern the province and command the pilgrimage. So well did the joint appointment work that, from this time onward, the two offices remained united until the fall of the Ottoman Empire in 1918. No longer, it was hoped, would the initiative in provincial affairs rest in the untrustworthy hands of local officials. Now the pilgrimage—and, by extension, the province of Damascus—would be closely supervised from the imperial center of Istanbul.

By the time Nasuh Paşa appeared on the scene, the gradual transformation of the administrative structure of Damascus had proceeded for nearly twenty years. Nasuh was well known as a valorous and determined servant of the Ottoman state. Probably no better appointment to Damascus could have been made. Very little is known about Nasuh's early career. Born in Güzelhisar, near Manisa in the province of Aydın on the west coast of Anatolia, Nasuh made his first impression in Istanbul through effective leadership of a janissary "suicide squad" (*yeniçeri serdengeçti*) in the *sancak* of Içel.[117] From that post, Nasuh was promoted to administer the tax farm (*muhassıl-lık*) of Aydın in 1703. He retained it until his death in 1714, leaving deputies in Aydın while he governed Damascus.[118]

[116] *Nusretname*, II, 2, p. 236; Râşid, *Tarih*, III, 225-226. For the biography of Yusuf Paşa, see *SO*, IV, 661.

[117] *Nusretname*, II, 1, p. 9. For a brief biography of Nasuh Paşa, see *SO*, IV, 557. A brief but well-grounded study of the man and his career, which emphasizes the wealth Nasuh amassed in his lifetime, is Akalın, "Nasuh Paşa'nın hayatına ve servetine dair."

[118] Çağatay Uluçay, *Eşkiyalık ve halk hareketleri*, p. 274.

During the early eighteenth century, the province of Aydın resembled Damascus in its troubles with tribesmen (in this case, Turkman) who won the sympathy of a populace seeking escape from taxation. Tax collection in the province was vested in a *muhassıl* (not the governor) who resided in Saruhan, one of the province's *sancak* capitals. His deputies or *mütesellims* were stationed in other *sancaks*, which they administered,[119] a pattern similar to the provincial centralization of Damascus, which took completed form after Nasuh's arrival. As in Damascus, the *muhassıl* maintained a large retinue with which to contain rebel tribesmen and the assertive local aristocracy (*ayans*) who attempted to supplant the central government, although with no success until after 1750.[120] It is noteworthy that three eighteenth-century Aydın *muhassıls* became governors of Damascus: Nasuh (1708-1714), Aydınlı Abdullah (1730-1733), and Çelik Mehmed (1760-1761). (One might add Rağıb Mehmed—for four days in 1757—but his case was exceptional because he never went to Damascus). All were renowned for their toughness and administrative skills, but their zeal seems only to have fanned the flames of rebellion and led to an increase in banditry and the flight of Aydın's population to areas controlled by the tribes.

Nasuh Paşa succeeded in 1706 in destroying a small but effective group of bandits from the Kündeşli tribe. He sent the rebels off to exile on the island of Lemnos.[121] The immediate cause of this incident was the failure of local officials to collect income from the *haremeyn vakıfları*, the pious endowments established in the area for the benefit of the poor of Mecca and Medina. Because the Kündeşli were attacking farms and stealing crops, the income from the endowments had dropped drastically. Nasuh's success in correcting the situation no doubt earned him some favor with the *kızlar ağası*, the chief of the sultan's harem and an important power behind the throne, who could make or break grand vezirs. The *kızlar ağası* was also the superintendent of the *haremeyn vakıfları* for the whole

[119] Ibid., pp. 12ff, 56.

[120] Ibid., p. 17.

[121] Ibid., pp. 105-106.

empire. Each year, he organized and dispatched the income of these endowments to Arabia along with the pilgrimage caravan. Because of both his control over these endowments and his influence in appointments to the grand vezirate, the *kızlar ağası* would have much to say about Damascus, whose administration, as we have seen, became increasingly tied to that of the pilgrimage. On 18 August 1708, Nasuh Paşa was assigned the governorship of Damascus. In taking note of this event, the chronicler Râşid refers to Nasuh as a man celebrated for his severity and daring, well suited to command the pilgrimage and to control the province of Damascus.[122] Nasuh's severity, however, was to become tyranny and his daring, open rebellion. No wonder a local Damascus chronicler called this many-sided man "one of the wonders of the world."[123]

Upon arrival in Damascus, Nasuh Paşa quickly set out to restore Ottoman rule in conformity with his mandate. No detail was too small to escape his attention. A shortage of grain and cereals in the provincial capital was effectively dealt with by imports from Aydın. Within a short time, Nasuh created a surplus.[124] In addition, Nasuh's role in weeding out unfit members of the local janissary corps (*yerli kulları*) and in improving communications between Damascus and the Holy Cities of Arabia was of the greatest importance to the restoration of Ottoman authority. The tribes were dealt a particularly severe blow when Nasuh executed Kulayb, who had served for some years as the chief of the tribes that operated in the Syrian desert. It was he who was responsible for the death of Firari Hüseyin Paşa two years before. Known as the *Şam urbanı şeyhi*, and formally appointed by imperial *firman* from Istanbul, Kulayb had abandoned his duties to assist the pilgrimage commander and to transport provisions to the for-

[122] Râşid, *Tarih*, III, 248-249. For the date of Nasuh's appointment, see *Nusretname*, II, 2, p. 245.

[123] Ibn al-Qārī, "al-Wuzarā'," p. 76. Ibn al-Qārī and Haydar Aḥmad al-Shihābī incorrectly refer to Nasuh as "Nāṣīf." Ibn Jum'a, "al-Bāshāt," p. 52, uses the correct name. For Ḥaydar Aḥmad al-Shihābī, see his *Kitāb al-ghurar wa al-ḥisān*, pp. 752-754.

[124] Ibn Jum'a, "al-Bāshāt," p. 52.

tresses along the pilgrimage route. Furthermore, he attacked the caravan on Nasuh Paşa's first pilgrimage. On the pretext of offering to start negotiations, Nasuh lured the beduin chief to a conference tent pitched in the desert between the opposing camps. When Kulayb entered the tent, Nasuh, with a single and brutal stroke of his sword, eliminated the most serious local threat to the pilgrimage,[125] Nasuh's other military operations during his six-year term—against the settled beduin of Balqā and Karak (in Jordan), against the Masā'ūdī beduin, and against the Druzes of the Matn region of Lebanon—resembled his campaigns in Aydın.[126]

As the years passed, the central government became concerned with the unruly behavior and excesses of Nasuh's troops and the high-ranking members of his retinue. What had begun as a campaign of law and order had become a reign of terror. Loath to lose a capable, though cruel, administrator, the state chose to retain Nasuh Paşa and renewed his term of office five times. With each successive renewal, Nasuh demanded and received additional *sancaks* of the province to be placed under his own control or under that of members of his retinue, thus extending the control from Damascus that had begun so tentatively some twenty years before.[127] By 1713, he was governor of Damascus, commander of the pilgrimage, governor of Jidda, and had direct rule, through his retinue, over the *sancaks* of Jerusalem, 'Ajlūn, Gaza, Nablus, Ṣafad, Ba'albak, and Payās near Iskenderun. In the first months of 1713, Nasuh demanded control over the provinces of either Tripoli or Sidon, or, preferably, both. The central government had had enough, however. In December 1713, it ordered Topal Yusuf Paşa, governor of Aleppo and Rakka, to prepare an army to march on Damascus and to execute Nasuh Paşa.[128] These orders must have remained secret, for it was

[125] Ibid.; Ibn al-Qārī, "al-Wuzarā'," p. 76; Râşid, *Tarih*, III, 281-283.

[126] Ibn Jum'a, "al-Bāshāt," p. 53; Shihābī, *Kitāb al-ghurar*, p. 754.

[127] For his last renewal of office, Nasuh obtained the *sancaks* of Jerusalem and Nablus for his son and 'Ajlūn for his top aide, Suleyman. See BA-Cevdet/Dahiliye 1394, dated 7 Cemaziyelevvel 1125 (1 June 1713).

[128] The foregoing details on Nasuh's overextension of his powers are con-

not until two months later, on his return from Arabia with the pilgrimage caravan, that Nasuh learned of the impending attack.[129] He was unable to persuade his troops to make a stand against the 15,000 men—mainly Kurdish and Turkman tribesmen—whom Topal Yusuf had assembled. Nasuh Paşa then gathered a few loyal followers and whatever portable valuables he could and crossed the Jordan River. He hoped to reach the Mediterranean port of Yāfā (Jaffa) to make his escape by sea, but the pursuing army was already close behind him. Within sight of Yāfā, Nasuh was dislodged from his horse when he struck a low-hanging tree branch; he was immediately murdered by Topal Yusuf's troops.

Nasuh was not, as might be supposed, one of the many Ottoman governors who, over the centuries, had launched abortive regional rebellions that failed to establish permanent roots. From the point of view of the Ottoman state's overall policy of reorganizing Damascus—by limiting its governor's functions and by centralizing its affairs—Nasuh Paşa succeeded brilliantly, perhaps too brilliantly. He had, nevertheless, brought to fruition the administrative reorganization begun haltingly some thirty years before. Where once there had been separate appointees governing each of the *sancaks* of the Damascus province—and a separate pilgrimage commander—there was now a single appointee who had direct control over nearly half the *sancaks* and who commanded the all-important pilgrimage as well. That later so many governors were unequal to the task of maintaining the new structure is indicative of the success that Nasuh Paşa attained. Regional forces that could and did create serious problems were to be contained by an administrative framework controlled by the state: the local janissaries, through reduction of numbers and reassignment of duties and the tribes, through mili-

---

tained in the draft order of his execution, an extremely long document in BA-Cevdet/Dahiliye 4305, dated beginning Zilhicce 1125 (19-28 December 1713). A summary of the order is contained in Râşid, *Tarih*, IV, 9.

[129] This account of Nasuh Paşa's downfall is drawn from the following sources: *Nusretname*, II, 2, pp. 312-315; Râşid, *Tarih*, IV, 14-18; Ibn al-Qārī, "al-Wuzarā'," p. 76; Ibn Jum'a, "al-Bāshāt," pp. 54-55.

tary pressure and financial temptation to cooperate in the pilgrimage. Without Nasuh Paşa's legacy, his well-known successors, the 'Aẓms, even with their local roots and long years in office could not have succeeded to the extent they did.

Retrospect: the 'Aẓms and the Governorship of Damascus

The 'Azms' administration of Damascus has been regarded as a virtually unbroken sixty-year monopoly of power, a view encouraged by a narrow focus on that family and the simple arithmetic of accumulated years in office.[130] Somewhat more distinct cases of "dynastic succession" in the Iraqi provinces were the *mamlūk* family of Ahmed Paşa in Baghdad and the Jalīlīs of Mosul. Similarly, the dramatic enfeeblement of the Ottoman governorship of Egypt during the eighteenth century was complemented by the rise to near total power of the local *mamlūk amīrs*. These phenomena have encouraged the generalization that the Arab provinces of the Ottoman Empire, including Damascus, gradually slipped away from Istanbul's control during the eighteenth century. This interpretation is no longer an adequate explanation for events in that province. Indeed, a good argument can be made that the 'Azms were appointed to Damascus precisely because they possessed the qualities that the Ottoman state required for its attempt to reorganize the province. That the manner in which they ruled was often not to the central government's expectations does not justify invoking the broad interpretation of Ottoman decline to explain events in Damascus.

The thesis of Ottoman decline and the corresponding rise of the 'Aẓms has its best representative in Shimon Shamir, who offers two possible causes of the 'Azms' dominance. He considers, first, whether the Ottomans began a new program of provincial appointments during the early eighteenth cen-

[130] Cf. Gibb and Bowen, *Islamic Society*, I, 1, p. 219, among others. Shamir has been the major proponent of this view, which he states succinctly in "As'ad Pasha al-'Azm and Ottoman Rule in Damascus."

tury and, second, whether the rise of the 'Azms "was brought about by contemporary circumstances over which the Ottomans had little control and of which they were scarcely aware."[131] Opting for the latter interpretation, Shamir concludes that the 'Aẓm phenomenon, "a constructive measure by external appearance, was actually another manifestation of the decay endemic in the central government."[132] Shamir has apparently been compelled to accept this thesis because of the weight of his evidence, which focuses narrowly on the 'Aẓm family and on upheavals and disorders in the province of Damascus and its neighbors. His evidence concerning the motives and policies of the central government is understandably less detailed. A broader focus—taking in the preceding two centuries of Ottoman rule in Damascus—would yield a similar pattern of disorders and troubles, these being the stuff of local chronicles, even of the Ottoman court histories. Such a focus would attempt, among other things, to account for these events by seeking the central government's view of provincial affairs, rather than taking refuge in the comfortable assertion of general decay and decline in order to exclude the central government as an actor in provincial affairs.

This discussion of changing patterns in the governorship of Damascus requires a review of the 'Aẓms' place in those patterns. The phenomenon of governors of local origin was by no means a new development, and the 'Aẓms should be regarded less in this light than as a group of governors whose background and skills fit well with Ottoman plans for reorganizing Damascus. Two important points are involved here: first, the disputed ethnic origins of the 'Aẓms and second, the "dynastic" aspects of their history.

For many years, historians have debated the mystery of the 'Aẓms' origins. In spite of contradictory and generally unsatisfactory evidence, students of the problem have allowed themselves to be locked into one of two explanations. The first favors the "Turkish" or Anatolian origin of the 'Aẓms. They are alleged to have been *sipahis* of Turkman extraction

[131] Shamir, " 'Azm Wālīs," p. 250. [132] Ibid., p. 251.

living in Konya. Honored by Sultan Murad IV (reigned 1623-1640) for their part in the Baghdad campaigns, they are said to have settled in Maʿarra, due south of Aleppo. The second explanation holds that the family stemmed from the Banū ʿAzīm tribe of the northern Ḥijāz, served the Ottomans in the sixteenth century by protecting the Damascus-Medina caravan route, and later migrated to Anatolia, then to Maʿarra.[133] What is not in dispute is the fact that the ʿAzms resided in Maʿarra immediately prior to their rise to power in Damascus. The difficulty lies in the family's history during the seventeenth century and its ethnic identity or orientation.

Both Shamir and Rafeq attempt to attach ethnic tags to the family. The former comes to the following conclusion:

> Although none of the views is supported by definite proofs, the latter [that is, the beduin theory] seems to be more acceptable. In the realities of Syria in the seventeenth and eighteenth centuries, it is more likely that a Beduin family in the Ottoman service should become partly turkicized and live for a while in Anatolia than that a Turkish family should seek to derive prestige by falsely attributing its origins to a Beduin tribe.[134]

The difficulty with this assertion is that there is no proof that the ʿAzms themselves claimed to be of beduin origin. In fact, a local origin was attributed to them by local chroniclers in what may have been a post facto "adoption" of the ʿAẓms by the Damascenes.[135]

After carefully reviewing the available evidence, Rafeq opts

[133] Scholarly discussions on these theories of origin are: ibid., pp. 22ff, and Rafeq, *Province*, pp. 85-90, in favor of the local or beduin origins; ʿAbd al-Qādir al-ʿAzm, the family historian, who takes a noncommittal position and briefly presents both theories in his *al-Usra al-ʿAzmiyya*, pp. 3-4; and a brief defense of the Anatolian theory by Mücteba Ilgürel, in his review of Rafeq, *Province*, in *Tarih Enstitüsü Dergisi*, I (1970), 275-276.

[134] Shamir, " ʿAzm Wālīs," pp. 23-24.

[135] Ibn al-Qārī, "al-Wuzarāʾ," p. 77, calls the first ʿAẓm a *fallāḥ*, or peasant, with a noticeable touch of the city man's disdain for people from the country such as the ʿAzms of Maʿarra. Mikhāʾīl Burayk (Breik) refers to the ʿAzms as *awlād al-ʿArab*. See his *Tārīkh*, p. 36.

for the local-origin theory without committing himself to the beduin part. He cites an early eighteenth-century local chronicler, Ibn Mīrū, who states that Ismail Paşa's father was a soldier who settled in Ma'arra during the second half of the seventeenth century. We might add that the alleged migration of the 'Aẓms from Anatolia to Ma'arra and their military background, as attested to by Ibn Mīrū, would seem to conform to a trend that had prevailed since the Celalî revolts of 1595-1606. At that time, a number of rebellious *sipahis* from central and eastern Anatolia migrated to northern Syria. The arrival of an imperial janissary force in Damascus in 1660 to check the power of the local janissaries was another instance of population shift that threw together many ethnic groups in Syria. In this light, it seems that the process that Shamir suggests—a beduin family's move to Anatolia—would have been highly unlikely.

Rafeq presents important evidence regarding the eighteenth-century 'Aẓms as a local family of rural notables. He cites Ibn al-Qārī's description of the family as peasants (*fallāḥīn*), as well as French consular reports from Sidon that state that Süleyman liked rural life; that the family, after Ismail's dismissal in 1730, was only too glad to return to the countryside; that Sadeddin was "un autre pacha arabe de nation"; and that Mehmed was of an Arab family.[136] The Christian chronicler, Breik, states that the 'Azms were "Arabs" (*awlād al-'Arab*) from the Arab lands (*al-bilād al-'Arabiyya*), by which he means the territory extending from Antioch to 'Arīsh in Sinai.[137] This is important contemporary evidence that shows that the 'Aẓms were regarded as a local patrician family. Rafeq rightly treats these statements with great caution, especially the epithet "Arab," which he takes to mean "local" as opposed to Ottoman.[138] According to Rafeq, it is in this sense that Mehmed Rağıb Paşa, who briefly succeeded Esat Paşa (al-'Aẓm) in Damascus before being called to the grand vezirate, is said to have referred to Esat, then governor of Aleppo,

[136] Rafeq, *Province*, pp. 89-90.
[137] Burayk (Breik), *Tārīkh*, pp. 35-36.
[138] Rafeq, *Province*, pp. 88-89.

as "a peasant, son of a peasant" (*fallāḥ ibn fallāḥ*), when the latter allegedly refused to sell him some provisions needed for the pilgrimage.[139] Rafeq's evidence for this incident is derived from a single source, Patrick Russell, a doctor resident in Aleppo.[140] What probably transpired was as follows: when Rağıb Paşa became grand vezir, he wished to dislodge Esat entirely from Syria, sensing the danger that a jealous Esat might pose to Mekkizâde Hüseyin, the new governor of Damascus. In an order dated one week after Rağıb became grand vezir, Esat was instructed to go to Egypt as its new governor and to dispatch that province's annual tribute (the *Mısır irsaliye hazinesi*) to Istanbul. For this purpose, a ship from the Mediterranean branch of the imperial fleet was to dock at Iskenderun, Aleppo's seaport, and to take Esat to Alexandria.[141] Esat refused to go and remained in Aleppo until he was dismissed some months later. Mehmed Rağıb's angry epithet probably referred less to Esat's rural origins than to Rağıb's belief that Esat had ceased to uphold the Ottoman ruling class ideal of service to the faith and to the state. This incident, if true, seems to indicate that the central government regarded the 'Azms as part of the Ottoman establishment, notwithstanding their local roots.

As stated at the outset, the evidence of ethnic origins is extremely sketchy and does not justify total acceptance of either of the theories developed. We may speculate, however, that the 'Aẓms expertly manipulated both stories to their own advantage. There is evidence, for example, that, in spite of Süleyman's love of country life, he knew not a word of Arabic;[142] whereas Mehmed was apparently thoroughly

[139] Ibid., p. 87.

[140] For a description of Russell's *A Natural History of Aleppo*, see Hachicho, "English Travel Books about the Near East," pp. 48-50.

[141] BA-Cevdet/Dahiliye 1360, memorandum to the sultan, approved on 15 Cemaziyelâhır 1170 (7 March 1757). Rağıb Paşa became grand vezir on 8 Cemaziyelâhır. See Itzkowitz, "Mehmed Rāghib Pasha," p. 141. The memorandum stated that it was appropriate to transfer Esat to a faraway post (*baid bir mansıb'a nakl ve tahvil muktaza olmak*. . .).

[142] Shamir, " 'Azm Wālīs," p. 71, n. 2: the French consul in Sidon "reported that he could not dispatch the *dragoman* of Acre with a message to

Arabized.[143] Possessing a deep knowledge of provincial affairs and extensive local connections with all levels of society—the religious elite, the minorities, and the European merchants and diplomats—the 'Aẓms were also exposed to the Ottoman way—the high culture, connections, and ethos of the empire's ruling elite. The order appointing Esat to Damascus makes the latter point quite clear: Esat was regarded as the product of an Ottoman education provided by his father (Ismail) and uncle (Süleyman), which led him to acquire the precepts of Islam, win the right to bear responsibility, and the right to achieve the vezirate.[144] He did not, by implication, win this right through dynastic inheritance, but was, instead, put to the test by his masters in Istanbul. This evidence leads directly to the question of dynastic succession.

Three characteristics marked the alleged dynastic hold of the 'Azms on the Syrian provinces of the Ottoman Empire: local roots that provided an independent base of power; long tenure of office; and appointments of members of the family to the neighboring provinces of Sidon and Tripoli, in addition to Damascus.[145] Based on these characteristics, Shamir maintains that the 'Aẓms became so paramount in provincial affairs that their hold on office was established virtually by right of inheritance. In the broader perspective of Ottoman provincial administration, however, the 'Aẓms do not stand out as a unique group of autonomous governors, but are representative of developments in the structure of the Ottoman ruling elite over the preceding two centuries. Without denying the family's special character—its skillful blend of Ottoman and local traditions—it is possible to rectify the distortion with which the 'Aẓms have been viewed.

Shamir infers from the fact of local origins that the 'Aẓms

Sulaymān because Sulaymān did not speak Arabic (which was the *dragoman's* proficiency)."

[143] Murādī, *Silk*, IV, 97-102.

[144] BA-Cevdet/Dahiliye 5468, draft appointment letter (*berat*), dated 25 Receb 1156 (14 September 1743). A similar passage appears in Sami, Şakir, and Subhi, *Tarih*, folios 222b-223a.

[145] Shamir, "As'ad Pasha al-'Azm," p. 2.

had a golden opportunity to establish themselves in the area, unlike other Ottoman governors who, during their careers, moved rapidly from province to province throughout the empire. Although there is no question that this inference is correct, it cannot suggest that the dynamics of Ottoman political life did not apply to the 'Azms. On the contrary, Shamir unintentionally calls attention to the fact that they were compelled—just like other Ottomans—to seek patronage and protection in Istanbul and elsewhere. For example, Esat Paşa early in his career secured the tax farm of Ḥamā with the support of Bekir Paşa, then governor of Jidda.[146] The latter was a man of great influence at court: when he retired from Ottoman service, he proceeded to Istanbul and was received there by the grand vezir and the imperial council. His son Iskender Paşa was named to succeed him at Jidda.[147]

The case of Bekir Paşa's son and his appointment bears a striking resemblance to that of the 'Azms. In fact, it suggests that we should regard the 'Azms as simply another successful family of Ottoman governors within the Ottoman tradition. In this connection, one may ask whether previous governors of Damascus had traditions of family rule. It is interesting that, although the individuals cited admittedly lacked comparable tenure of office, the results meet—to a certain degree in every case—Shamir's criteria of local origin or connections and appointments of relatives to Tripoli or Sidon. Ahmed Paşa, the governor of Damascus in 1697-1698, was the son of Arap Salıh, also a governor of Damascus (1685-1686). The latter came from a prominent Tripoli family of Albanian origin.[148] He began his career as a *beylerbeyi* and rose to be governor of Tripoli and commander of the pilgrimage before his promotion to Damascus, whereupon he appointed his son as *mutasarrıf* of the *sancak* of Nablus and made him commander of the pilgrimage. A similar case is Arslan Mehmed Paşa's. From Jabala in Tripoli province, he held the Damascus and

[146] Ibid., p. 3. For a biography of Bekir Paşa (Abū Bakr ibn Ibrāhīm al-Rūmī), see Murādī, *Silk*, i, 49.

[147] Samı, Şakır, and Subhı, *Tarih*, folio 179a.

[148] *SO*, iii, 203-204; *Nusretname*, i, 3, p. 330.

pilgrimage posts several times at the end of the seventeenth century. His brother Kaplan Paşa simultaneously held the Sidon governorship and succeeded him as commander of the pilgrimage.[149] Nasuh Paşa's appointment of his fifteen-year-old son as *mutasarrıf* of Jerusalem also shows that the ʻAzm phenomenon was not unique by any means.[150] Similarly, Çerkes Osman, the immediate predecessor of the first ʻAzm governor of Damascus, had his son Ali Bey appointed in charge of the relief force that escorted the pilgrimage caravan on its return to Damascus.[151]

This series of cases fits with the general Ottoman pattern of elite careers. By the eighteenth century, important factors in the pattern were *hemşehrilik* (nepotism among those from a common place of origin), *intisap* (patron-client relationships), and the succession of sons in the footsteps of their fathers. These phenomena have been acknowledged for the bureaucratic and religious careers and the janissary segment of the military career.[152] Their gradual extension to the governorship was a natural development, as was the rise of the ʻAẓms as a family of governors. Shamir's undue emphasis on Esat's succession to the governorship of Damascus "both by right of inheritance and his own merit" (a translation of an Ottoman chronicler's phrase, *irsen ve iktisaben*) is misplaced.[153] Although the phrase can mean "by right of inheritance," it may also be taken to mean "by heritage." In other words, Esat's appointment recognized his membership in the Ottoman elite; it also recognized his competence.

The ʻAzms were logical instruments to continue the Ottoman reorganization of the province of Damascus that began in the late seventeenth century. That they tended to serve themselves more than the state was partly the reason for the

[149] *Nusretname*, II, 1, p. 18; Râşıd, *Tarih*, II, 478-479. For the biography of Arslan Mehmed, see *SO*, I, 320.

[150] *Nusretname*, II, 2, pp. 312-315.

[151] Âsım, *Âsim Tarihi*, pp. 95-96.

[152] Itzkowitz, "Ottoman Realities," pp. 91-93.

[153] Shamır, "Asʻad Pasha al-ʻAzm," p. 5, citing Sami, Şakir, and Subhı, *Tarih*, folio 223a. Cf. BA-Cevdet/Dahıliye 5468, cited in Note 144 above.

failure of Ottoman policy by the mid-eighteenth century. Rather than a sign of provincial autonomy, the rise of the ʿAẓms was more nearly representative of trends among the Ottoman ruling elite. The ʿAzms may have dominated the scene during their long years in office, but this was due to their service in the execution of policies determined outside Damascus and spanning a period far longer than their own.

TWO

CONTAINMENT OF PROVINCIAL GROUPS: NOTABLES, JANISSARIES, AND TRIBESMEN

THROUGHOUT most of its history, the Ottoman state employed both direct and subtle forms of persuasion, such as mass deportations, direct military measures, and financial or personal inducements, to control influential groups in the provinces. These methods produced different effects, an example of which is offered by the following incident. A young Ottoman officer once received command of one of several military units engaged in containing rebels in the Ḥawrān area of Syria. In his heart, he opposed destruction of villages and extortion of tax "arrears" from the population—methods much favored by his fellows and superiors. Through his courage, quick thinking, and personal diplomacy, he won the respect and sympathy of many rebels. One day, the Ottoman camp at Buṣrā, a large town in the Ḥawrān, was busy with military training exercises. Suddenly, a large rebel force attacked the camp. The Ottoman commander, although expert at repressive measures, did not have time to prepare a defense. He asked the young officer what to do. "Continue your exercises," the latter replied. "But don't you see, they're attacking us," cried the dumbfounded commander. "Yes, I see," the former said, "but I know these people; they are honorable. They will not attack those who do not use their weapons." Taking his subordinate's advice, the commander was astonished when the rebels halted their attack. When peace talks were proposed, the young officer represented the Ottoman side. He befriended the rebel chiefs and defused a potentially explosive situation.

For centuries, incidents such as that at Buṣrā had been the

stuff of the daily lives of Ottoman administrators. In this case, however, the situation was different. The year was 1905, the Ottoman Empire was close to collapse, and the Ottoman officer was no ordinary man. His name was Mustafa Kemal, later known as Atatürk.[1]

It is useful to remember that the maintenance of public order was a more or less constant preoccupation of Ottoman provincial governors and their retinues throughout the history of the empire, not just during the sixteenth century, when Ottoman power was at its peak. Right from the beginning, for example, the Ottoman conquest of Syria was more difficult and tiring for the Ottoman army than is generally believed.[2] During the late seventeenth and early eighteenth centuries, however, the number and intensity of violent incidents in the Syrian provinces rose sharply. The once well-ordered local janissaries (*yerli kulları*), assimilated descendants of some of the Ottoman soldiers who conquered Syria, clashed with their imperial counterparts (*kapı kulları*), newcomers who occupied the Damascus citadel after 1660. Turkman tribes created disturbances north of Damascus. And, to the south and southeast, large numbers of beduin moved in from the Arabian peninsula to threaten the peasant population as never before. The widely accepted interpretation of these events has stressed the weakness of Ottoman control as the principal cause for the high rate of violence and disturbance. It is taken for granted that there was a vacuum at the center of the empire that encouraged regional forces to assert themselves and to compete for the power supposedly relinquished by the state. Istanbul, then, had little to say or do in dealing with local groups. It was a "constant" in a field of change in the

[1] Ataturk's experiences in Syria, where he participated in forming the *Vatan ve Hürriyet* movement after the Buṣrā incident, are contained in Âfet (A. Âfetınan), "Atatürk'ü dınlerken: Vatan ve Hürriyet." An account of disturbances in the Hawrān during this period is contained in Saliba, *Wilāyat Sūriyya, 1876-1909*, pp. 154-217 passim.

[2] Haydar Çelebı, *Haydar Çelebi Ruznamesi*, pp. 99ff. For details of resistance in Syria to the Ottoman conquest, see Bakhit, "Ottoman Province," pp. 13ff and especially pp. 16-17.

provinces, rather than an entity that was also capable of change, and of action.

The argument here attempts to shed new light on the role of the central government in containing provincial groups in the Damascus of the first half of the eighteenth century. Disturbances in the province may thus be seen as symptoms—among others—of the struggle to revise the structure of government in an important Ottoman province, rather than merely as the "decay" of the order of centuries or simply as the rebelliousness that preceded Ottoman reform and the "impact of the West" during the following century. In order to make secure the changes they effected in the provincial governorship of Damascus and the reorganization of the annual pilgrimage, the Ottomans were compelled to come to terms with three substantial provincial groups: the notables, the janissaries of the major towns, and the tribes in the countryside. These attempts worked with mixed success until the pilgrimage disaster of 1757 and began to show distinct signs of failure thereafter. The patterns of violence in the province stemmed in large part from competition of local groups for favored places in the revised provincial order during a period of recurrent economic and social instability. Rather than rebelling against the Ottoman state, local groups were, instead, trying to assert their place in the provincial system. After the middle of the century, as the central government increasingly failed to maintain the system designed for Damascus, local groups came gradually to displace the representatives of central authority and to challenge them successfully in government functions.

The Notables: Provincial Patricians

The notable estate has attracted a good deal of attention in recent years, as scholars have sought the Ottoman background of the nineteenth and twentieth-century history of the Arab lands. The notables have been regarded as the seedbed of new political ideas and regional political developments. This "backward" projection of notable strength from the end to the beginning of the eighteenth century obscures the attainment by that estate of resources and continuity to match those of the central authority. As available evidence indicates, this attainment took place in the last two decades of the eighteenth century, not before. In light of this fact, it is necessary to make some distinctions between the notable estate of 1700 and its much strengthened counterpart of 1800. A brief review of the historical literature on the notables is therefore in order.

Sustained interest in the notable estate has developed in the last thirty years. Several influential scholars— I. H. Uzunçarşılı, H.A.R. Gibb, Harold Bowen, and, most recently and cogently, Albert Hourani—have attempted to give general accounts of the rise of the notables in the late seventeenth and eighteenth centuries.[3] In the process, a good deal of confusion has arisen as to the relative strength and weakness of this group in various times and places and the terminology applied to it. Notables, *ayans*, and *derebeys* are the terms most frequently used, although now it is believed that the *derebeys* were openly rebellious, and the *ayans* were more like "overmighty subjects." In this respect, the prominence of Ẓāhir al-'Umar, a leading tax farmer and rural political leader in northern Palestine (then part of Sidon province) and the attempts by Damascus governors to dislodge him (which finally succeeded in 1775) may be explained: Zāhir was more like a rebel than an "overmighty subject," and was beyond the reach of the state for the better part of his career. The distinction is not absolute, but it has some significance, as we shall see later.

Uzunçarşılı argues that the *ayans* had long existed as a recognized entity in Islamic societies. In Islamic literatures, especially Arabic, they were treated as proper subjects of great biographical dictionaries. Here, the all-inclusive term *ayan* did not denote a distinct social group, but, instead, worthy and well-known persons—most often ulema, but not always

[3] Uzunçarşılı, "Ayan," *IA*, II, 41-42; H. Bowen, "A'yān," *EI*², I, 778; Gibb and Bowen, *Islamic Society*, I, 1, pp. 198-199, 211, 256-257, 303; Hourani, "Ottoman Reform and the Politics of Notables," pp. 41-64.

so—who were recognized for their pious manner of life and literary fame. In the Ottoman Empire, before the end of the seventeenth century, notables were recognized simply as famous men, or notables in the broadest sense. The common phrase employed in official correspondence was *ayan-ı vilayet ve is erleri*, or "notables of the *vilâyet* and elders of affairs."[4] They were allegedly appointed by imperial rescript after selection within their towns of residence, although the process of selection is still unknown. According to Uzunçarşılı, the *ayans* came to prominence as a distinct political and social force towards the end of the seventeenth century when the central government, hard-pressed to raise revenue for war, began to reorganize tax farms in the provinces and to grant them in increasing numbers to the *ayans* for life (as *malikâne*). The *ayans* benefited from this arrangement, Uzunçarşılı says, because they alone had the financial resources to make the substantial down payments to secure the tax farms. With large incomes at their disposal, the notables could also hire mercenaries to establish their claims to local administration and to deflect any attempt by provincial governors to bring them under control. By the late eighteenth century, several local notables in the Balkan provinces actually became provincial governors and ruled those provinces virtually independently of central authority. The same process prevailed to a greater extent in nearly the whole of Anatolia. Sultan Mahmud II (1808-1839), in a series of campaigns, largely succeeded in bringing these notable "dynasties" under central control. It is significant that the individual *ayans* cited by Uzunçarşılı were active at the end of the eighteenth century, particularly after 1792. Uzunçarşılı's focus on the late eighteenth century seeks to explain the particular situation of the notables of that period and after: a local group roughly equal in standing to central authority and indispensable to its financial and military strength.

Harold Bowen, in his brief encyclopedia article, largely repeats Uzunçarşılı's ideas. With Gibb, he goes somewhat fur-

[4] Gibb and Bowen, *Islamic Society*, I, 1, pp. 198 and n. 9.

ther. He attributes the flight of the peasant population and desertion of landholdings to the greed and rapacity of the *ayans* in their tax-collecting functions.[5] He seems to assume that this occurred throughout the eighteenth century. Other scholars have used Uzunçarşılı's and Gibb and Bowen's ideas in their own research. They accept them and seem to feel that the history of the *ayans* in the Ottoman Empire has been thoroughly worked out. In fact, although scholars have made some valuable studies of individual *ayans* in specific areas, they have shed little light on the changing relations between the *ayans* and central authority on a broad, comparative scale.[6] These relations are still assumed to have been one-sided or nonexistent, as the case may be, in that provincial notables acted more or less as they pleased, whereas the central government did little or nothing to check their growing power.

Albert Hourani, on the other hand, has recently attacked the problem more concretely. According to Hourani, three conditions are necessary for the rise of what he calls, after Max Weber, the "patriciate." The first occurs "when society is ordered according to relations of personal dependence—the artisan in the city producing mainly for patrician patrons, and the peasant in the countryside, whether nominally free or not, also producing mainly for a landowner, either because he cannot otherwise finance himself or because the landowner holds the key to the urban market."[7] When the notables enjoy the political backing of their respective urban areas and can dominate the hinterland, the second condition is fulfilled. Finally, if the urban areas are either self-governing or influence a larger political entity—usually a monarchy—the notables

[5] Ibid., pp. 198-199, 256-257.

[6] Two studies that focus partly on these problems are Uzunçarşılı, *Meşhur Rumeli ayanlarından*; and Sadat, "Ayan and Ağa," which deals with the career of Osman Paşa Pasvanoğlu.

[7] Hourani, in "Ottoman Reform," p. 45, presents both a program for future research and a model for the historical evolution of the notable estate. But here too the emphasis is on the period from 1760 to 1860, and especially from 1820 onward, with such developments as the provincial councils and the role of the notables in modernization of political ideas.

have "freedom of political action."[8] In other words, the notables of the Ottoman Empire fulfilled an intermediary role between the central government and the provincial population. They taxed the peasantry and derived social and political power from the urban areas. At the same time, they derived their positions, their authority, from the central government.

Hourani divides the notable estate into three broad categories. First, there were the members of the local religious establishment, who, by dint of their membership, had strong connections with their counterparts throughout the empire and, by marriage, with the merchants of the major towns and cities. Second, there were the janissary garrison chiefs, who had communication channels to Istanbul independent of provincial governors and who derived strength from their hereditary positions, the support of local auxiliaries, and marital ties with local families. Third, there were the "secular notables," who were not formally on the state payroll as religious, bureaucratic, or military officials, but whose past family history included either such positions or the "control of agricultural production through possession of *malikanes* or supervision of *waqfs*."[9]

Albert Hourani's model has yet to be widely applied to individual provinces of the Ottoman Empire. From what is generally known, however, it seems that the second and third categories of notables—military officers and "secular notables"—were far stronger in the Balkan provinces during the late eighteenth century and influenced events in Istanbul to a much greater degree than did their counterparts in, say, Damascus or Aleppo. On the other hand, the Anatolian *derebeys* would have to be excluded from the category of notables, by Hourani's definition, because they did not serve as intermediaries between state and society but sought to displace the state on the local level.[10] Hourani finds the "purest" form of

[8] Ibid.

[9] Ibid., p. 49.

[10] The assumed exclusion of the *derebeys* is not widely accepted. For instance, see J. H. Mordtmann and Bernard Lewis, "Derebey," *EI*², II, 206-208. The prime example of a *derebey* given in this article is Alemdar Mustafa Paşa, a Balkan *ayan*. This terminological problem needs further exploration.

notables in the cities of Syria and the Hijāz, with which he is intimately acquainted as a historian. In those cities, the notables served the state as buffers for the grievances and complaints of urban society. As Hourani writes elsewhere, "It was only through the mediation of [the notables] that the Ottoman Empire was still able to keep some sort of moral and material hold on its subjects."[11]

In summary, the notables of the Ottoman Empire increased their political power at the end of the eighteenth century and into the nineteenth century as the central government struggled to adjust itself to the twin threats of external pressure and internal disintegration. But, during the first half of the eighteenth century, the central government contained the notables' political ambitions in the province of Damascus. This containment was an important part of the Ottoman policy that reorganized the provincial governorship and the pilgrimage. Seen in this light, the long-accepted, artificial distinction between periods of "strong" and "weak" Ottoman rule—between the age of Süleyman the Magnificent and the centuries that followed—becomes inadequate. Instead, the following chronology for Damascus might provide a better historical sense of the notables' evolution: (1) from 1516 to 1595 might be considered the "classical" age, during which the notables conformed to the norms established by Süleyman the Magnificent;[12] (2) 1595 to 1699 constituted a long period of flux during which the notables first tested their strength vis-à-vis the central authority and won important tax concessions and increased control of imperial *vakıfs*;[13] (3) 1699 to 1758 was a period of resurgent Ottoman control that witnessed a revived provincial governorship that attempted to check notable strength; (4) the period from about 1760 onward was characterized by Istanbul's waning influence and increasing dependence on the notables as semiindependent surrogates

[11] Hourani, "The Ottoman Background of the Modern Middle East," p. 47.

[12] Inalcık, *The Ottoman Empire*, p. 161.

[13] Suggested in ibid., p. 148.

rather than as intermediaries, in the provinces.[14] Even this last phase, however, does not justify assuming an absence of central control in Damascus or the total autonomy of its notables. As Hourani writes,

> On the one hand, Ottoman authority remained real; it *had* to be a reality, because its legitimacy, in the eyes of the Muslim world, was bound up with its control of the Holy Cities and the pilgrim routes, and also because it was control of the Fertile Crescent which determined that Istanbul, not Cairo or Isfahan, should dominate the heart of the Muslim world. Although this authority might appear to be ceded to a local group, as with the 'Azms in Damascus throughout most of the eighteenth century, it could be taken back, either by the time-honored method of setting one governor against another, or by direct military methods: the imperial road to Syria and the Hijaz lay open.[15]

There were, however, more subtle methods than the encouragement of petty feuds between governors or military attack. If it is agreed that the notables' power stemmed as much from recognition by the central government as from local support, then the former requires further investigation. Two aspects of the role of Damascene notables in the first half of the eighteenth century should be considered. The first is the means employed by the central government to limit the influence of that estate. The second concerns the notables' political activity, illustrated by the career of Fethi Efendi. Of all the Damascus notables of the period, the latter came closest to es-

[14] Suggested by Karpat, "The Transformation of the Ottoman State." Prof. Karpat (p. 245) contrasts what he calls the "conflicting group ideologies" of the *ayan* and the "bureaucratic order," by which he means the central government. These ideologies "formed . . . the central dynamics of the internal transformation which occurred in Ottoman society in the eighteenth and early nineteenth centuries. . . ." and resulted in a dichotomy between state and society.

[15] Hourani, "Ottoman Reform," p. 52.

tablishing the independent provincial power base characteristic of successful notables in the Balkans during the later eighteenth century.

In the Damascus of the first half of the eighteenth century, the Ottoman state employed three methods to limit the notables' power: (1) inducements of state income and positions; (2) encouragement of the gradual ascendancy of the official Ottoman religious rite, the Ḥanafī, at the expense of the local, traditional rite, the Shāfiʿī, the effect of which was to limit the local autonomy of the religious establishment; and (3) in extreme cases, exile and imprisonment of troublesome notables.

Appointment to state posts implied relations of dependence that, although not absolute, gave office holders both status and some freedom of action locally. This problem merits brief discussion, if only for clarification. Because of their intermediate status, neither wholly Ottoman nor entirely regional, Damascene notables varied widely in their cultural orientation and notions of self-identity. A working definition of an Ottoman—a person with the highest status in society—emphasizes three fundamental traits: service to the Muslim faith, service to the state in a post conferring an income and tax exemptions, and the practice of Ottoman language and customs.[16] In respect to the third trait, the notables of Damascus were not wholly faithful, and understandably so. They were, first and foremost, Arabic speaking, and they were far from Istanbul, the center of Ottoman Turkish culture. Nevertheless, a significant proportion of Damascene notables—especially those in the religious establishment—were familiar with the "Ottoman way" (*edeb-i Osmanî*), either through education, knowledge of Turkish (less so of Persian), travel, or through correspondence. The number of such people is perhaps less impressive on first sight than are their actual accomplishments.

Several examples illustrate the degree to which Damascus notables participated in the intellectual, religious, and political life of the Ottoman Empire. Abū Bakr ibn Bahrām al-

[16] Itzkowitz and Mote, *Mubadele*, p. 11.

Dimashqī, a native of Damascus and an outstanding mathematician, obtained the favor of one of his students in Istanbul, the future grand vezir, Köprülüzâde Fazıl Ahmed. He joined the religious establishment with a teaching post in the Süleymaniye mosque in Istanbul. After serving briefly as *kadi* of Aleppo, he returned to Istanbul, where he taught until his death. Another of his outstanding pupils was Kara Mustafa Paşa, who, as grand vezir, led the second siege of Vienna (1683). Abū Bakr is best remembered for his translation of the *Atlas Major*, a geographical work first published in 1662 in the Netherlands, and for his work in completing Kâtip Çelebi's *Cihannümâ*, an Ottoman geographical survey.[17] Another born Damascene (though by family origin from Aleppo) was Ibrāhīm ibn Muṣṭafā al-Ḥalabī (d. 1776). After receiving his education in Damascus from 'Abd al-Ghanī al-Nābulsī (d. 1731)—probably the most famous scholar in Syria during Ottoman times—Ibrāhīm moved to Egypt, where he led a chorus of complaints against Süleyman Paşa (al-'Aẓm), governor of Egypt (1738-1741) and twice governor of Damascus. To make his point more forcefully, Ibrāhīm traveled to Istanbul and met with the chief of the chancery bureaus (*reisülkuttap*), Mehmed Rağıb Efendi, a future grand vezir (1757-1763). He so impressed the scholars of Istanbul that he remained in the capital until his death. Among his students were Mehmed Rağıb and several future *şeyhülislams*, or chief jurisconsults of the empire.[18]

The two examples cited so far concern men of Damascene origin who earned their fame outside their home city. It may be argued that such men were exceptions and that the vast majority of notables—particularly those in the religious establishment—remained bound by the Arabic culture of Damascus. There is no question that Damascene notables had a sense of contrast between their own regional cultural tradi-

[17] Adıvar, *Osmanlı Türklerinde Ilım*, pp. 137-140, 152. Adıvar regrets that no reliable biography of Abū Bakr is available. However, see Murādī, *Silk*, I, 50-51, from which we learn of Abū Bakr's influence on Köprülü and Kara Mustafa.

[18] Murādī, *Silk*, I, 37-39.

tion and that of Istanbul. The biographer Murādī, for instance, always took pains to emphasize that contrast by referring to Ottoman practice with the phrase, "as was their custom." In the notice about his uncle, Ibrāhīm, whose promising career in Istanbul was cut short by an early death, Murādī states; "he did not advance in the schools [as a teacher], as was their custom [that is, the Ottoman *medrese* system], because he died."[19] Murādī refers to the Ottoman "graduation" process (the *çıkma*) in the same manner. "As was their [the Ottomans'] custom, he graduated with a post in the *hacegân* [the top rank of bureau chiefs]."[20] Murādī's emphasis on the difference between the Damascus religious establishment and that of Istanbul does not, however, warrant the generalization by Gibb and Bowen that "even the aristocratic families among the *'ulemâ* of Damascus, though in frequent relations with the Turkish *'ulemâ* and inter-marrying with Turkish families, resented the introduction of Turkish usages, and only those who had studied in Constantinople were familiar with the Turkish language."[21] Gibb and Bowen's evidence consists of two biographies in Murādī that neither explicitly nor implicitly indicate any such resentment,[22] much less the fact that Damascene scholars could not learn Turkish in Damascus. In fact, there is evidence from the early eighteenth century that shows the opposite is true. Ibrāhīm ibn Ṣārī Haydar taught Turkish and Persian to the children of Damascene notables.[23] A Medinese scholar, Ibrāhīm al-Khiyārī, stopped in Damascus during a trip to Anatolia and met with Sulaymān al-Maḥāsinī, notable, historian of the

[19] Ibid., II, 25. On the *çıkma*, see Inalcık, *The Ottoman Empire*, pp. 84-85.

[20] Murādī, *Silk*, II, 60, biography of Hüseyin Maanoğlu, son of Fakhr al-Dīn II, prince of Lebanon. Hüseyin was captured by the Ottomans and trained in the Ottoman tradition. He became ambassador to India and an important Ottoman historian. Naima's account of Maanoğlu's life does not refer to a post in the *hacegân*. See the text translated in Thomas, *A Study of Naima*, p. 30, and M. Cavid Baysun, "Ma'n," *IA*, VII, 271-272.

[21] Gibb and Bowen, *Islamic Society*, I, 1, p. 211.

[22] Murādī, *Silk*, II, 98 (Khalīl al-Himṣānī), and II, 187 (Shākir al-'Umarī).

[23] Murādī, *Silk*, I, 8.

city, and preacher at the Umayyad mosque. Of him, al-Khiyārī wrote:

> His chanting delivery in sermons follows that of Rūm [that is, Turkish-speaking Anatolia and Istanbul]. This is the first sermon we heard that differed from that of our own land [that is, the Holy Cities of Arabia] and which was contrary to tradition. . . . In Damascus and Rūm and adjacent lands, they chant the sermon well and are known for it. But they do not know the meaning of linguistic purity and eloquence.[24]

In light of this evidence, it appears that the cultural orientation of Damascus was neither exclusively Ottoman nor Arab, but was inclined to both traditions. What this implied for intellectual life is still not known. Research concerning the role of Arab scholars in the Ottoman world is still in its initial stages. Nevertheless, it is clear that the cultural window on the Ottoman world was of great importance for the strength and influence of the notable estate. It reinforced the notables' intermediary status while not imposing cultural uniformity. Aside from scholarly activity, the other major source of Ottoman orientation—with all its political implications—was income from state revenue designated for the support of individuals in the provincial bureaucracy and religious establishment. Although there were not enough posts to go around, there were sufficient numbers to attract several hundred individuals.

The primary evidence of state income inducements for the notables is just beginning to be made available. It is scattered through that portion of the Ottoman archives open to researchers, as well as through the vast volumes of the local law courts of Damascus, which were opened to scholars in 1974.[25] In the Ottoman archives, there are several registers

[24] al-Khiyārī, "Tuḥfat al-udabā' wa silwat al-ghurabā'," p. 302. al-Khiyārī journeyed to Istanbul and was awarded a high-paying post in Egypt by Sultan Mehmed IV; see Murādī, *Silk*, I, 251.

[25] See the descriptive article by Rafeq, "Les registres de tribunaux de Damas comme source pour l'histoire de la Syrie," which supersedes and

containing names of Damascene recipients of state incomes. Additional documents provide extensive evidence of the degree to which notables sought to obtain such incomes during the first half of the eighteenth century. In 1746, for example, the provincial treasury of Damascus spent 1,310,238 *akçes* from its budget to support a total of 334 positions (shared by approximately 350 persons). This represented an increase from 75 positions recorded during the first quarter of the century. The treasury also spent 855,520 *akçes* for 146 positions held by residents of Mecca and Medina, 937,260 *akçes* for 124 needy or worthy persons in Mecca and Medina, 19,710 *akçes* for 9 persons in Jerusalem, and 78,130 *akçes* for 14 persons—all scribes and apprentices—who worked for the provincial treasury of Damascus.[26] Incomes in the first and largest category ranged from 1 *akçe* per day up to the 70 paid to Shaykh Luṭf Allāh, who held an endowed teaching chair in the Umayyad mosque.[27] There was some variation in the number of days for which individuals received pay. Shaykh Luṭf Allāh, for example, was given 14,700 *akçes* per year, which translated to 210 days' pay, whereas Shaykh Aḥmad

brings up to date most of the information in Mandaville, "The Ottoman Court Records of Syria and Jordan." Prof. Rafeq has informed me that, for any given year in the eighteenth century, there are three registers with up to 1,000 pages each and at least three entries per page. This amounts to nearly one million entries for the whole century. There is no index yet to these records.

[26] BA-Kepeci 2346, a register of 15 folios, dated the last day of Zılhicce 1159 (the end of the year)/12 February 1747 and signed by the *defterdar* of Damascus, Muḥammad ibn Farrūkh (for whose biography, see Murādī, *Silk*, IV, 38). The second, undated, register (BA-Kepeci 2408), signed by the *defterdar* "Sayyid Muḥammad," is probably from the early eighteenth century. There is corroborating evidence for four persons listed in the register: Shaykh Muḥammad ibn Jum'a (probably the author of "al-Bāshāt"), who died after 1753; Sayyid Fatḥī ibn Sayyid Muḥammad, son of a *defterdar*, and the future *defterdar* of Damascus (d. 1746; Murādī, *Silk*, III, 279); Şeyh Murad-ı Şamī, probably Murādī's great-grandfather and eponymous founder of the family (d. 1720; Murādī, *Silk*, IV, 130); Sayyid 'Abd al-Qādır al-Şamādī (d. 1702; Murādī, *Silk*, III, 60). None of these identifications is certain.

[27] The income is confirmed by Murādī's biography of Luṭf Allāh, who died two years after the register in question was compiled. Murādī, *Silk*, IV, 15.

ibn al-Faqīh, whose daily income was 40 *akçes*, received 14,400 *akçes* in 1746, or 360 days' pay (a 6-day bonus over the 354 days in the Islamic lunar year).[28]

Positions included scholarships for students, readerships of the Qur'ān in mosques, subsidies for food for dervish convents, and teaching positions and administrative posts for charitable endowments established in mosques or at the tombs of famous men, such as Abū al-Dardā, a companion of the Prophet Muḥammad and first *kadi* of Damascus.[29] Most striking is the fact that many individuals shared positions, and that many others held more than one. Also significant was the extent to which notable families held on to, shared, and inherited incomes of even the lowest-paying posts. Shaykh Luṭf Allāh's brother, for instance, enjoyed an income of 8 *akçes* per day; Ismā'īl al-Nābulsī, son of the famed 'Abd al-Ghanī, held 4 positions paying 22, 4, 3, and 8 *akçes* per day.[30] On the other hand, a whole family, consisting of four brothers and two sisters, shared an income of only 6 *akçes* per day.[31] In view of the fact that the cost of living in eighteenth-century Damascus far outstripped such paltry incomes—many of which had been established in the sixteenth century—why did families retain them with such tenacity? Although concrete evidence of individual motives is so far scarce, it seems that what made these positions so desirable were the prestige, contacts, and influence they conveyed. There is firm evidence, however, that notables paid out considerable sums to obtain and keep state incomes. One official who received 30 *akçes* per day from the revenues of an endowment supporting the Umayyad mosque paid 18.5 *kuruş* (or 2,220 *akçes*) in clerical fees for registration of his appointment, another 18.5 *kuruş* as a fee for preparing a payment authorization voucher in the central government's finance bureau, and 5.5 *kuruş* (or 660 *akçes*) as the cost of his appointment certificate. The total cost of an office conferring

[28] BA-Kepecı 2346, folio 1a.

[29] Ibid. The tomb was ınside the Damascus citadel. See al-'Adawī (d. 1623), *al-Ziyārāt bi-Dimashq*, p. 78.

[30] BA-Kepecı 2346, folios 1a, 2b.

[31] Ibıd., folio 2b.

10,620 *akçes* per year was 5,060 *akçes*, nearly half a year's income.[32]

Every notable on the state payroll was, perforce, involved with the local Ottoman administrative establishment. He had to ask the provincial treasurer (the *defterdar*) to draw up a petition to the central government requesting his appointment. He also had to ask the local magistrate (*kadi*) to notarize a request for any change in either payment or beneficiary. If an office holder died or wished to ensure that his family retain his income, the *defterdar* could submit appropriate petitions. If a post became vacant, the *defterdar* could submit a request on behalf of other individuals.[33] Similarly, notables attempted to increase their incomes by obtaining more favorable exchange ratios between the *akçe* (a unit of account) and the *kuruş*, a coin that more accurately reflected inflation and the cost of living. For example, in 1733, Shaykh Aḥmad al-Ṣaydalī, who enjoyed an income of 20 *akçes* per day from the Sidon customs revenues, at a ratio of 160 *akçes* to the *kuruş*, requested and was granted a ratio adjustment to 120 *akçes* to the *kuruş*.[34] The

[32] TKS-E. 10467/1, undated list of appointment fees received; TKS-E. 10467/3, identical in script, style and arrangement of material as TKS-E. 10467/1 and 2, is dated 1157 (1744). Fees for registration of the appointment and clerical work are referred to as *arzları tetabbuk ve ruüsu'na*, the authorization voucher, *tezkiresiçin Anadolu halifesine harç*; and the diploma fee, *harç-ı berat*.

[33] For the appointment of a son to succeed his father, see BA-Emiri/III Ahmed 5740, petition by Damascus *defterdar*, dated beginning Şaban 1116 (29 November to 8 December 1704), registered in the finance bureau in Istanbul on 5 Zilhicce (31 March 1705), and approved on 18 Zilhicce (13 April). For the transfer of a position from a father to his sons and their families during the father's lifetime, see BA-Emiri/III Ahmed 17854, two appointment diplomas with statements of surrender on the back, witnessed by the *kadi* of Damascus and attached to the *defterdar*'s petition, dated 5 Rebiyülevvel 1125 (1 April 1713). The families still held the position, along with several others, in 1746. BA-Kepeci 2346, folio 1a. For the acquisition of a vacant position, see TKS-E. 505/7, appointment diploma authorizing an income of two *akçes* per day from the Sidon customs revenue, dated 18 Muharrem 1156 (14 March 1743).

[34] TKS-E. 505/19, diploma dated 19 Rebiyülevvel 1146 (30 August 1733). The ratio adjustment was referred to as *tebdil*. For the *para* as the unit of common currency (three *akçes* made one *para*), see Budayrī, *Hawādith*, p. 4.

powerful position of the provincial treasurer in forwarding all these requests to Istanbul can be readily appreciated. It was partly this bureaucratic control of imperial patronage that nearly allowed the *defterdar* Fethi Efendi to succeed in seizing full control of Damascus from the 'Azms in the 1740s.

The inducements, prestige, and preferential treatment[35] afforded the notables on state incomes were, then, one means of state control, albeit indirect. Another was the state's inceasing patronage in the eighteenth century of the official Ottoman religious rite, the Ḥanafī, at the expense of the local, Shāfi'ī tradition. The four "orthodox" (Sunnī) Muslim rites—the Ḥanafī, Mālikī, Shāfi'ī, and Ḥanbalī—represented divergent views of Islamic law, each of which nevertheless "recognized the orthodoxy of the others and tolerated their divergences of detail."[36] The Ottoman state, in line with its Turkish predecessors, opted for the Ḥanafī rite, probably because of "the desire of the Turkish rulers to retain as much freedom as possible in their political and executive authority. . . ."[37] In regard to the concept of *ijmā'*—consensus of any generation of jurists—the Ḥanafīs qualified "authority of Traditions and strict *qiyas* [analogical reasoning]. . . . *Ijmā'* represents, in a sense, the contradiction of ash-Shāfi'ī's thesis; for it tolerates those variations which it had been ash-Shāfi'ī's aim to eliminate."[38]

At the outset, it should be stated that there is no direct evidence of an official Ottoman policy in eighteenth-century

---

Budayrī calls the *para a miṣriyya*, plural *maṣārī*, used in the sense of "money" in eighteenth-century Damascus as well as today. *Para* has the same sense in modern Turkısh.

[35] For example, notables who traveled to Istanbul on state business were entitled to special escort and comfortable lodgings. BA-Cevdet/Dahilıye 452, *yol hükmü* or travel order to all government officials between Istanbul and Damascus to provide protection and services to Seyyıd Ahmed, *türbedar* or guardian of the tomb of Abū al-Dardā' (see Note 29 above) in Damascus, who traveled to Istanbul on business. The order was dated end Zilhicce 1147 (14-23 May 1735).

[36] Gıbb and Bowen, *Islamıc Society*, I, 2, p. 115.

[37] Inalcık, *The Ottoman Empire*, p. 181.

[38] Coulson, *A History of Islamic Law*, p. 80.

Damascus that clearly preferred the Hanafī rite. To have openly espoused an official rite would have had grave social and political consequences: a Muslim's rite (*madhhab*) governed not only his recourse to Islamic law, but also the intimate details of religious ritual. Hence, a man's *madhhab* governed his social and religious obligations. As with the inducements of imperial patronage, the apparent Ottoman encouragement of the Ḥanafī *madhhab* was subtle and indirect. John Voll's careful study of changes in the major notable Damascus families who dominated the religious establishment during the eighteenth century shows that "it is possible to discern an increasing integration of primarily parochial families into the larger structures of Ottoman religious affairs, as well as continued strong influence of Istanbul politics in local Damascene religious affairs."[39] The caution with which Voll approaches his subject is worth keeping in mind. The evidence, nonetheless, shows an unmistakable trend: posts in the religious establishment were more readily available to those who switched to the official Ottoman rite.

Voll documents the apparent preference of the Ottoman state for "cosmopolitan" Damascenes—that is, those with contacts and experience outside Damascus—for appointees to the offices of *khaṭīb* (preacher) of the Ummayad mosque. *muftī* (jurisconsult) of the Ḥanafīs, and *naqīb al-ashrāf* (head of the league of descendants of the Prophet Muḥammad). In regard to the latter office, Voll shows that two families—Ḥamza and 'Ajlānī—switched from the Shāfi'ī to the Ḥanafī rite in order to qualify for office. Of sixteen major notable families who were represented in the religious establishment around 1650, eight were Shāfi'ī, six Ḥanafī, and two Ḥanbalī. By 1785, two families were no longer represented, twelve were Ḥanafī, and only two were Shāfi'ī. Furthermore, a considerable number of instructorships held by Shāfi'īs until 1700 were in Ḥanafī hands by 1750. Voll suggests that this gradual transfer took place by "cumulative attrition."[40]

[39] Voll, "Old 'Ulama' Families and Ottoman Influence," p. 48.
[40] Ibid., pp. 56-58.

Preference for the Ḥanafī rite worked effectively to bring Damascene notables into the empire's religious affairs and to deflect them from excessive preoccupation with parochial concerns. Voll contrasts this general situation with what he regards as the contemporaneous "growth [in the eighteenth century] of local politico-military despotism," such as that represented by the 'Aẓms.[41] Perhaps this contrast is far too sharp, in view of the fact that changing patterns in the governorship of Damascus (a "politico-military despotism") were designed to strengthen Ottoman control of the province. The parallel attempt to influence the notables was also designed for that purpose. As early as 1691-1692, the Ottoman state had begun to take direct action to that end. An Ottoman chronicler's description of the notables leaves little doubt as to the state's view of their activities. "Some of the *ayans* of Damascus, because of the favor of the requisites of good fortune and an abundance of followers and riches, burst forth from subjection and obedience and ascended the summit of rebellion."[42] At roughly the same time, the state was reorganizing the structure of the annual pilgrimage to Mecca and Medina, which originated in Damascus, and was expanding the authority of the provincial governor.

On a number of occasions, the state saw fit to confront notable power directly. But the rarity of this third, and most extreme, policy of containment—exile or imprisonment—speaks strongly of the state's desire to first employ other means. In the few known cases of exile, the state nearly always had to back down and allow prisoners to return to Damascus. There were basically two reasons for exile: the commission by a notable of an act contrary to the state's best interests and the loss of favor in Istanbul to the benefit of a rival on the local scene. In either case, the governor of Damascus had to request an order of banishment from the central government. Two instances illustrate these processes. In the first, three notables were exiled for failing to fulfill a bargain they had struck with the governor Baltacı Süleyman

[41] Ibid., p. 59.

[42] Râşıd, *Tarih*, II, 173.

Paşa. As commander of the pilgrimage in 1707, the latter ran short of funds on his journey with the pilgrims to Arabia. He halted the caravan at Muzayrīb, the first major stopping place outside Damascus, and negotiated a loan of 40,000 *kuruş* with three notables, As'ad al-Bakrī, 'Abd al-Raḥmān al-Qārī, and Sulaymān al-Maḥāsinī. In turn, the notables were instructed to raise the loan from Damascene merchants and from fines collected by local grievance courts (*maẓālim*).[43] The merchants, however, refused to raise the money, and the ensuing delay in the pilgrimage infuriated the governor. He wrote to Istanbul and demanded the exile of the three notables to Cyprus. When the order authorizing the banishment arrived, the notables were sent to the port of Sidon to await a ship that would take them to Cyprus (27 March 1707). In the meantime, a storm of protest caused the central government to countermand the exile order. Release instructions were sent to the governor of Cyprus in the event that the notables had already arrived by ship. They had not. Upon their return to Damascus (they left Sidon on 16 June 1707), they were greeted by a large demonstration of popular support. Furthermore, the governor personally and publicly apologized for his action.[44] In spite of the fact that the notables ultimately won their freedom, they no doubt realized that their failure to assist the governor in the state-supported enterprise par excellence—the pilgrimage—was not to be forgotten. Exile was also a means by which the state showed favor to one notable at the expense of another. In 1758, when Çeteci Abdullah Paşa took over Damascus after the disastrous pilgrimage of the preceding year, he dismissed the local *naqīb al-ashrāf* and replaced him with a member of a rival family. The former

[43] For *maẓālim*, see Gibb and Bowen, *Islamic Society*, I, 2, p. 126.

[44] The only account of the incident is in the biography of As'ad al-Bakrī, in Murādī, *Silk*, I, 224. The release order, addressed to the governor of Cyprus, is in BA-Ibnulemin/Dahiliye 1949, dated beginning Safer 1119 (4-13 May 1707). This document, which clearly cites the collusion of the three notables and the governor (*ittifakile*), modifies the view of Rafeq (*Province*, p. 35) that the three "were exiled . . . for opposing the governor's attempts to exact money from the Damascenes." Here again is a case in which the evidence—largely self-justifying—is hard to evaluate.

naqīb, Sayyid Ḥamza, was exiled to Cyprus at the governor's request. 'Alī al-'Ajlānī, a bitter rival, took over the post and kept it until his death some twenty years later.[45]

The Ottoman state's attempt to contain the notables was less successful than its efforts to reorganize the pilgrimage and the governorship of Damascus. Because the notables had so much freedom of action locally, and because they had influential friends at court in Istanbul, they could not be confronted directly. Instead, the state preferred to apply pressure to limit the notables' control over charitable endowments and institutions of learning and to prevent the development of cozy relations with provincial governors. The power of patronage and their restrictive role as intermediaries imposed limits on notables' political activity. Yet, within these limits, the notables managed to flourish. The pages of Damascus chronicles are filled with constant references to the notables' mediation between the two major janissary corps. With each outbreak of factional violence between the local and imperial janissaries, the notables hoped to gain strength and prestige, in the eyes both of their Ottoman masters in Istanbul and of their fellow Damascenes as well. The greatest danger to which they exposed themselves was in calling for the removal of a governor. One example will serve as an illustration. Much has been made of the fact that Khalīl al-Ṣiddīqī, the Ḥanafī *muftī* of Damascus, led the popular revolt in 1725 that overthrew the hated governor Çerkes Osman and brought Ismail al-'Aẓm to power in Damascus.[46] This assertion of local power has been emphasized at the expense of the fact that the *muftī* enjoyed considerable leverage with the religious establishment in Istanbul. Although mentioned in passing, the significance of

[45] The incident is described in Budayrī, *Ḥawādith*, p. 218, and in Murādī, *Silk*, III, 207 (biography of 'Alī al-'Ajlānī). A summary of the governor's request for a banishment order is in BA-Emiri/III Mustafa 3624. Appended to the summary is the banishment order, dated 3 Cemaziyelâhır 1171 (12 February 1758). Budayrī states that Sayyid Hamza was exiled to Jerusalem (al-Quds), although the banishment request and appended order mention Cyprus (Qubrus/Kıbrıs). Budayrī may have mistaken Qubrus for Quds.

[46] Rafeq, *Province*, pp. 83-85; Shamir, " 'Azm Wālīs," p. 17.

this leverage has not been seen. Without it, the revolt might have proved fruitless and the appointment of the first 'Aẓm governor of Damascus might not have taken place. In fact, shortly after these events, al-Ṣiddīqī returned to Istanbul, where he rose in the capital's scholarly circles. After brief appointments as *kadi* of Tripoli, Jerusalem, and Damascus, he returned to Istanbul, where he died as *kadiasker* of Anatolia (the third-highest rank in the Ottoman judicial system).[47] Here was, yet again, that peculiar combination of local origins and local support, balanced by cosmopolitan aspirations and favor, that characterized so many Damascene notables.

The remarkable career of Fethi Efendi (al-Sayyid Fatḥī ibn al-Sayyid Muḥammad al-Falāqinsī), *defterdar*, or chief of the provincial treasury of Damascus, posed, by far, the greatest threat by a notable to Ottoman control in Damascus during this period.[48] More than any other notable, Fethi came closest to securing a position comparable to the Anatolian *derebeys* of the later eighteenth century. In other words, he nearly broke out of the pattern of intermediary activity to which the notables customarily confined themselves. At one point, he enjoyed political power based on control of local endowment (*vakıf*) revenues (most of which were beyond the reach of state officials) and the support of the notables and local military establishment. Above all, and for reasons we still do not know, Fethi was protected by Koca Beşir Ağa, the chief of the imperial harem in Istanbul. Fethi's ambition—to govern Damascus—was crippled, however by the death of his patron, Beşir Ağa, in 1746 and by his blatant, and ultimately, fatal contempt for his fellow notables.

A weaver from the town of Falāqins near Himṣ, Fethi's grandfather migrated to Damascus toward the end of the seventeenth century. His sons, by means still not known, obtained positions in the local treasury (*defterdarlık*). Fethi's father became chief treasurer of the province in the early years

[47] Murādī, *Silk*, II, 84.

[48] An extensive biography is found in Murādī, *Silk*, III, 279-287. Excellent accounts of Fethi's career are those by Shamir, " 'Azm Wālīs," pp. 97-109; and Rafeq, *Province*, pp. 149-154 and 164-169.

of the eighteenth century.[49] Fethi inherited the administration of local charitable endowments (*vakıfs*). Over the years, he extended his influence with local groups that formed the base of his political power. As a *şerif*, or descendant of the Prophet Muḥammad, he won friends among the ulema. As the grandson of a weaver, Fethi could appeal to the sentiments of the local janissaries, who doubled as craftsmen and members of Sufi orders, and to musicians and even comedians.[50] The more unruly local janissaries—known as *zorab* (for the Turkish *zorba*, meaning bully or rebel)—enjoyed Fethi's protection from the reach of the law. They responded with their support and intimidated the rest of the population. Finally, Fethi's patronage and protection included the expanding French merchant community in Damascus.[51]

After becoming provincial treasurer in 1736, Fethi redoubled his efforts to undermine the 'Aẓms. He conducted great public celebrations on various occasions, which gave him the chance to show off his popularity. When Süleyman Paşa al-'Aẓm was transferred from Damascus to Egypt in 1738 and a new governor arrived in Damascus, Fethi became briefly *mütesellim*, or interim governor.[52] In spite of the fact that he did not take an active role in this brief period of political authority, Fethi unmistakably showed the direction he wished to take: from the relatively sheltered and dead-end position of provincial treasurer to the summit of provincial power, the governorship. When Süleyman died in 1743 during his brief second term as governor of Damascus, Fethi quickly moved to confiscate the latter's estate in accordance with Ottoman practice. Fethi's enthusiasm and zeal for this task angered many of the notables who had supported the 'Aẓms. When Esat Paşa al-'Azm assumed the governorship, he and Fethi began a three-year struggle for power. Steadily and surely, the tide turned against the ambitious treasurer. For several years, Fethi had bribed imperial messengers and one gover-

[49] His signature appears on the undated register cited in Note 26 above: BA-Kepecı 2408.

[50] Murādī, *Silk*, III, 280.

[51] Rafeq, *Province*, p. 123.

[52] Ibid., p. 132.

nor, Ali Paşa Maktuloğlu, to prevent delivery of letters of complaint from Fethi's growing number of opponents in Damascus.[53] The sudden death of Beşir Ağa in 1746 deprived Fethi of his patron in Istanbul. Far worse for him, a certain Ahmed Ağa, whom the treasurer had once offended, and who was now a *paşa* close to the grand vezir, was prevailed upon by Esat Paşa to deliver a petition to the sultan upon the deposit of "security" in the amount of 500,000 *kuruş*.[54] The petition, signed by the large and growing number of Damascenes affected by Fethi's corrupt practices, was a scathing indictment of the treasurer. It was signed by the cream of the notables: forty-six members of the religious establishment and fifty-four local janissaries and *timar* holders.[55] After some time had passed, Esat Paşa received an imperial rescript that ordered Fethi's execution.[56] On 15 Cemaziyelâhır 1159 (5 July 1746), during a visit to the governor's residence, Fethi was confronted with the rescript and was abruptly executed. His ambition to be governor of Damascus had failed. His seemingly unbeatable coalition of support fell apart under the strain of his corruption, intimidatory tactics, and his loss of protection in Istanbul. On the provincial scene, Fethi, a local notable and bureaucrat, could not duplicate what his counterparts in Istanbul were increasingly able to achieve: a promotional leap from the rank of *efendi* (membership in the *kalemi*

[53] Murādī, *Silk*, III, 287; Ibn Jum'a, "al-Bāshāt," p. 64.

[54] Murādī, *Silk*, III, 287.

[55] BA-Emiri/ı Mahmud 316, undated. The document refers to a plague that struck Damascus "one and a half years ago." According to Budayrī, Hawādith, p. 56, the plague occurred toward the end of 1156 (December 1743-January 1744), which would date the document some time during the middle of 1158 (June-July 1745).

[56] On 23 Safer 1159 (17 March 1746), the notables of Damascus petitioned the central government for orders to Esat Paşa that would allow the execution of Fethi's supporters among the *zorab* and the confiscation of their property. The notables offered 15,000 *kuruş* as a reward. BA-Emiri/ı Mahmud 9077. In response, the central government issued a rescript to that effect, addressed to Esat Paşa. BA-Emiri/ı Mahmud 14192, dated Rebiyülevvel 1159 (24 March-22 April 1746). (The actual date of the month is illegible because of ink smudges on the document).

or bureaucratic order) to *paşa* (membership in the *seyfi*, or military-administrative order).[57] The bureaucrat in Istanbul, close to the center of power, advanced or fell with his patron through the social tie known as *intisap*. He could rise to the top ranks of the bureaucracy and then, with luck, make the shift to a provincial governorship or a military command. But, in the Damascus of the first half of the eighteenth century, a provincial treasurer did not become provincial governor: the *efendi* did not turn *paşa*.

The Janissaries

If the notables of Damascus were contained with relative ease, the janissaries of the provincial capital proved somewhat more troublesome. Divided between local and imperial corps, and competing with separate groups of mercenaries who served the governor, the Damascene janissaries were a constant headache to the Ottoman state during the eighteenth century. After the first decade of that century, the governor of Damascus ceased to lead the provincial military forces on campaigns outside the province. The result of this change in imperial policy was the presence in the provincial capital—more than in the other major towns of the province—of military groups that competed furiously for the benefits of their state-conferred privileges, for economic gain, and for social prestige.

The origins of the problem are to be found in the establishment of a provincial janissary force shortly after the Ottoman conquest of Syria in 1516. As in other parts of the empire, the provincial janissaries moved quickly to take over local crafts and to engage in commerce and money changing.[58] In Damascus, this was complemented by a reverse process that developed during the sixteenth century, whereby

[57] "Beginning with an occasional figure in the late seventeenth century, however, and then with greater frequency in the eighteenth century, professional bureaucrats [those not trained in the sultan's palace school] were elevated to the rank of vezir."—Itzkowitz, "Mehmed Rāghib Pasha," p. 121.

[58] Inalcik, *The Ottoman Empire*, p. 51; Rafeq, *Province*, pp. 26-27.

local merchants and craftsmen joined the corps to enjoy its privileges. During the 1650s, the Damascus janissaries supported the revolt of Abaza Hasan, governor of Aleppo. In 1658-1659, the grand vezir Mehmed Köprülü dispatched a new group of janissaries to Damascus. A purge of the leadership of the older corps led to the triumph of the newer; it "took control of the citadel, the gates of the city, and other public services which had been in the hands of the Janissaries."[59] Now the older corps became known as the local janissaries (*yerli kulları*, or *dawlat Dimashq* in local parlance), and the newer corps became known as the imperial janissaries (*kapı kulları*, or *dawlat al-qal 'a*).

After 1660, then, two corps existed side by side in the city; in contrast, in Aleppo at that time, a single corps was maintained.[60] The social and economic implications of increasingly complex local janissary corps were nonetheless serious for the empire as a whole: in 1685, thirty-six major towns had 13,793 garrison janissaries; in 1723, that number had increased to 30,560, and by 1750, it had reached 53,966.[61] Not only did Damascus have to absorb two competing janissary corps; it also had to absorb irregular mercenary units that did not come under the control of the central government but, instead, served governors of the province: *delis (dālātiyya), levends, Mağrıblıs (Maghāriba), sekbans*, each of which had its own organization and system of governance.[62] Like the two formally sanctioned janissary corps, these mercenary units put down roots in the local economy and society. Their leaders—the *shaykhs* of each group—were responsible only to the governor. Yet, this additional military presence—augmented during the eighteenth century by an influx of new members—only added to the state's administrative problems.

The Ottoman government's response to this situation was to temporize: to control the mercenaries through the provin-

[59] Rafeq, "The Local Forces in Syria," p. 278.

[60] For Aleppo's janissary establishment in a later period, see Bodman, *Political Factions*, pp. 55-78.

[61] Uzunçarşılı, *Kapıkulu Ocakları*, I, 329-330.

[62] Rafeq, "The Local Forces in Syria," pp. 283-287.

cial governor; and to tinker with the numbers, composition, leadership, and duties of the two janissary corps. In 1660, it did not abolish the old corps, but imported a competitor, the *kapı kulları*. From time to time, it would purge the leadership of the local corps, as in 1688-1689, or add to the numbers of the *kapı kulları*, as in 1706-1707 and on later occasions.[63] Once the state had committed itself to the maintenance of the local janissaries, it could not disturb these arrangements without widespread social and economic dislocation. Nevertheless, the state still had ways to contain the local military. In addition to frequent checks of muster rolls (*yoklamas*), the state attempted to assign duties to these sedentary garrisons, especially after the governors of the province ceased to participate in imperial campaigns. The fact that the administration of Damascus was closely linked to management of the pilgrimage made it possible for the state to send out a portion of the local janissary force to garrison the forts along the road to Arabia. As for the imperial janissaries, the state assigned them the duty of purchasing supplies for the pilgrimage escort force, which, incidentally, was composed of mercenaries in the governor's employ. Some of the imperial janissaries also defended a number of the pilgrimage route forts.[64] In this manner, the state attempted to divert the military establishment from deadly internecine warfare for at least that part of the year when Damascus was caught up in preparation for the pilgrimage. This attempt met with only mixed success.

Perhaps the boldest move to control the Damascus military establishment in the first half of the eighteenth century occurred between 1740 and 1746, when the *kapı kulları* were forcibly removed from Damascus by decree and by public demand.[65] In 1740, Muhassil Osman Paşa, the governor, wrote a private letter to the sultan in which he complained specifi-

[63] Rafeq, *Province*, pp. 34-35.

[64] For details of these measures, see Chapter Three below. Our evidence indicates that the janissaries did, in fact, perform their duties on the pilgrimage. This contrasts with Rafeq's view that they by and large did not. Rafeq, "The Local Forces in Syria," p. 279.

[65] Shamir, " 'Azm Wālīs," p. 232; Rafeq, *Province*, pp. 140-141.

cally that two *ortas* (companies) of imperial janissaries were not fulfilling their duties. The contents of this remarkable letter[66] deserve some description. Osman Paşa complained that, for some time, unreliable and untrustworthy guildsmen—such as bakers and greengrocers—had entered the imperial janissary corps with the understanding that they would assist the governor in obtaining provisions for the pilgrimage escort force. Because the chiefs, or *ağas*, of the corps had been dismissed frequently on charges of corruption, these unruly elements found it easy to form a *sofa*—in janissary parlance, a group of youths who sauntered about and enjoyed themselves (*gezip tozmakta*) instead of doing their jobs. The authorized punishment for such behavior had been public flogging, removal from the payroll, and dangerous assignments on campaign.[67] As this last punishment (combat duty) was no longer part of the experience of either of the Damascene janissary corps—except at pilgrimage time—the state was forced to consider other options. Osman Paşa advised the authorities in Istanbul that it would be useless to dismiss this unruly group and replace it, simply because those expelled would form their own force, a force that could not be controlled. The only solution was to disband the *kapı kulları* altogether. Once the imperial rescript arrived, the expulsion of the janissaries took place quickly: "Those of them who had families and proved that they were of good conduct, not *zorab*, as judged by the city notables who reviewed each at the door of his house, were permitted to stay, provided they gave up their uniforms and other privileges and became ordinary inhabitants [*reaya*]."[68] Others escaped to the hinterland to await the opportunity to return. This action in effect ratified the social reality of the *kapı kulları*—as local craftsmen and guild mem-

[66] TKS-E. 12169, undated letter signed by Osman Paşa. The imperial rescript in response to this petition arrived in Damascus in July 1740. Rafeq, *Province*, p. 141. We did not find in the Ottoman archives a petition from the notables of Damascus that accompanied Osman Paşa's letter.

[67] *TDS*, III, 244.

[68] Rafeq, *Province*, p. 141, citing Ibn Jum'a, "al-Bāshāt," p. 68, on the *reaya*, or nonprivileged sector in Ottoman society.

bers—while taking away their privileged Ottoman status. Fethi the *defterdar* moved right into the power vacuum created by this corps' departure. Shortly before his losing struggle with Esat Paşa, Fethi had to contend with the return of the *kapı kulları*, who now squared off for combat with the local janissaries, their old enemies and the backbone of Fethi's grand alliance.

Because the local janissaries had extensive roots in Damascus, their containment and control proved to be more difficult for the Ottoman state. Its members had supported themselves by collecting certain customs duties and other local taxes (see Appendix III). In theory, the *ağa* of the corps, through his deputy, the *kul kethüdası*, was entrusted with the collection duty. In 1706, however, the governor of Damascus, Baltacı Süleyman Paşa, complained to the central government of pilferage and waste of supplies bought with these revenues by the leaders of the corps. As a result, the poorer members of the corps were hard-pressed to make ends meet. Baltacı Süleyman recommended the conversion of these tax collections into *malikâne*—or purchased life-leaseholds—to be administered by the provincial treasurer. The result of this change in administration was the purchase of the new tax farms by nonjanissaries, especially notables.[69]

Just three years after the local janissaries' tax collection duties were taken away, the state began the long process of reducing the numbers in the corps. It is significant that those dismissed from the corps still received their pay from the provincial treasury.[70] By removing the unfit, the state was able to ensure a more manageable local janissary corps, even at the price of sacrificing tax revenues (for a summary table of

[69] BA-Cevdet/Askeri 44575, petition dated 24 Cemaziyelevvel 1118 (3 September 1706), approved 14 Cemaziyelâhır 1118 (23 September 1706). A similar collection problem existed in the *kapı kulları* corps, which held the tax farm for tax seals placed on bolts of cloth produced in Damascus (*mukataa-ı damğa akçesi*). Some members of this corps attempted to prevent their chief from managing the collections. BA-Emiri/I Mahmud 16488, undated, approved on 5 Rebiyülevvel 1156 (29 April 1743).

[70] BA-Cevdet/Askeri 5261, order to the governor of Damascus dated 15 Cemazıyelâhır 1131 (5 May 1719).

corps complements, see Table 2). By requiring a substantial portion of the corps to defend the pilgrimage fortresses in alternate years, the state tried to ensure that restless troops would be occupied with duty that served the state. In fact, several unruly members used this opportunity to restore their good standing with the authorities rather than face punishment or dismissal for bad behavior.[71]

In spite of the Ottoman state's efforts to control the military establishment of Damascus, the provincial capital continued to suffer from periodic outbursts of factional warfare. Discovery of the underlying social and economic causes of these incidents is a task scarcely undertaken by historians concerned with the local history of Damascus. At present, interpretations of this problem range from the general—local groups were competing to fill the power vacuum created by the "decline" of central authority—to the specific—the groups were fighting for economic and social gain.[72] In order to conduct more sharply focused research in local history, these two interpretations—"decline" and "greed"—might best be set aside. At this stage of our knowledge and in relation to the arguments of this study, we may suggest a working hypothesis from the broader perspective of Ottoman history.

From the time of the Celalî rebellions of the late sixteenth century, members of the Ottoman military establishment, whether in the capital or the provinces, faced two major problems. The first was economic pressure that resulted from the treasury's inability to keep military pay commensurate with inflation. It was this pressure that encouraged the janissaries to engage in crafts and commerce, which, in Damascus and other provincial towns, led to their identification with the

[71] BA-Ibnülemin/Dahiliye 2531, clemency order for two members of the *yerli kulları* who acquitted themselves well in service on the pilgrimage. The document is dated middle Rebiyülevvel 1121 (21-30 May 1709).

[72] For a sketch of these interests and of the problem of factional warfare, see Shamir, "Belligerency in a Disintegrating Society." For the general interpretation linking violence to the decay of central authority, see, for example, Gibb and Bowen, *Islamic Society*, I, 1, p. 206.

TABLE 2
COMPLEMENTS OF DAMASCUS JANISSARY CORPS, 1693-1746

Year	*Local corps*	*Imperial corps*
1693-1694	1,004[a]	—
1701-1702 (?)	—	268[b]
1706	1,231[c]	—
1709	1,231[d]	413[f]
	913[e]	
1710	—	641[g]
1719-1720	750[h]	
	80 added for pilgrimage fort duty[i]	—
1721-1722	833[j]	
	90 added for pilgrimage fort duty[k]	—
1727-1728	923[l]	—
1734-1735	—	413[m]
1735	—	641[n]
1740	—	Corps disbanded
1746		Corps restored

[a] BA-Maliye 2816, p. 27.
[b] BA-Kepeci 2408, p. 5. See Note 26 above regardıng the approximate date of this register.
[c] BA-Cevdet/Askeri 44575, dated 14 Cemaziyelâhır 1118 (3 September 1706).
[d] BA-Malıye 2816, p. 74.
[e] Ibid., p. 13.
[f] BA-Emırı/ııı Ahmed 6205/1,2, dated 15 Rebiyülâhır 1122 (13 June 1710).
[g] Ibıd.
[h] BA-Maliye 2816, p. 76.
[i] Ibıd., p. 87.
[j] Ibid., p. 95.
[k] BA-Maliye 6676.
[l] BA-Malıye 314.
[m] BA-Cevdet/Askerı 16492, dated 7 Şaban 1148 (23 December 1735).
[n] Ibid.

local population. The fact that janissaries began to inherit their positions reinforced this process of localization. The second difficulty was an increase in the number of men seeking military careers, particularly after the diminution of the levy (*devşirme*) of non-Muslim males—long the principal source of the Ottoman sultan's military manpower. At the close of the sixteenth century, large numbers of peasants driven from their land wandered through the countryside of eastern Anatolia, burned crops and villages, and lived off the land as bandits. It was from this group—known as *sekbans*—that mercenary units were first formed and attached to the households of provincial governors and other high officials. Immigrants from the North African provinces (particularly those who settled in Syria) added to the numbers in competition for privileged status under state auspices, whether this meant employment in mercenary units or in the regular provincial janissary corps. Although each military group in Damascus had strong ethnic roots—such as the Anatolian *sekbans*, Kurdish *tüfenkcis* (fusiliers), and the North African *Maghāriba*—it was the strong sense of *'aṣabiyya*, or feeling of social solidarity, rather than ethnic differences that appears to have given each group its identity. Some of the mercenary groups had members from several ethnic backgrounds; nevertheless, each group had its own internal organization, dress, and separate barracks.[73] The mercenaries struggled furiously for the patronage of the state, provided through the provincial governor, especially with respect to escort duty for the pilgrimage. Even outside Damascus, the mercenaries who made up the army of Ẓāhir al-'Umar proved to be unreliable, for they supported the Ottoman force that destroyed Ẓāhir in 1775. Later, Cezzar Ahmed Paşa's reintroduction of Egyptian-style *mamlūks*, whose loyalty to their master was somewhat more dependable, represented an attempt to eliminate uncertainty in the provincial military.

Rather than greed, decline of central authority, or ethnic

[73] Rafeq, "The Local Forces in Syria," pp. 283ff. For a very detailed, but indigestible, monograph on the mercenaries, see Cezar, *Osmanlı tarihinde Levendler*.

tension, the explanation for intermittent factional warfare in Damascus is to be sought in the social solidarity of military groups and in their competition for state patronage. The latter element has been rather cynically regarded as the state's way of "playing off" one group against another, but the evidence we have presented above indicates that, in contrast, the central government was interested in maintaining an equilibrium between the elements of the military establishment, an equilibrium that would allow for peace in the province. It had faced this problem for well over a century and, in the Damascus of our period, it moved quickly to contain serious outbreaks. The fact that the solutions devised often proved ephemeral indicates a reluctance to introduce sweeping changes in the military establishment. This policy remained in effect until the reform period of the early nineteenth century. Because of the heavy concentration of scholarly attention on the latter century and its momentous events, it has been easy to regard the preceding century as a period of stagnation and decline. The state was only too painfully aware of what was going on in the Damascus military establishment during the eighteenth century, and its attempts to contain the groups that made up that establishment were not without success even when they did not provide for permanent solutions.

The Tribes

The first half of the eighteenth century witnessed important changes in the relationship between the Ottoman state and the Arab, Kurdish, and Turkman tribes in the province of Damascus. Concomitant with the Ottomans' revision of the provincial governorship, organization of the pilgrimage, and attempts to contain the notables and janissaries, state policy sought to absorb the tribes into the Ottoman system. Settlement of the tribes along major communications routes and their employment in the escort and provisioning of the pilgrimage were the key elements of this policy. In other words, the state held out the same inducements of patronage that it offered the notables and janissaries.

These changes in Ottoman policy gain significance when compared to the events of the preceding two centuries, which saw the gradual exclusion of the tribes from settled areas and an increase in raids and banditry. This dangerous situation threatened the long-standing arrangements between central authority and the tribal masters of the countryside, particularly among the beduin. From early Islamic times onward, successive states adopted different methods to deal with nomads.[74] In the first few centuries of the Islamic era, the tribes of Syria seem to have been controlled with relative ease, although "they were not included in the registers (*dawāwīn*) and as such did not receive regular pay, a privilege that was limited to those who abandoned their nomadic way of life and joined those who were settled in the *amṣār*."[75] With the decline of the 'Abbāsid Caliphate and its division into tributary states, the Syrian tribes came under the patronage of the Hamdānids of Aleppo. It was not till the age of Saladin that formal arrangements were made to bring the tribes under central control. Saladin's precise administrative methods are not fully known, but the basic understanding between all parties concerned was that the governor of Damascus acted as arbiter of tribal disputes, as paymaster for services rendered, and as tax collector. The office of *imārat al-'Arab*, or "principality of the Arabs," was created and formally incorporated into the state system by the later Ayyūbids.[76] It was the Mamlūks, however, who recognized the necessity of organizing the tribes in order to deal with them. In other words, if the tribes were left outside the system, without an *amīr* responsible to central authority, they would be a constant threat to communications and especially to the pilgrimage. In return for "fiefs" (*iqṭā's*), the *amīr* rendered service to the state and paid taxes on cattle and sheep. He was regarded as a state official—specifically as one of the "men of the sword" (*arbāb al-suyūf*)—with a rank commensurate with lesser provincial governors and the recognition of such rank in state corre-

[74] This section of the discussion is based on the extensive research of Hiyārī, "The Origins and Development of the Amīrate of the Arabs."

[75] Ibid., p. 510.

[76] Ibid., pp. 512-514.

spondence. Furthermore, officials of the central government manned a new department "whose main concern was the management of the tribes. That department was called *al-mihmindāriyya. . . .*"[77]

The arrival of the Ottomans in Syria did not change the official status of *amīr al-'Arab*, who continued to receive an *iqṭā'* in the amount of 7,193 *akçes*.[78] In other respects, however, there appear to have been important changes in the organization and settlement patterns of the tribes, although "available sources neither explain the prerogatives or the functions . . . of the *amīr* nor do they shed any light upon his status in the administration of Syria."[79] The office was hereditary but was contested by Āl Ḥiyār and Āl Faḍl. On the other hand, the tribes were included in the land registry and population surveys (*taḥrīr*) that the Ottomans conducted after the conquest. In Gaza, for example, four tribes paid taxes (*âdet*), mainly on households and agricultural produce, and one tribe had a *timar* of 26,800 *akçes*.[80] Tribes in Balqā and Ḥawrān were also included in the *taḥrīr*, but no reference was made to the tribes of Karak-Shawbak, farther to the south.

One as yet unexplained development in the early years of Ottoman rule was the apparently sudden prominence of Turkman tribes in Syria. In the Ḥawrān, south of Damascus, there were no fewer than 25, counting 1,410 households, 36 bachelors, and 29 *imams* during the reign of Süleyman the Magnificent (1520-1566). This number increased to 1,651 households, 133 bachelors, and no *imams* in 1569. Their tax obligations (*tekâlif-i örfiyye*) rose from 194,964 *akçes* in 1529 to 225,000 *akçes* in 1545, and to 250,000 *akçes* in 1569.[81] In Ḥamā, near Aleppo, there were 8 Turkman tribes, with 240 households and 46 bachelors paying taxes of 22,411 *akçes* during the reign of Süleyman. The Turkmans of the Palestinian coastal region of 'Athlīth comprised 32 households and 4 bachelors paying 23,080 *akçes* in taxes.[82] What is perhaps

[77] Ibid., pp. 521-522.
[78] Bakhit, "Ottoman Province," pp. 232-233.
[79] Ibid., p. 233.
[80] Ibid., pp. 223-225.
[81] Ibid., p. 268.
[82] Ibid., pp. 265-266.

most striking is the distribution of 101 *timars* between 1549-1551 to an organized Turkman *sipahi* ("feudal" cavalry) regiment in Ḥawrān, which was subject, as were other *timar*-based regiments, to the sultan's call to serve in imperial campaigns. Each *timar* had a revenue of 2,000 *akçes*. The Turkman lands included two hundred and sixty *mazra'as*, or farms, and the total revenue was 267,000 *akçes*, of which 65,000 accrued to the sultan as personal income (*hass*). According to the Damascus administrative regulations (*kanunname*) of 1589, the Turkmans were considered part of the *reaya*, or that large, nonprivileged part of the Ottoman population that engaged in agriculture, crafts, and commerce.[83]

Accompanying what appears to have been the deliberate settlement of Turkman tribes in Syria—perhaps in conformity with Ottoman procedure following conquest of new territory—was the employment of tribesmen as *sancakbeyis* and local administrators. For example, Nāṣir al-Dīn ibn al-Hanash administered the Biqā', Beirut, and Sidon briefly after the Ottoman conquest. Ṭarabāy ibn Qarājā, in his capacity as governor of Ṣafad, was given responsibility for the roads that led from Damascus to Egypt and Jerusalem.[84] Other tribesmen were put in charge of the pilgrimage and competed vigorously for that privilege. Around the middle of the sixteenth century, however, about thirty years after the Ottoman conquest, Ottoman officials almost entirely replaced tribesmen employed in provincial administration. Toward the end of the century, the tribesmen who organized and commanded the pilgrimage were also replaced.[85] At the same time, the beduin were subjected to economic boycott by the state. Although not entirely successful, this measure seems to indicate an attempt to whittle down tribal economic power. The state also tried, in 1567, to confiscate from Damascus bazaars all heavy arrows, bows, and daggers that the beduin might purchase and then use against the settled population.[86] All of these events at the end of the century—settlement of

[83] Ibid., pp. 266-267.
[84] Ibid., p. 236.
[85] Ibid., pp. 236ff.
[86] Ibid., pp. 255-258.

Turkman tribes as apparent foils to the beduin, displacement of tribesmen from provincial administration and command of the pilgrimage, and attempts to cut off sources of arms and income—represent the "second stage" of Ottoman conquest as described by Halil Inalcik for the Balkan lands. In the first stage, the Ottomans would retain local institutions and personnel. After a considerable lapse of time, the state would displace them and substitute centralized Ottoman forms: "The Ottomanization of a conquered region was not a sudden and radical transformation, but a gradual development."[87] There were, however, in Syria, several important departures from this norm. In the first place, unlike the Ottoman conquests in Europe, the Arab lands contained a largely Muslim population whose control of the sources of wealth could not be easily broken. Within several weeks of their occupation of Damascus, the Ottomans tried to seize control of property deeds, especially of the vast *vakıf* (endowment) holdings that were administered by the local notables. This attempt naturally met with great opposition.[88] In the second place, the geographic and ethnic composition of the land did not permit as extensive or as easy a distribution of military "fiefs," or, more correctly, *timars*, which were the backbone of Ottoman administration in Anatolia and the Balkans. The security of communications between Syria and Arabia, Egypt, Iraq, and Anatolia made accommodation with the nomadic tribes imperative. This had its effects on the administrative divisions of the province of Damascus. From an unwieldy giant in the 1520s, Damascus was reduced considerably over the years (see Table 3). The larger, peripheral units to the north, such as Aleppo and Adana, were split off into separate provinces. Tripoli followed in the 1570s, while Sidon-Beirut shuttled between separate status and inclusion in the *paşa sancağı*, the provincial unit of Damascus in which the governor resided. Ḥamā and Ḥimṣ were drawn off to the newly created neighboring provinces of Aleppo and Tripoli respectively, al-

[87] Inalcik, *The Ottoman Empire*, p. 14. Inalcık's ideas are more fully presented in "Ottoman Methods of Conquest."

[88] Bakhit, "Ottoman Province" pp. 161-162.

TABLE 3
FORMAL DIVISIONS OF THE PROVINCE OF DAMASCUS, 1527-1641

1527[a]	*1568-1574*[b]	*1578-1588*[c]	*1632-1641*[d]
Damascus	Damascus	Damascus	Damascus
Jerusalem-Gaza	Jerusalem	Jerusalem	Jerusalem
	Gaza	Gaza	Gaza
Nablus-Şafad	Nablus	Nablus	Nablus
	Şafad	Şafad	Şafad }
	Sidon-Beirut (separated from Damascus)	(abolished)	Sidon } separate after 1660
			Beirut }
Şalţ-'Ajlūn	'Ajlūn	Şalţ-'Ajlūn	'Ajlūn
	Karak	Karak	Karak
	Lajjūn	Lajjūn	Lajjūn
	Tadmur (Palmyra)	Tadmur	Tadmur
	Şalkhad	(abolished)	
Tripoli	(separate province)		
Aleppo	(separate province)		
Adana	(added to Aleppo)	(separate province)	
Ḥamā-Himṣ	Ḥamā	Ḥamā (added to Aleppo)	
	Himṣ	Himṣ (added to Tripoli)	
	Ma'arra (to Aleppo)		
Uzeyrili, Antep, Sis	(separated from Damascus)		
Tarsus, Birecik	(added to Aleppo)		
Akrād	Akrād	Akrād	(added to Rakka)

NOTE: The divisions here are by *sancaks*, although the province was not so subdivided until 1521. See Bakhıt, "Ottoman Province," p. 44.

[a] Kunt, *Sancaktan eyalete*, p. 129, citing TKS-D. 5426.

[b] Ibid., p. 141, citing BA-Malıye 563.

[c] Ibid., p. 158, citing BA-Kepecı 262.

[d] Ibid., p. 189, citing BA-Kepecı 266.

though in the eighteenth century, their tax revenues were part of the income that Damascus governors devoted to the pilgrimage. Of interest to us in regard to the tribes is the appearance of four units, all of which were in the desert or on its edge: Karak, Lajjūn, Tadmur, and Ṣalkhad. The latter, exposed as it was on the edge of the Syrian desert,[89] was abolished within only a few years of its establishment. As a result of these shifts in provincial divisions, which were probably caused by tribal pressure and administrative difficulties, the province of Damascus in the seventeenth century could boast only 128 *zeamets* and 868 *timars*, whose beneficiaries were theoretically supposed to muster 9,065 *kılıç*, or armed retainers, as well as equipment and provisions for the empire's wars.[90] One consequence of a relatively weak *timar* system in Damascus was the very proliferation of provincial janissaries and mercenaries discussed above. The central government had to make satisfactory arrangements to secure the cooperation of and, with luck, the settlement of the tribes.

It is difficult to know precisely when, how, and why the tribes moved as they did. But it is obvious that, by the end of the seventeenth century, tribal encroachments threatened two areas of Syria: the vast plain around Ḥamā and Ḥimṣ, and the land bordered on the west by the Jordan River and on the north by Damascus. In both areas, apparent shifts of the tribal population had caused disruption of road communications and much jeopardy to the settled population. Banditry and imposition of "taxes" were commonplace tribal abuses. The effect of the tribal population shifts was threefold. First, the pilgrimage route from Damascus to Medina was seriously threatened, calling into question the Ottoman state's suze-

89 For references to Ṣalkhad in medieval Arab geographical literature, see Le Strange, *Palestine under the Moslems*, p. 529.

90 These figures are supplied without attribution by Evliya Çelebi in *Evliya Çelebi Seyahatnamesi*, IX, 530-531. For a number of reasons, Evliya's figures should be treated with skepticism. He includes Sidon, Beirut, and Ṣafad as *sancaks* of the province of Damascus, although, in fact, these *sancaks* had become a separate province in 1660, twelve years before Evliya's journey to Syria. This apparent error may mean that Evliya relied on figures given in 1609 by Ayn-i Âlî. See: *Osmanlı imparatorluğunda eyalet taksimatı*.

rainty over and access to the Holy Cities. Second, a decline in the sedentary population along the way jeopardized the trade routes that passed eastward from Anatolia through Aleppo and to the Persian front. In normal times, that population would have provided supplies for the Ottoman armies that fought several wars with Persia during the eighteenth century.[91] Third, the province of Damascus was caught in a vise between displaced Arab, Turkman, and Kurdish tribes from the north and the great movement of Arab tribes from the south that threatened the whole of the Fertile Crescent. In both areas—the northern and southern halves of Syria—the transhumant pattern of tribal life caused great difficulty to settled agriculture. The Turkmans spent the winter in the plains around Antioch as well as in the countryside of Hamā and Ḥimṣ; they moved in summer as far away as Elbistan in eastern Anatolia.[92] As for the Arab tribes, the 'Anaza confederation, which had begun to migrate from Arabia toward the Euphrates around the end of the seventeenth century, spent the spring and summer between Hadiyya (in the Ḥijāz) and Aleppo, and the autumn and winter in remote eastern parts of the Syrian Desert.[93]

The causes of these great shifts in the nomadic population may never be known. There is no evidence, for example, that drastic changes of climate were responsible for the movement of Arab tribes into more fertile regions. The very size of the forces that attacked the pilgrimage caravans of 1732 and 1757

[91] This is specifically stated in BA-Cevdet/Dahiliye 13477, dated middle Cemaziyelevvel 1146 (20-29 October 1733).

[92] Hasluck, *Christianity and Islam under the Sultans*, II, 480. Cf. the orders sent out in the early eighteenth century to control the Turkman, Kurdish, and Arab tribes in the western Fertile Crescent and eastern Anatolia: BA-Emiri/III Ahmed 5660, order to the governor of Damascus, dated beginning Zilhicce 1125 (19-28 December 1713); copies of this order were sent to the governors of Sidon, Beirut, Adana, Diyarbekır, Karaman, Anadolu, Sıvas, Tripoli, and Maraş. At a later date, the state again ordered the removal of wandering tribes to areas in which they had previously been confined: BA-Cevdet/Dahiliye 3989, dated 7 Şevval 1150 (28 January 1738), and addressed to the governors of Kütahya, Adana, Sıvas, Erzurum, Damascus, and Rakka.

[93] E. Gräf, " 'Anaza," *EI²*, I, 481-483.

may indicate population pressure by tribes against settled areas. Five hundred to two thousand beduin had been involved in some of the attacks of previous years.[94] Two other possible causes of the beduin migration have been advanced: the decline of the Mawālī beduin of the Aleppo region, which left a power vacuum into which the ʿAnaza moved from the south, and pressure from other tribes in Arabia proper, especially after the rise of the Wahhābīs in the later eighteenth century.[95] Already, by 1699, the ʿAnaza were providing transport and supplies for the pilgrimage.[96]

The response of the Ottoman state to the tribal threat was to encourage settlement in the north, prevent migration southward from Aleppo to Damascus, and to engage selected Arab tribesmen from the Damascus-Medina region to participate in the pilgrimage under the leadership of the *Şam urbanı şeyhi*, the chief of the Damascus beduins, an institution roughly equivalent to the *imārat al-ʿArab* of previous Islamic states.[97] Although the last measure had long been part of Ottoman policy, it appears to have been better organized and more extensive in the first half of the eighteenth century. The system was designed to contain the tribes and to make them compete for the lucrative state contracts provided by the pilgrimage commander.

The signs of the defeat of Ottoman policy were apparent in the pilgrimage attack of 1757, as well as in the years that followed. An important distinction is in order here. The evidence seems to indicate that the Ottomans were relatively successful in dealing with the tribes until the mid-eighteenth

[94] Shamır, "Asʿad Pasha al-ʿAẓm," p. 23.

[95] Gräf, " ʿAnaza," *EI*².

[96] Rafeq, *Province*, p. 71, n. 6; BA-Kepecı 1677, a register of payments (*sürre*) made to Arab tribes between 1695 and 1703. A total of 120,018 *kuruş* was dıspensed durıng that period to 3,170 ındıviduals. Payments to each trıbesman ranged from 8 to 500 *kuruş*.

[97] The earlıest known date for the existence of the *Şam urbanı şeyhi* is the early 1690s. BA-Ibnülemin/Dahiliye 2105, an order to three tribesmen whose clans shared the position, dated beginning Şaban 1103 (18-27 Aprıl 1692). This does not, of course, rule out the possibilıty that the posıtıon existed previously.

century, but that they lost the initiative after that date. Because the evidence is not as full as would be desirable, this distinction requires testing through further research. Professor Rafeq, relying on the evidence of European travelers of the late eighteenth and early nineteenth centuries, is convinced that the Ottomans paid "protection money" in return for services: "Not all tribes along the route [to Arabia] received such a payment—only the militant ones that could cause trouble and obstruct the passage of the Pilgrimage. The sums paid to these tribes were intended mainly to procure a safe passage through the regions they dominated. This also implied that the Beduin acted as guides to the Pilgrimage along the desert route."[98] The evidence presented here, however, suggests something rather different: the Ottomans increased their patronage in relation to the tribes and attempted to bring them into the network of dependence in which the notables and janissaries were involved. By opening urban markets to the beduin and by providing them with cash with which to purchase goods, the Ottomans hoped to draw the beduin into increased dependence on settled areas. In two respects, however, the Ottomans gravely miscalculated the effects of their policy. First, it was impossible to control the desert environment in which the beduin lived and it was impossible to limit their population growth and their movements. Second, the beduin used a large portion of their income from the state to purchase arms—illegally—from, among others, Ẓāhir al-'Umar (d. 1775), whose own prosperity, based on the intelligent sale of cotton crops to the French in Palestine, made it possible for him to purchase arms from Europe to sell to the beduin.[99] The effects of these miscalculations were increasingly felt as Ẓāhir's power grew during the third quarter of the eighteenth century.

During the first half of the eighteenth century, then, the Ottoman state was fully aware of the problems it faced in the province of Damascus from provincial groups. In response, it

[98] Rafeq, *Province*, pp. 70-71.
[99] Cohen, *Palestine*, p. 15.

developed and refined policies that would contain the three groups discussed: notables, janissaries, and tribesmen. Keeping each group within its system of patronage and dependence helped the Ottoman state revise the administrative structure of the province of Damascus.

THREE

THE PILGRIMAGE: CENTERPIECE OF OTTOMAN RULE IN DAMASCUS

INSIDE the harem of the Topkapı Palace in Istanbul, there is a tiny, dark vestibule. Little more than a passageway, it once served as a prayer room for the sultan's mother. On the walls are two beautiful tile panels dating from 1667. They show, respectively, the Prophet's mosque in Medina and an encampment of pilgrims near the Meccan sanctuary that was the focus of the pilgrimage. Elsewhere in the palace, there are large chambers where the key to that sanctuary and some of the personal effects of the Prophet are now exhibited. These bear witness to the Ottoman Empire's heritage of sovereignty over the Holy Cities. From 1517 to 1917, each Ottoman sultan tenaciously and jealously guarded his prerogative as servant of the holy sanctuaries (*khādim al-ḥaramayn al-sharīfayn*).[1] The major pilgrimage to these cities—the *ḥajj*—took place in the month named for it, Zilhicce, whereas the lesser one—*al-'umra*—could be performed at any time of the year. Like their predecessors in Islamic history who had assumed responsibility for the pilgrimage, the Ottoman sultans showed continuous, deep concern for the piety and orderliness of the pilgrimage, and for the security of the thousands of pilgrims who journeyed into the heart of Arabia.

The pilgrimage provided the Ottoman state with the annual opportunity to demonstrate its temporal authority, to show its colors, to assert its identity as the paramount Islamic state. The long and majestic journey through difficult terrain, the rituals of the pilgrimage, the commerce and trade that accompanied it, and the necessity for tranquility, piety, and order all required elaborate administrative preparations well

[1] *TDS*, I, 703; and Inalcık, *The Ottoman Empire*, pp. 33-34.

in advance of the departure of the two major caravans from Egypt and Syria.[2]

Although it by no means overshadowed its Egyptian counterpart, the Damascus caravan was of considerable importance in Ottoman times. This was, in part, because high Ottoman officials and members of the sultan's family, in addition to thousands of ordinary pilgrims from Rumeli, Anatolia, Iraq, and Persia traveled to Arabia along this route. One of its names is the "Imperial Way."[3] The preservation of this lifeline to the Holy Cities loomed as large in Ottoman self-awareness as, for example, did the route to India in the minds of British imperial planners in the nineteenth and twentieth centuries. "The most important of the exalted state's affairs" is a phrase that occurs often in Ottoman correspondence concerning the pilgrimage.

When lesser officials from the province of Damascus failed to lead and protect the caravan in the late seventeenth century,[4] the state saw fit to turn over command of the pilgrimage to the governor of Damascus. This was a regular practice after 1708. Like his Egyptian counterpart, the governor of Damascus was assigned the prestigious title of commander of the pilgrimage (mirülhac; Ar., amīr al-ḥajj). Because it was led by a vezir ranking high among provincial governors, the pilgrimage became the centerpiece of Ottoman rule in Damascus in the eighteenth century.

A host of administrative problems came to rank with religious concerns in the eyes of the Ottoman state. For example,

---

[2] For other routes, most of which flowed into the Damascene and Egyptian routes, see Uzunçarşılı, *Mekke*, p. 57.

[3] *Tarik-i Sultanî*. Mehmed Edib ıbn Mehmed Derviş, *Menasik-i hacc-ı şerif*, p. 247. A French translation by Bıanchi, *Itinéraire de Constantinople à la Mecque*, is incomplete and ınaccurate. An autograph copy of this work is preserved ın the Chester Beatty Library in Dublin, under the title, *Behcet'ül-menâzil*. See V. Minorsky, *The Chester Beatty Library*, pp. 98-99. Mehmed Edib went on the pilgrımage in 1779.

[4] Low-ranking Ottoman officials from the *sancak* of Damascus and tribal shaykhs from Nablus held the post of *mirülhacc* from the mıd-sixteenth to the late seventeenth centuries. See Bakhıt, "Ottoman Provınce," pp. 117-118.

adequate supplies of fodder for pack animals and food for the military escort were subjects of considerable correspondence. So important was the pilgrimage that it figured in most eighteenth-century requests from the grand vezir to the sultan to renew the terms of Damascus governors. Such requests referred to the pilgrimage as a vital duty and stated whether or not the commander in question had performed it properly.[5]

This chapter analyzes several aspects of the pilgrimage that related to Ottoman rule in Damascus, (1) the financial base that generated tax revenues for the pilgrimage, and which required extensive tax gathering and administrative effort by the governor; (2) the safe transport and delivery of money and food, raised from the sultan's personal treasury and from the income of pious foundations, to the poor of the Holy Cities (these were known as *sürre*; Ar., *ṣurra*); (3) the maintenance of a network of fortresses and garrisons along the route from Damascus to Arabia; (4) the organization of the caravan itself, with special attention to the military escort and transport of essential supplies; and (5) the safe return of the caravan to Damascus, particularly in the last stages, for which a special escort (the *cerde*; Ar., *jarda*) was provided.

Financial Base

As with its wars in Persia and Europe, the Ottoman state in the eighteenth century took great pains with the financial and military organization of the pilgrimage. Because the provinces of Damascus, Tripoli, and Sidon were expected to provide funds for this annual equivalent of a military campaign, tax collection and land tenure in these provinces came to acquire a special character. As related in the preceding chapter, military functions within the province, and especially in the major cities, were shared by mercenaries, local forces, and regular janissary troops. The cost of paying for the upkeep of these units, and the additional cost of paying for pilgrimage

[5] See, for example, BA-Cevdet/Dahılıye 14768, dated 29 Rebıyülevvel 1146 (10 September 1733), reappointment of Aydınlı Abdullah Paşa.

escort duty, created great strains on the economic and social fabric of the Syrian provinces in spite of efforts by the authorities to minimize expenses. Although the Syrian provinces participated less and less in the empire's wars, an Ottoman "campaign" involving thousands of troops was conducted each year at pilgrimage time. It is in these terms that a chronicler remarks that one governor of Damascus "conquered" or "opened up" the pilgrimage route (*fataḥa ṭarīq al-ḥajj*). He did so by strengthening the fortress network, subduing uncooperative tribes, and maintaining the roads. A further reference to the military character of the pilgrimage is found in an inspection of muster rolls (*yoklama*) of the local janissary forces in 1722. In it, those troops assigned to perform escort and garrison duty for the pilgrimage are called "campaigners."[6] To conduct the pilgrimage effectively required organized central control. This was provided by the governors of Damascus. It is understandable, then, that command of the pilgrimage, which was previously in the not so competent hands of lesser officials, was continuously assigned to governors of Damascus in the eighteenth century.

To raise sufficient funds required an effective system of tax collection. This, in turn, implied a detailed knowledge of the potential sources of wealth—the financial base of the Syrian provinces. A complete analysis of the Damascus tax structure is beyond the scope of this study. Amnon Cohen's recent study of Palestine is a sound and important contribution to the study of Ottoman fiscal history. Yet, it leaves open many questions about the pilgrimage's financial base. There is evidence, for instance, that the costs involved far exceeded the 300,000 *kuruş* that Cohen claims on the basis of evidence in annual tax registers. This is a good example of the pitfalls of research in the fiscal history of an Ottoman province. No tax register, or set of registers, however impressive and complex, can be regarded as complete. Additional registers, or even individual documents, may reveal revenues or expenditures not contained in a supposedly complete register. The present dis-

[6] *Seferliyân*. BA-Malıye 314, p. 18.

cussion attempts only to understand the way in which the pilgrimage was financed, not to analyze the whole fiscal system of the province of Damascus.

Sources of revenue for the pilgrimage, as far as can be determined with available evidence, were included in an annual pilgrimage budget, the account books of the provincial treasury, and the governor's personal record books. There was no single budget kept for all expenses, but the governor had the responsibility for coordination and expenditure.

Tax assessments for the pilgrimage were made first in Istanbul, normally during the month of Rebiyülevvel, seven months in advance of the pilgrimage caravan's departure from Damascus in the month of Şevval. The chief financial officer of the empire, the *başdefterdar*, would draw up a detailed budget, called a *tertib defteri*. He would list potential sources of income and calculate projected expenses for the pilgrimage, with the exception of the cost of actually raising the taxes, the pilgrimage fortress expenses, and the return escort costs. At the end of the budget, the *başdefterdar* would inform the grand vezir that the estimated figures had been recorded in the registers pertaining to each source of income. These registers were kept in the chief comptroller's office, the *başmuhasebe*. The *başdefterdar* would then request the grand vezir to issue the necessary documents that would authorize the governor of Damascus, with the assistance of the governors of Tripoli and Sidon, to collect taxes for these purposes. His petition usually followed this example:

> To ensure the safe departure and return, with God's help, of the joyful pilgrims who will travel in 1162 [1749] on the Damascus pilgrimage route under the supervision of the present governor of Damascus and commander of the pilgrimage, the honorable vezir, Hacci Esat Paşa [As'ad al-'Aẓm], the following expenses are recorded: wages and extras for 1,500 mercenary footsoldiers and cavalrymen; camels and other expenses; rental of camels for 400 Damascus local troops; basic and supplementary payments to Arab tribes; adding up to 309,341 *kuruş*. Of this sum,

94,040.5 *kuruş* are set aside as *ocaklık* [revenues raised for special purposes, usually for fortress and garrison maintenance]. . . . Besides this, there is also the sum of 215,300.5 *kuruş* itemized and raised by promissory note [*havale*] from the areas named [below]. Accordingly, upon your excellency's approval, these will be recorded in the chief comptroller's office and the necessary certificates, copies, and orders pertaining to the stated sums will be written. Orders to proceed are requested from your excellency.[7]

Once the necessary papers and orders were drawn up and approved, they were issued and sent to the governor of Damascus. He would then collect the taxes, either in cash or, occasionally, in kind. Theoretically, he was supposed to transmit the money to Istanbul for verification against the income side of the budget and the entries made in the registers of the chief comptroller's office. But, in practice, monies collected for the pilgrimage would be deducted from the net total sum sent annually to Istanbul from the province (the *irsaliye*). Given the very considerable expenses of the pilgrimage, "only a very small portion [of the revenues] was sent directly to the treasury itself."[8] Several reasons account for this departure from administrative routine. First, the time and trouble to move money over the great distance between Damascus and Istanbul, then back again in time for the pilgrimage, was too great and too risky. Second, there was the danger that funds raised for military purposes (*ocaklık*) might be embezzled by Istanbul janissary officers.[9] Third, the funds devoted to specific purposes and raised in the area would be spent right there. Here was a good sign of the central government's flexibility in dealing with a difficult enterprise. There were other signs of flexibility as well. These are worth consideration here.

For example, Osman Paşa Muhassil, a former governor of Damascus (1739-1740), was dismissed from the Sidon gover-

[7] BA-Emırı/ı Mahmud 352, dated 25 Rebıyülevvel 1161 (15 March 1749).
[8] Cohen, *Palestine*, p. 228. [9] Ibıd., pp. 229-230.

norship for failing to remit to Damascus badly needed pilgrimage revenues for the year 1746. He was transferred—in effect banished—to Jidda, and his successor was ordered to make up the arrears with the assistance of the governors of Damascus and Tripoli.[10] Osman Paşa's failure was not due solely to the troubled internal political situation in Sidon, where dissension among members of the semiautonomous Shihāb family made tax collection difficult. Osman Paşa was also engaged in a feud with Esat Paşa (al-'Azm), then governor of Damascus. He may have believed that, by withholding tax revenue, he could jeopardize his rival's position as commander of the pilgrimage and prevent him from assigning the Sidon governorship to one of his own men with the help of friends in Istanbul. If it was Osman Paşa's belief that the central government would accept his excuse of political rivalries and disorder within Sidon province, he was greatly mistaken. In fact, the grand vezir sent him a private letter of warning that contained an elaborate statement of Ottoman political ideas on provincial administration. The letter asserted that (1) governors were appointed to oversee the good government of their provinces; (2) governors should cooperate with one another in spheres of critical importance to the state; and (3) the finances of the pilgrimage should not become a means for conducting personal vendettas.[11] Osman Paşa's dismissal followed soon after.

Another example of the central government's flexibility with respect to pilgrimage finances was its willingness to draw on funds from other sources when circumstances required it. There is evidence that this was a well-established practice. For example, in 1742, a deficiency in pilgrimage revenues was made up from money raised in the eastern Anatolian province of Urfa.[12] In 1770, the chief Muslim jurisconsult

[10] Ibid., p. 232.

[11] BA-Cevdet/Dahiliye 11054, *kayime* (letter from the grand vezir) dated 15 Cemaziyelâhır 1162 (3 June 1749). For the situation in Sidon, see Rafeq, *Province*, pp. 189-192.

[12] TKS-E. 3439, dated end Şaban 1155 (late October 1742), a letter in Arabic to the governor of Damascus, which specifies the sum of 14,000 *kuruş*, its source, and the method of transferring it to Damascus from Urfa.

of the Ḥanafī rite (the *muftī*) in Damascus received an order from the central government that referred to a massive deficiency in pilgrimage revenue, probably due to the Egyptian invasion of Syria in that year. The invasion struck first at Gaza, then at other parts of Palestine before threatening Damascus.[13] The order to the Damascus *muftī* noted several precedents for raising pilgrimage revenues from other sources. It allowed the governor of Damascus, Gürcü Osman Paşa, to use the revenues of the Damascus tobacco customs for the preceding two years—which amounted to 423,380.5 *kuruş* out of a total of 472,957 available—to make up the deficit.[14]

Further evidence of the central government's ability to deal with the unexpected is found in the budgets for the pilgrimage in the years 1733, 1749, and 1764 (see Appendix IV). The variety of sources of income is noteworthy, although two broad types of taxes may be identified. The first was *mal-ı miri*, or *miri*,[15] taxes on land held under various forms of tenure; the second was the *cizye* (Ar., *jizya*), the poll tax on non-Muslim male heads of households. The areas affected were the provincial subunits (*sancaks*) of Damascus, Ḥimṣ, Ḥamā, Ma'arra, Jerusalem, 'Ajlūn-Lajjūn, Gaza-Ramla, and Nablus and the provinces of Sidon-Beirut and Tripoli. When required, there were also assessments on the poll tax of Aleppo, on the standing debts and confiscated inheritances (*muhallefât*) of Ottoman officials in the province, and on other sources.

On the expense side of the budget, the relatively stable outlay over the period spanned by our three examples was broken only by several thousand *kuruş* for additional fortress protection. On the income side, a slight decline in *ocaklık* revenues (monies expressly devoted to military expenses) were

[13] Rafeq, *Province*, pp. 225-257.

[14] TKS-E. 2382, dated 1184 (1770) by the archivist.

[15] That is, the tax on land calculated "from the beginning of March of one year until the end of February the following year," although in the registers in Istanbul, "it was regarded as covering a single *hijrī* year." Cohen, *Palestine*, p. 204.

made up by a sharp increase in the poll tax and revenues from the tax farms (*mukataas*) of Ḥamā, Ḥimṣ, and Sidon. The first two of these areas were usually the personal responsibility of Damascus governors, who received them along with their governorships. Sidon, which, in the eighteenth century, underwent considerable economic development under the stimulus of foreign trading centers, provided an expanding tax base. However, in the pilgrimage budgets, this is not immediately apparent, for total *net* income rose over the thirty-year period to meet only a minor increase in fortress maintenance. In every case, the budget was balanced, at least on paper.

Several entries on the income side of the budget deserve brief consideration. They suggest important trends in patterns of land-tenure, trends to which we can refer only in passing. The *mal-ı miri* of Damascus, also called the *bedeliye*, was raised within the *sancak* of Damascus, that is, the administrative subunit of the province in which the governor resided (the *paşa sancağı*). The sum of 12,000 *kuruş* remained fixed throughout the eighteenth century. It was levied in lieu of military service by beneficiaries of *timars* and *zeamets*. In the classical Ottoman provincial system, the state had sustained military reserves by providing provincial governors, their subordinates, and lesser figures in the military (*askeri*) class with *timars* and *zeamets*,[16] usufruct on specific lands in return for military service in the empire's wars. In addition to administrative duties, beneficiaries were expected to reside in the areas whose income they enjoyed; and they were to be fit to provide military service. The precise manner in which this system deteriorated rapidly in the Syrian provinces is still not understood.[17] We do know, however, that two disastrous

[16] For an excellent description of this system, see Inalcık, *The Ottoman Empire*, pp. 108ff; for further details, see Gibb and Bowen, *Islamic Society*, I, 1, pp. 46ff.

[17] We know, for example, that the provinces of Sidon and Tripoli largely retained a pre-Ottoman system of tax farms, or *mukataas*, which eventually supplanted the Ottoman system in other parts of Syria. In the later seventeenth century, a refinement of the *mukataa*, known as *malikâne*, was in-

trends developed. First, beneficiaries unfit for military service and frequently absent from their assigned lands began to receive *timars*. Second, the military service requirement in the Syrian provinces was reinforced because beneficiaries had to provide escort either for the outward journey of the pilgrimage or for the return. This required the beneficiaries' absence from their lands for up to four months of every year. During the early decades of Ottoman rule in Syria, this requirement was strictly enforced, with loss of tenure the punishment for failure to comply.[18] By the eighteenth century, only a few beneficiaries in the Palestinian *sancaks*, for example, were required to perform military escort duty. On most occasions, they failed to do so, fearing to leave home because rivals on the scene might usurp their rights and also because they lacked the proper equipment with which to perform their tasks.[19] The general practice of payment of a sum of money in lieu of service was instituted. This payment became known as the *bedel* or *bedeliye*.[20] As the eighteenth century progressed, beneficiaries had difficulty in paying even this sum. *Bedels* of 3,000 *kuruş* for the *sancak* of Jerusalem and of 8,000 for Gaza, Nablus, and Lajjūn were not paid after the second decade of the eighteenth century.[21] *Timar* and *zeamet* holders of the *sancak* of Damascus were more conscientious, probably because the governor could put pressure on them more easily. In one case, the beneficiaries were unable to produce the sum. They appealed to the central government, complaining that they were suffering from repeated crop failures and the flight of the peasant population. They begged to be relieved of their obligation so that their villages could be rebuilt. They also asked for an inspection of land registers to verify the names of the

troduced. It was a life leasehold given under special terms to individuals who often did not reside in the areas under their assumed supervision. See Gibb and Bowen, *Islamic Society*, I, 2, pp. 22-23.

[18] Bakhit, "Ottoman Province," pp. 121-122.

[19] Cohen, *Palestine*, pp. 298ff.

[20] The *bedel* is thought to have been first introduced in 1659. See Harold Bowen, "Badal," *EI*², I, 855.

[21] Cohen, *Palestine*, p. 307.

proper beneficiaries. Apparently the central government refused to accept this appeal and reconfirmed the *bedel* obligation.[22] On another occasion, later in the century, the governor of Damascus was compelled to accept less than the full tax.[23]

Two other types of income in the pilgrimage budget deserve brief consideration. The *avarız*, also known as the *avarız-ı divaniye*, of Damascus were originally extraordinary taxes raised under the jurisdiction of state-appointed magistrates (*kadis*) and were applied for special purposes, usually for wars.[24] In practice, the *avarız* became additional annual taxes. It permitted the Ottoman state "to secure the performance of certain services and the supply of certain commodities free (so to speak) by . . . exempting those peasants and townsmen who could furnish such assistance from the payment of these taxes."[25] There were many other ramifications of this levy. In two of the pilgrimage budgets referred to, it appears that the *avarız* were used to make up what would otherwise have been a deficit. In the third budget, no such entry exists. Finally, the sums included in the budgets for tax farms of the *defterdarlık* and *kethüdalık* of Damascus were the annual fees paid by the holders of these two offices (chief treasurer and chief lieutenant, respectively) for lands whose usufruct they enjoyed.[26]

Informative as they are, the budgets do not give a full picture of the financial base of the annual pilgrimage. Because the expense side of these budgets showed a remarkable stability over a thirty-year period during which there was rampant

[22] BA-Emirı/III Ahmed 7374, dated 23 Rebıyülevvel 1134 (12 January 1722).

[23] TKS-D. 3073, folio 2b, where the amount collected in 1186 (1772) was 2,413 *kuruş* short of the full 12,000.

[24] Gibb and Bowen, *Islamic Society*, I, 2, pp. 2-4.

[25] Ibid., pp. 3-4.

[26] For the provincial *kethüda*, the governor's second in command, see Shamir, " 'Azm Wālīs," p. 222. That the *defterdarlik* and *kethüdalık* were tax farms is confirmed in BA-Emirı/I Mahmud 12852 and 12853 (dated 11 Safer 1165/31 December 1751), which contain promissory notes that specify sums to be raised for the pilgrimage and to be drawn from these tax-farms and the *avarız* of Damascus.

inflation, the governors of Damascus clearly had to raise other revenues to make up deficits. No further information is available as to why the budgets did not account for all income and expense. It may be that this was a device employed by the central government to hold down projected expenses for wages of the escort troops and their provisions, the largest items in the budget. Even in 1795-1796, the total revenues listed in one source for the pilgrimage were 311,316 *kuruş*,[27] precisely equal to those assessed thirty-one years before in the budget for 1764. Consistent cost cutting in the budgets is explained not so much by the tax potential of Damascus and the surrounding provinces as by the long-standing liquidity crisis from which the Ottoman state had suffered since the later sixteenth century. The crisis was partly due to the influx of New World silver, to the state's vast military expenditures on standing armies, and the decline of the reserve cavalry that had earned its income on land.[28] There is substantial supporting evidence of this important trend in the empire's fiscal affairs in the case of the Damascus military establishment. Here, the attempts by the state to hold down expenses on military wages took the form of bookkeeping devices. Wages of both mercenaries for the pilgrimage and the regular forces scattered along the province's fortress network were calculated in *akçes* (aspers), the unit of account of the sixteenth century. In the records of the central government, when these *akçes* were converted into *kuruş* (piasters), that is, into real terms, the exchange rate was often fixed at the high rate of 160 *akçes* to the *kuruş*, rather than 120, which was the prevailing rate for most other transactions during the eighteenth century. This had the effect of reducing by about one-third the actual expenses in *kuruş*, thus limiting the outflow of hard cash. What stands out most sharply is that revenues raised for the maintenance of the provincial military were affected by the frequent use of this device. When these monies were assessed, they were calculated at 120 *akçes* per *kuruş*; and when

[27] Cohen, *Palestine*, p. 66, n. 133.
[28] Inalcik, *The Ottoman Empire*, pp. 49ff.

spent, at 160.[29] The state thus profited from both processes, calculation of income *and* expense. Dissatisfied with the precipitous decline in the real value of their wages, a segment of the Damascus military petitioned the central government in 1722 for an increase to offset these cost-cutting devices. This request was made by ninety local Damascus janissaries who were assigned to garrison duty along the pilgrimage route. They were initially granted an increase in the daily wage for this duty. Their pay was raised from 5 to 15 *akçes* per person. In current costs, this sum could buy only a dozen eggs.[30] One year's pay for one man came to 5,310 *akçes* and, for the lot, the total was 477,900 *akçes*. Converted at 160 *akçes* per *kuruş*, the sum came to 2986.75 *kuruş* and 5 *paras*.[31] Nevertheless, the central government revoked the wage increase in the following year. It cited the precedent set on three previous occasions for maintaining the 5-*akçe* wage (in 1693-1694, 1710-1711, and 1718-1719) and the danger that an increase might disrupt the tax structure.[32] The *firman* that was issued some months later officially revoking the increase, ordered the governor of Damascus to maintain proper records of recipients of pay for garrison duty and insisted that all recipients be paid equally. The purpose of this last injunction was to assure that all ninety men would go to their posts rather than only a few who might pocket the wages of the rest. Records were hence-

[29] For example, revenues intended for the pilgrimage and raised from the crown lands (*hasslar*) and tax farms (*mukataas*) of the province of Sidon-Beirut in 1744 and 1745 were calculated in *akçes* and then converted to *kuruş* at 125 *akçes* per *kuruş esedi* (or lion dollar). TKS-E. 3232/1, 17, dated respectively 2 Ramazan 1157 and 15 Cemaziyelevvel 1158 (9 October 1744 and 15 June 1745). The same device was in use earlier in the century, for example, in a document concerning the poll tax of the Syrian provinces. BA-Emiri/III Ahmed 209, dated 15 Rebiyülâhır 1131 (8 March 1719).

[30] Budayrī, *Ḥawādith*, p. 35 (1742 prices, but comparable in this case, even assuming a high rate of inflation in the interim).

[31] BA-Malıye 6676, p. 2, dated 20 Ramazan 1134 (4 July 1722). At a rate of 120 *akçes*, the cash outflow would have been 3,982.5 *kuruş*. The central government thus saved nearly 1,000 *kuruş* on this transaction.

[32] The wage increase "would damage revenue flow to the state," meaning that the tax structure would be upset. Ibid., p. 4, petition to the grand vezir, approved on 1 Rebıyülâhır 1135 (10 January 1723).

forth to be sent to Istanbul every year to verify that no established practice was violated.[33] This practice persisted until 1755.

One of the two other major sources of income for the pilgrimage was the provincial treasury of Damascus (*Şam defterdarlığı*). It appears to have laid out 82,000 *kuruş* for the pilgrimage, over half of its annual income. Most of this sum was devoted to supplies and transport for local janissaries escorting the pilgrimage caravan and for payments to Arab tribes and religious functionaries in the Holy Cities. The balance of the provincial treasury's annual revenues was reserved to pay the pensions of retired provincial employees, salaries of provincial clerks, wages of garrison troops in the province, and miscellaneous expenses.

The most striking trends in the two provincial account registers for 1741-1742 and 1759-1760 are the increase in pensions and the inclusion in the second register of garrison wages for the pilgrimage fortress network (these records were post facto accounts of actual collections and expenditures, see Appendix v). From a net profit of 2,502.5 *kuruş* in 1741-1742, the provincial treasury fell into a deficit of 4,751 *kuruş* in 1759-1760. In spite of an increase of 9,000 *kuruş* in revenue, the deficit occurred because of a jump of nearly 16,000 *kuruş* in expense. Income devoted to the pilgrimage remained constant at 82,000 *kuruş*, although, in the first register, an additional 5,000 was taken from the surplus for pilgrimage expense and reduced the total surplus to 2,502.5 *kuruş*. The sources of pilgrimage revenue in these registers were among the richest in the Syrian provinces. For example, the assessment of an average of 25,000 *kuruş* from Sidon-Beirut's tax farm in the budgets was supplemented by the 45,000 *kuruş* accruing to the Damascus provincial treasury. Tripoli contributed 29,350 *kuruş* over the average 45,000 assessed in the budgets.[34] If the

[33] Ibid., pp. 6-7; order approved on 4 Zilhicce 1135 (6 September 1723).

[34] The practice of distinguishing between the two accounts persisted throughout the century. See Cohen, *Palestine*, p. 226. In a register of income and expense for 1742, compiled by the governor and including both these accounts, the different assessments are kept separate. TKS-E. 2025/1, dated

average income raised according to the budgets is considered to have been 310,000 *kuruş*, the addition of revenue from the treasury of Damascus brings the total revenue for the pilgrimage to nearly 400,000.

The last source of additional revenue for the pilgrimage, the *dawra*, was the Damascus governor's personal contribution collected on his annual tour of the southern *sancaks* of his province. These *sancaks* included Nablus, 'Ajlūn-Lajjūn, Gaza, Jerusalem, and sometimes the Shūf (the mountainous area within the province of Sidon known at the time as Mount Lebanon). The *dawra* was probably begun when governors began to assume regular responsibility for the pilgrimage and when the chief tax farmers (*mutasarrıfs*) of the affected districts were no longer able to meet their tax obligations.[35] Then, the governors of Damascus took up those obligations when they became direct administrators of the districts. That the *dawra* was "in itself clear indication of the Porte's weakening hold over the *sancaks* and the collapse of the taxation system in the area"[36] is too strong a statement. After all, the central government had permitted responsibility to devolve on local officials in the classical system of Ottoman rule. When local officials failed to perform their tasks adequately, the central government transferred responsibility to provincial governors. Beginning in the eighteenth century, governors were appointed *mutasarrıfs* of several of the most troublesome *sancaks*. By no means did this necessarily imply a "weakening hold." Instead, it represented an attempt to come to grips with changes in local conditions. When all was said and done, the state managed to gather its taxes, either by obtaining what it had originally assessed, and often more with the governor's help, or by debiting governors' personal accounts for any arrears.

Not much is known about the organization of the *dawra*. However, from records kept of expenditure on this institution on one occasion, it cost approximately 65,000 *kuruş* to

end Muharrem 1156 (26 March 1743). Another example is a register for 1185 (1771-1772): TKS-D. 4364.

[35] Cohen, *Palestine*, p. 166.

[36] Ibid.

collect taxes in this way.[37] Collection usually began in the month of Şaban and sometimes as early as Rebiyülevvel. The governor would set out with a large column of troops, gather the taxes—often extorting more than was due—and return to Damascus by the month of Ramazan so that he could organize the pilgrimage caravan for departure the following month. His tour would last, therefore, from two to five months.[38] It was, no doubt, the most critical time of the year for the governor, aside from the pilgrimage itself. He had to ensure, first, that the revenues he raised would meet his obligations as tax gatherer of the areas for which he was *mutasarrıf* and, second, that they would provide sufficient revenues to finance the pilgrimage. In addition to financial pressures, the governor also had to contend with security problems, for several of the southern *sancaks* covered by the *dawra* were contiguous with the pilgrimage route. Two groups had to be kept in check there: first, any rebellious local chieftains who could and did try to prevent the effective collection of taxes or otherwise disturb the peace; and, second, any beduin tribes *not* in cooperation with the state who could raid villages and farms in these areas or, from these vantage points, attack the pilgrimage caravan on its return to Damascus.

During the eighteenth century, the total revenue raised on this tour ranged from 200,000 to 300,000 *kuruş* over and above the assessments made in the pilgrimage budgets. This may indicate that the budgets took into account the probability that the *dawra* would raise further revenue; hence, the very small assessments made on the *dawra* areas in the budgets. With respect to the total income reported by the governor of Damascus, we can point to the example of the year 1744-

[37] TKS-E. 2025/1, dated end Muharrem 1156 (26 March 1743). This is a register of income and expense compiled by the governor, Süleyman Paşa al-ʿAzm. His expenses on the *dawra* are given as 65,000 *kuruş*, which, by comparison, represents about one-fifth of the pilgrimage budget. In the same year, 16,620 *kuruş* represented the pay of soldiers who accompanied the governor. TKS-E. 2588/11, dated 5 Cemaziyelâhır 1156 (27 July 1743).

[38] Rafeq, *Province*, pp. 21-23; Shamir, " ʿAzm Wālīs," p. 33; Cohen, *Palestine*, pp. 165-166.

1745, when the governor accounted for total revenues from all sources amounting to about 700,000 *kuruş*.[39] Slightly less than half of this sum was raised to meet pilgrimage budget assessments, which provides direct confirmation that these were virtually all met in full. The remaining income was composed as follows:

1.	Surplus carried forward from 1743-1744	38,856 *kuruş*
2.	Revenue from debts paid and from the sale of soap, wheat, and other commodities	132,452 *kuruş*
3.	Sale of grain and fodder to various persons on the pilgrimage	39,004 *kuruş*
4.	Income from *zabit* of 'Ajlūn (local military official who helped governor on *dawra*)	4,843 *kuruş*
5.	Income from *dawra*, except Jerusalem	158,196 *kuruş*
6.	Income from Jerusalem	20,000 *kuruş*
7.	Additional revenue, from Jerusalem monasteries	9,900 *kuruş*

The second and third items above are not broken down further in this register, but they are evidence of the extensive dealings of provincial governors in the sale of essential commodities, the profits on which were helpful to the governor in meeting his obligations or, when possible, in amassing a fortune. Revenues of the *dawra* (items 4-7 above) are substantial here, adding up to about 190,000 *kuruş*. Expenses on the *dawra* for 1744-1745 were about 65,000 *kuruş*. By 1771-1772, that sum had reached 260,000 *kuruş*.[40] In that year, the *dawra* collection from Nablus was an especially remarkable 116,975 *kuruş*. Another large bloc of cash was collected from the "three monasteries of Jerusalem" (probably European Christian missions; cf. item 7 above)[41]—a sum that came to

[39] TKS-E. 2025/1.

[40] TKS-D. 4364; see Appendix VI.

[41] Rafeq, *Province*, pp. 22-23.

63,193.5 *kuruş*. Other districts paid fair-sized taxes either in cash or in kind.

To sum up, the financial base of the Damascus pilgrimage in roughly the first half of the eighteenth century probably exceeded 500,000 *kuruş*, 300,000 from budget assessments, 82,000 from the provincial treasury, and 135,000 from the *dawra* (a net figure that accounts for the cost of that mission). As indicated above, governors of Damascus reported at least 700,000 *kuruş* as income during this period. However, these only indicate revenues devoted to the governors' own local expenditure. There was also other income, from taxes on oil and tabacco, and from customs revenues, and income from taxes on livestock and crops that on occasion could be devoted to the pilgrimage. For example, the tobacco customs revenues of roughly 225,000 *kuruş* per year were an excellent resource in times of need.[42]

The pilgrimage's financial base was thus divided between the provincial governor and the provincial treasury, although the burden of collection fell on the governor. A rather unrealistic budget was drawn up every year with tax assessments and estimates of expenditure. The budgets reflected the fiscal conservatism of the central bureaucracy, for, with the help of various bookkeeping devices, the state managed to hold down theoretical expenditure to about 300,000 *kuruş*. Faced with far greater actual outlays, which he had to meet in order to secure a safe and orderly pilgrimage, the governor of Damascus drew an additional 82,000 *kuruş* from taxes accruing to the provincial treasury. He also went on a tour of the southern *sancaks* of his province to raise the balance of his needs and to attempt to ensure that the caravan would not be attacked when it returned from the Holy Cities. The financial management of the pilgrimage reflected two important aspects of Ottoman rule in Damascus: the central government's flexibility in handling revenue problems and its division of financial resources between the governor, the provincial treasury, and the *dawra*.

[42] TKS-E. 2382, dated 1184 (1770) by the archivist.

THE *Sürre*

Before the Ottoman state acquired sovereignty over the Holy Cities in 1516-1517, the sultan had followed the practice of sending gifts of money and provisions to the poor of Mecca and Medina on the occasion of the pilgrimage. Sultan Bayezid I and his son became the first Ottoman rulers to dispatch these gifts, known as *sürre* (literally, purse of money).[43] In some years, the *sürre* was provided to the poor of Jerusalem and Hebron—to those of Jerusalem because of its importance as the place from which Muḥammad ascended to heaven during his miraculous journey to Jerusalem, and to those of Hebron because it was the traditional burial place of the patriarch Abraham. When Sultan Selim I completed his conquest of the Mamlūk Empire in 1517, he received the key to the holy sanctuary in Mecca (the *Ka'ba*), as well as the relics of Muḥammad. They were symbols of Islamic sovereignty. For the next four centuries, the Ottoman sultan continued the tradition of dispatching the *sürre* to the Holy Cities every year at pilgrimage time. In addition to the poor, recipients came to include the Meccan *şerifs*, the semiautonomous rulers of the Hijāz who were members of the Hāshimite clan of Quraysh, the Prophet Muḥammad's clan and tribe. Rich notables also managed to get on the rolls of beneficiaries. The institution of the *sürre* developed to such an extent that a special administrative apparatus was created in Istanbul to manage its affairs. Safe delivery of the *sürre* became the responsibility of provincial governors along the route from Istanbul to Arabia. Governors of Damascus, as we shall see, were assigned responsibility for well over half that route during the eighteenth century. Until about 1714, Egypt was the main entrepôt for the procession carrying the *sürre*, which sailed from Istanbul to Egypt and then proceeded overland to Arabia through Sinai and southern Jordan or across the Red Sea. After 1714 the route shifted to Damascus for reasons still not clear.[44] How-

[43] Uzunçarşılı, *Mekke*, p. 13.

[44] Ibid., p. 35, citing an order in BA-Mühimme 122, p. 126, dated end Receb 1126 (2-11 August 1714).

ever, Egypt continued to be the funnel for money and provisions—also called *sürre*—whose beneficiaries included the Arab tribes around Medina.

Money for this pious purpose was raised from the Sultan's personal allowance and income from special pious foundations (*haremeyn vakıfları*). Administrative responsibility devolved on the chief of the sultan's harem, the *kızlar ağası*, who wielded great influence both in the sultan's household and in the empire at large. He was responsible for preparation of the *sürre* and the elaborate ceremonies that preceded its departure from Istanbul to Arabia.

Pious foundations, as mentioned, were an important source of funds for this institution as well as for other pious efforts. They were administered by a special bureau known as the bureau of accounts for the Holy Cities,[45] which was under the supervision of the grand vezir's office. But, on the whole, *sürre* revenues and their expenditure were managed by the *kızlar ağası*, who held the post of supervisor of the pious foundations for the Holy Cities.[46] He also controlled the revenues of foundations that provided salaries for religious functionaries throughout the empire. Once amassed, revenues for the *sürre* were deposited in a special treasury account located in the sultan's palace, and under the *kızlar ağası*'s supervision.[47] Because the pious foundations established specifically for the *sürre* were large in number and extended virtually over the whole empire, they enhanced the power and prestige of the *kızlar ağası*. In administering these accounts, he could hope to gain considerable information on local conditions in Ottoman provinces.[48] It was precisely such information that enabled the *ağa* to influence provincial appointments and dismissals.

[45] *haremeyn muhasebesi kalemi*. Uzunçarşılı, *Merkez ve bahriye*, pp. 346–347.

[46] *haremeyn vakıfları nezareti*. Uzunçarşılı, *Saray*, pp. 177-180. See also d'Ohsson, *Tableau*, III, 257ff.

[47] The special treasury was called the *haremeyn dolabı*. Uzunçarşılı, *Saray*, p. 181.

[48] For example, TKS-D. 4055 lists revenues from fifteen endowments in cities ranging from Trabzon to Edirne and from Istanbul to Damascus for the year 1160 (1747), to the amount of 25,446.5 *kuruş*.

Another important source of funds for the *sürre* was the sultan's personal treasury, specifically, that gained from income accruing to the sultan for his personal use.[49] For example, this source, along with some of the monies in the special treasury account, provided nearly half a million *kuruş* over the years 1711-1713.

Before considering the role of Damascus governors in the safe escort and delivery of the *sürre*, it will be useful to review the procedures by which the *sürre* was dispatched to Arabia and to demonstrate thereby its importance and the involvement of high Ottoman officialdom in its dispatch.[50]

On the twelfth of Receb every year, that is, three months before the departure of the pilgrimage caravan from Damascus, a special purse commissioner (*sürre emini*) was appointed in Istanbul. As representative of the state in this position of trust, the commissioner was normally chosen either from the *hacegân*, the upper bracket of Ottoman officials that included bureau chiefs; from trusted members of the palace bureaucracy; or, as was the practice in the late eighteenth and nineteenth centuries, from the ulema, religious learned men.[51] The commissioner had to be pious and honest by reputation—and wealthy. He was provided with a retinue that included water carriers (*saka başılar*) and a special official, the *müjdeci başı*. The latter's task was to bring to Istanbul the good news of the pilgrimage's safe return from Arabia to

[49] *Avaıd ve ceyb-i hümayun akçeleri*. TKS-E. 4415, dated 1 Rebiyülevvel 1125 (28 March 1713), a report to the sultan from the *kızlar ağası* concerning the income and expense from these sources.

[50] The following account of the *surre* ceremonies is derived from Uzunçarşılı, *Mekke*, pp. 35-40. Another good account is in *TDS*, III, 280ff, and in d'Ohsson, *Tableau*, III, 278-279.

[51] *TDS*, III, 283. For example, the *surre emini* for 1707 was a former chief comptroller (*başmuhasebeci*). In 1762, he was a chief doorkeeper (*kapıcıbaşı*) from the "outside service" of the palace (see Gibb and Bowen, *Islamic Society*, I, 1, p. 346). In 1731, the *sürre emini* was a former deputy to the grand vezir (*sadr-ı azam kethüdası*). See respectively BA-Cevdet/Dahiliye 8733, 1299, and 1223, dated respectively end Cemaziyelâhır 1119 (17-27 September 1707), 19 Cemaziyelâhır 1175 (16 January 1762), and beginning Rebiyulâhır 1144 (3-13 October 1731).

Damascus. After being given ceremonial robes at the offices of the grand vezir, the commissioner was sent to the *kızlar ağası* in the palace to receive another robe of honor. With the assistance of the chief of all Ottoman bureaus (the *reisülkuttap*), the keeper of the seal (*nişancı*), and the first deputy of the grand vezir (*sadaret kethüdası*), the commissioner would write out all the registers and certificates of *sürre* recipients. After preparation in the offices of the grand vezir, the customary imperial letter (*nâme-i hümayun*) to the *şerif* of Mecca on the occasion of the pilgrimage was brought to the palace. Then, all the registers were sealed in the offices of the *kızlar ağası*'s chief secretary inside the harem. After a meal given in honor of the commissioner, his retinue, and the religious functionaries of the palace, the whole group would leave the harem and proceed to the large courtyard in front of the domed chamber where the imperial council met. To the acclamation of all present, the sultan would then appear on horseback from his quarters and take his place in front of the domed chamber. From their repository in the harem, the purses of money and the royal letter were brought out for the sultan's inspection. After the money was counted, the registers were sealed inside special envelopes. These, along with the royal letter, were then handed to the sultan for his seal, following which the *kızlar ağası* presented them to the commissioner and his retinue. As prayers were said, the entire *sürre* was loaded on a convoy of camels and paraded around the courtyard by the master of the sultan's stable. Then the *kızlar ağası* was given the brocaded halter to lead the *mahmal* camel (the camel carrying the *sürre* registers and the imperial letter).[52] He, in turn, would pass the halter to the commissioner. At this point, one of the most critical parts of the ceremony took place. The *kızlar ağası* would approach the sultan, prostrate himself, and kiss the ground. By custom, this was the moment when the *ağa* would expect either dismissal from office or confirmation. After that test was endured, the *kızlar ağası* and the officials who managed the

[52] Uzunçarşılı, *Mekke*, p. 57.

affairs of the Holy Cities' endowments escorted the commissioner, his retinue, and the camel caravan to the palace gates, then returned to their quarters. From the palace gates, the procession was escorted by *baltacıs* (harem guards responsible to the *kızlar ağası*) past the Alay Köşkü, the ornate building at the edge of the palace grounds, from which the sultan could watch the procession unobserved, and down to the Kireç Iskelesi, the pier from which the procession boarded ship to be taken to the Asian side of Istanbul.

After petitioning the sultan and receiving permission to proceed with the journey, the commissioner set out for Damascus following the route through Kocaeli, Akşehir, Konya, Adana, and Ḥamā. Responsibility for the *sürre*'s safety was given to all officials (both governors and religious functionaries) of administrative units along the route. For example, the governor of Karaman was charged with protection of the *sürre* from Konya to Adana; the governor of Aleppo for the route from Adana to Ḥamā; and the governor of Damascus from Ḥamā onward.[53] Any changes in route had to be approved by the central government, which took great pains to plan any new routes in case of emergency.[54]

Upon arrival in Damascus, the *sürre* retinue took part in another ceremony with the participation of provincial officials, the military, and the populace. This involved the removal of the Prophet's banner (*liva-ı saadet* or *sancak-ı şerif*) from the Damascus citadel to the governor's offices in preparation for the pilgrimage journey.[55] An important symbol of Ottoman sovereignty, it had first been placed in the Damascus citadel by Selim I after his conquest of Syria and Egypt in

[53] BA-Cevdet/Dahılıye 15140 (twelve documents concerning protection of the *surre* of 1177/1763-64); BA-Emıri/ııı Ahmed 16827, dated end Receb 1128 (10-20 July 1716); and BA-Mühımme 160, p. 138, dated beginning Receb 1171 (11-21 March 1758).

[54] For example, on one occasion, the *sürre* had to take a long detour through eastern Anatolia because the bridge at Mesıs (first stop after Adana) was destroyed. The purse commıssioner and his retinue conferred and agreed to an alternate route, which was approved by the grand vezır. BA-Cevdet/Dahılıye 1804, undated.

[55] Uzunçarşılı, *Mekke*, pp. 40-41, 58.

1516-1517. This banner enhanced the significance of the pilgrimage to Damascus. The governor assumed care of it on the long journey to and from Arabia. From Damascus onward, the commissioner was under the protection of the governor of Damascus. He received, according to custom, a change of camel relays in that city, for which orders from Istanbul to Damascus were provided.[56] Upon arrival in Mecca, the commissioner presented the imperial letter to the *şerif*, who kissed it, burned off the seal, opened the letter, and had it read to the public. Then, the *sürre* registers were presented and the money distributed under the supervision of the *şerif*, the custodian of the meccan sanctuary, and the magistrate (*kadi*) of the city. Money for recipients shown to be dead or not present was returned to Istanbul with the commissioner. All transactions were recorded and reported back to the central government.[57] At the conclusion of the pilgrimage, the commissioner rejoined the Damascus caravan, carrying with him a letter of reply to the sultan from the *şerif*. He also carried gifts from the *şerif* to all major and minor Ottoman officials who had participated in preparation of the *sürre*.[58]

What was the governor of Damascus' role in this important aspect of the pilgrimage? We have mentioned the governor's escort and protection duty and the obligation to provide for the commissioner's needs. His responsibility began once the procession reached Ḥamā, and it continued through Damascus and well into the Ḥijāz, usually to Madā'in Ṣāliḥ or al-'Ulā (150 miles north of Medina), and sometimes as far as Medina.[59] From that point onward, the *şerifs* of Mecca usually took responsibility. A representative of the state, either the

[56] For example, BA-Cevdet/Dahiliye 1299, petition from the purse commissioner, approved 14 Cemaziyelâhır 1175 (11 January 1762); order isssud 19 Cemazıyelâhır 1175 (16 January 1762).

[57] So concerned was the sultan for the equitable distribution of the *surre* that this instruction was included in the imperial letter. See, for example, BA-Nâme 6, pp. 29-30, dated middle Cemazıyelevvel 1115 (22 September to 2 October 1703).

[58] A register of such gifts for the years 1146-1147 (1734-1735) is TKS-D. 2330.

[59] BA-Cevdet/Dahiliye 1223, dated beginning Rebıyulâhır 1144 (3-13 Oc-

commissioner or a special messenger (*mübaşir*), reported to Istanbul on the quality of the *şerif*'s performance. It is important to state in this respect that the Meccan *şerifs* were, like the Crimean Tatars, theoretically autonomous. But they held their positions at the pleasure of the Ottoman state, which regarded this escort service as probably the most important aspect of the position next to the just distribution of the alms.[60] As for the governor of Damascus, he continued to be responsible for the safety and good order of his caravan even when it arrived in the Holy Cities and fell under the jurisdiction of the *şerif*. His duties were, first, to protect the *sürre* from attack by beduin tribes or from embezzlement;[61] second, to be sure that his retinue's marching order and protocol were maintained and that no official attempted to take a more exalted place than was his due;[62] and, third, to prevent disorders once the caravan reached the Holy Cities.[63] In sum, the institution of

---

tober 1731); and BA-Emırı/ııı Ahmed 3643, draft ımperıal letter, dated begınnıng Rebıyülevvel 1131 (22-31 January 1719).

[60] It was "among the most ımportant of the Exalted State's affaırs and among the foremost and ındispensable conditions of the . . . *şerif*'s emırate." BA-Cevdet/Dahılıye 1223, dated begınnıng Rebıyulâhır 1144 (3-13 October 1731).

[61] On one occasıon, a governor attempted to take money from the purse commissioner on the pretext of a road tax (*farz-ı tarik*). He was dısmıssed from office, probably as a result of thıs act. A very strong order was sent to the next purse commıssıoner. It ordered hım to take all necessary steps to see that the treasure got through to the poor of the Holy Cities intact. By no means was the commıssioner to pay any road tax, not even to the pılgrımage commander. BA-Cevdet/Dahıliye 8733, dated end Cemaziyelâhır 1119 (17-27 September 1707). Unfortunately, the local Damascus chronıcles do not gıve dırect evıdence of thıs event. The governor concerned was eıther Mehmed Paşa Kurd-Bayramzâde, dismıssed from office on 20 Rebıyulevvel 1118 (3 July 1706) or Baltacı Süleyman Paşa, dismıssed some tıme ın 1707. The chronıcles are not ın agreement on the dates of the latter's tenure. See Ibn Jum'a, "al-Bāshāt," p. 51; and Ibn al-Qārī, "al-Wuzarā'," p. 76.

[62] Uzunçarşılı, *Mekke*, p. 41, citıng BA-Mühimme 132, p. 293, dated mıddle Ramazan 1137 (24 May to 3 June 1725).

[63] For example, ın 1726, a race to see whether the Egyptıan or Syrıan *mahmal* (lead camel in the *sürre* and pılgrımage processıon) would be presented first to the *şerif* led to disorders between the mılıtary escorts of both groups. These dısorders were strongly condemned ın a sharp order from Istanbul to

the *sürre* provided the state with yet another means of supervising governors of Damascus, who were judged by their assistance and protection. Accurate intelligence gathered by the commissioner and his retinue enabled the Ottoman state to maintain a close watch over affairs in the province of Damascus.

The Pilgrimage Fortress Network

Communications, trade, and religious interests combined to make the pilgrimage route from Arabia through Damascus one of the three main clusters in the Ottoman Empire of road networks that ultimately converged on Istanbul. The other clusters were the Balkan highways from Albania, Serbia, and the lower Danube, and the Anatolian routes from Iran.[64] Within southern Syria, the pilgrimage route was complemented by two major roads: the coastal highway from Beirut to ʻArīsh in Sinai and the inland route to Cairo from Damascus through Palestine. Like other routes in the empire, the pilgrimage route was protected by a network of fortresses that served as halting places (*menzils, kervansarays*) for pilgrims and traders.[65] The pilgrimage fortresses were more modest in scope than the huge urban establishments (*imarets*) of Anatolia, the Balkans, and the more frequently traveled road from Aleppo to Damascus.[66] Nevertheless, the typical Ottoman caravansaray, including the pilgrimage fortresses, was characterized by towers and walls that either enclosed or adjoined a complex of buildings that could include market stalls, a mosque, a public bath, fountains, and sleeping quarters. During the classical age of the Ottoman Empire, gen-

both sides and to the Meccan *şerif*. BA-Cevdet/Dahılıye 619, dated end Rebiyülâhır 1139 (14-24 December 1726).

[64] Inalcik, *The Ottoman Empire*, pp. 146-147.

[65] See Bakhit, "Ottoman Province," p. 99, for sixteenth-century fortresses constructed along these highways.

[66] For large urban establishments (*imarets*), see, for example, Barkan, "Edirne bılançolari." For the caravansarays between Antioch and Damascus, see Sauvaget, "Les caravansérails syriens."

erally regarded as the period from 1300 to 1600, the Ottoman sultans, wealthy officials, and local notables created religious endowments for the maintenance of the larger establishments along well-traveled routes. Due to the pilgrimage fortresses' remoteness from major urban centers, the Ottoman state in the sixteenth century encouraged people to settle in and around these halting places by compensating them with specific tax exemptions. In Syria, this practice was welcomed as a continuation of the "old Mamlūk *darak* system by which the security of the roads was entrusted to local people."[67]

In several respects, the Ottoman conquest of Syria and Egypt in 1516-1517 brought changes to the old Mamlūk communications route to Arabia. The most visible change was the increased importance of the Damascus pilgrimage route—long overshadowed by its Egyptian counterpart—which originated in Cairo and extended through Sinai to the Gulf of 'Aqaba and south along the Ḥijāz coast. Although not perceptibly diminished in importance after the fall of Cairo as an imperial capital, the Egyptian route began to feel greater competition from Damascus. Ottoman control of the Arab lands required consolidation of communications between Istanbul and Arabia through Syria. To this end, Sultan Selim I (1512-1520) ordered, during the last four years of his reign, the construction of forts at Sanamayn, Muzayrīb, and Tall Far'ūn, all within one hundred miles south of Damascus.[68] They were built to provide secure lodging places, at shorter intervals than had previously been available, for the increased number of pilgrims from the Anatolian and European parts of the Ottoman Empire who used the Damascus route. Selim's successor, Sultan Süleyman I, took over the task of consolidation and extended Ottoman control of the pilgrimage route

[67] Bakhıt, "Ottoman Province," pp. 99-100, 107-108. For *mamlūk* communications, see Sauvaget, *La Poste aux chevaux dans l'empire des mamelouks*. For Ottoman communications, see Orhonlu, *Osmanlı imparatorluğunda derbend teşkilatı*, pp. 24-25.

[68] Mehmed Edib, *Menasık*, pp. 65, 66; Kâtip Çelebi, *Cihannümâ*, p. 538; and Sabrı, *Mir'ât'ül-Haremeyn*, III, 235. See Appendix VII for a list of the fortresses along the pilgrimage route.

all the way to Medina. Several of the forts were built at the request of local officials to increase local security and stimulate trade. By 1563, six forts were added to the three built by Sultan Selim: Qaṭrāna, Ma'ān, Dhāt Ḥajj, Tabūk, Ukhayḍir, and al-'Ulā, all on the pilgrimage route.[69] Four more forts—at the district capitals of 'Ajlūn, Ṣalṭ, Karak, and Shawbak—were constructed as alternative halting places. They lay close to the eastern banks of the Jordan River, parallel to, and west of, the main route.[70]

It is significant that this relatively slow Ottoman consolidation (over some fifty years) resembled, in method, the first Ottoman penetration of Europe from Anatolia. In 1354, the Ottomans, in temporary alliance with a claimant to the Byzantine throne, had crossed the Straits and taken the fortress of Tzympe (Cinbi) on the Gallipoli peninsula. They refused to evacuate it, despite Byzantine pleas, and quickly converted it into a base for campaigns against neighboring Byzantine fortresses and against Gallipoli itself. This tactic contributed to successful Ottoman penetration into Europe.[71] Similarly, just after the conquest of Syria, the Ottomans under Selim I secured for the pilgrimage three major stopping places immediately south of Damascus. Under Sultan Süleyman, they completed the process southward. Ottoman communications with the Ḥijāz—for pilgrimage and trade—were firmly established by the middle of the sixteenth century. During the rest of that century, the pilgrimage fortress network was further strengthened with the construction of forts at 'Unayza (just before Ma'ān) and Hadiyya (forty-two hours' march from Medina). The latter was built in 1576 and the former, at probably the same time, by a Süleyman Paşa, possibly the governor of Damascus by that name in 1583-1584.[72] Kâtip Çelebi (d. 1656) mentions these forts in his geo-

[69] Bakhıt, "Ottoman Provınce," p. 105; Kâtip Çelebı, *Cihannümâ*, p. 539; Sabrı, *Mır'ât*, ııı, 237-241 passim. For 'Ulā, see Mehmed Edıb, *Menasik*, pp. 80-81.

[70] Bakhit, "Ottoman Provınce," p. 105.

[71] Inalcik, *The Ottoman Empire*, p. 9.

[72] For the date of Hadiyya's construction, see Bakhit, "Ottoman Prov-

graphical work, *Cihannümâ*, thus confirming their existence prior to the early seventeenth century.[73] A proposed castle at Buṣrā, southeast of Muzayrīb and off the main road, was never actively used, because maintaining its garrison proved too difficult.[74]

In contrast with the methodical consolidation of fortresses south of Damascus, there was very little construction along the route to Aleppo in the north during the sixteenth century. The Ottomans, rather, concentrated on the route south of Damascus—the pilgrimage route proper—because it was, by virtue of terrain, climate, and sparse population, far less secure at the time than the route to the north. Major fortress repair and construction between Damascus and Aleppo was not to come until the end of the sixteenth century and the beginning of the seventeenth. There was, however, one significant exception. To the northwest of Aleppo, and just east of the strategic Cilician Gates, Sultan Süleyman built the fort of Baylān in 1552-1553. He sought thereby to control communications between Anatolia and Safavid Persia, his deadly enemy, and southward to the Arab lands. During the late sixteenth and early seventeenth centuries, the following fortresses were built on the northern route: Qal'at al-Muḍīq, al-Rastan, Hasiyya, al-Nabk, and al-Quṭayfa.[75] The forts of Kara-Mughurt and Jisr al-Shughr were built during the reign of Murad IV (1623-1640) and the grand vezirate of Köprülüzâde Fazıl Ahmed (1661-1676) respectively.[76] Of far greater architectural importance than the southern forts, those in the north were larger, better built, and consistently maintained, probably because they were in use throughout the

---

ınce," p. 119, n. 114. Suleyman Paşa, not further identified, is credited with construction of both forts by Mehmed Edib, *Menasik*, pp. 70 and 82. For the Suleyman Paşa who was governor of Damascus, see Ibn Jum'a, "al-Bāshāt," p. 19.

[73] Kâtip Çelebı, *Cihannümâ*, p. 539.

[74] Bakhıt, "Ottoman Provınce," p. 105.

[75] Sauvaget, "Les caravansérails syriens," pp. 108ff. For Baylān, see *EI²*, I, 1134.

[76] See Sauvaget, "Les caravansérails syriens," pp. 108ff.

year, unlike the forts along the pilgrimage route, which had heavy traffic for only part of the year.

Local Damascus chroniclers make no reference at all to construction or maintenance along the pilgrimage route proper during the seventeenth century. According to one source, only the fortress at Tabūk is said to have been repaired, in 1654.[77] In addition, at Sha'b al-Na'āma, a well shaft was ordered dug by the mother of Sultan Ahmed I (1603-1617); the site became known as Valide Kuyusu.[78] An alarming sign of the network's decay was reported in 1694 by 'Abd al-Ghanī al-Nābulsī, the famed Damascene mystic (d. 1731). He reported that, on his return from Arabia, he found the old Ayyūbid fort at al-Mu'aẓẓam in ruins and its garrison massacred by beduin.[79] Further research is required to explain this pattern of neglect during the seventeenth century.

A turning point in Ottoman administration in Syria was the appointment in 1708 of Nasuh Paşa to the governorship of Damascus and the command of the pilgrimage. During his first three years in office, Nasuh succeeded in effectively neutralizing the beduin tribes that had attacked pilgrimage caravans with impunity over the previous twenty years. He also succeeded in improving communications along the route to Medina, especially between Damascus and the first several fortresses to the south, for which he was granted an increase in funds to support a special courier corps.[80] To secure a base of operations deep in the Ḥijāz, Nasuh Paşa repaired the fortress at Hadiyya (in Turkish sources, Hediye Eşmeler, meaning water holes), four halting places from Medina. Hadiyya was thereafter to serve as the point where the *cerde*, the two thousand-man relief force sent from Damascus, would meet and escort the returning caravan. Within six months of his

[77] F. Buhl, "Tabūk," *EI*¹, IV, 593-594.

[78] Mehmed Edıb, *Menasik*, p. 82. Kâtıp Çelebı does not mention thıs well in the *Cihannümâ*.

[79] Cited in Musil, *The Northern Ḥeğâz*, pp. 330-331.

[80] BA-Emiri/III Ahmed 4374, dated 15 Cemazıyelevvel 1121 (24 July 1709). Nasuh was given extra funds for the courier service (*bargirân-ı ulak*) from the revenues of Sidon.

appointment, Nasuh's first petition for funds to carry out repairs at Hadiyya was approved in the amount of 15,000 *kuruş*.[81] So extensive were the repairs that more funds were needed and, in the following year, 9,122 *kuruş*, drawn from the poll tax of Damascus, were granted under contract to Nasuh Paşa.[82] His other major construction effort along the pilgrimage route was the digging of a well shaft at Nakhlatayn, sixteen hours' march from Hadiyya in the direction of Medina.[83] This was important—and perhaps critical—because the nearest safe drinking water was either at Valide Kuyusu, some twenty-eight hours' march to the north, or at Abyār Ḥamza, twenty-six hours' march to the south, just before Medina.[84] Hadiyya's water supply, though plentiful, was not safe to drink.[85]

Available evidence indicates that the next Damascus governor to undertake fortress construction and repair was Aydınlı Abdullah Paşa (1730-1733). He is credited with repairing several forts and with building a castle and two cisterns at Jughaymān (also known as al-Mudawwara), twenty-eight hours' march south of Ma'ān.[86] In addition, he built the bridge that carried pilgrims across Wādī al-Hasā, which was prone to serious flash floods.[87] The halting place of al-Ḥasā

[81] BA-Emiri/III Ahmed 4343, voucher (*tezkire*) dated 27 Cemaziyelevvel 1121 (5 August 1709). The 15,000 *kuruş* were raised from the Damascus treasury and the Aleppo tax farm, 9,122 *kuruş* and 5,878 *kuruş* respectively. As mentioned at the beginning of this Chapter, in the section on pilgrimage financial base, the Damascus treasury raised and spent some 130,000 to 140,000 *kuruş* per year, of which 82,000, at a minimum, were set aside for the pilgrimage. The Aleppo tax farm contributed irregularly to the pilgrimage.

[82] BA-Emiri/III Ahmed 10547, voucher dated 1 Rebiyulâhır 1122 (30 April 1710) and contract granted 6 Rebiyulâhır 1122 (5 May 1710).

[83] Mehmed Edib, *Menasik*, pp. 82-83.

[84] For marching times between the forts, we have relied on Mehmed Edib, *Menasik*, pp. 65-82 passim.

[85] Its "water is from water holes and causes diarrhea." Kâtip Çelebi, *Cihannümâ*, p. 539. Mehmed Edib also makes the same remarks in *Menasik*, p. 82.

[86] Mehmed Edib, *Menasik*, p. 72; Ibn al-Qārī, "al-Wuzarā'," p. 77.

[87] Mehmed Edib, *Menasik*, p. 69. The site was also known as Tabut Korusu, the "burial grove" of a man named Celaleddin Halveti.

was eleven hours from Qaṭrāna and about twenty-five miles southeast of the end of the Dead Sea. Finally, Abdullah Paşa undertook two very ambitious projects: first, paving the road from Damascus to Qunayṭra, which diverged slightly from the pilgrimage route but whose condition was nevertheless important for the caravan's security as an alternate route; and, second, construction of strong embankments along the river-banks between Ṣanamayn and Muzayrīb, another flood protection measure to keep the pilgrimage route open.[88]

It is somewhat surprising that the 'Aẓm governors appear to have done so little themselves to maintain the forts during their long terms as governors and effective pilgrimage commanders. With the exception of the forts built respectively by Mehmed Paşa at Zumurrud (about 1779), and by Esat Paşa at Madā'in Ṣāliḥ,[89] there is, as yet, no evidence of major construction along the network by the 'Aẓms. Only routine and minor repairs were carried out, such as those at 'Unayza and Hadiyya in 1736-1737 at Süleyman Paşa's request.[90] The cost was less than 600 *kuruş*.

The most ambitious program of fortress building since the Ottoman conquest was initiated by Gürcü Osman Paşa (known locally as Kurjī 'Uthmān, al-Ṣādiq), who began his career in the retinue of Esat Paşa (al-'Aẓm) and was later governor of Damascus (1760-1771).[91] His efforts best represent the revival of the fortress network after what appears to have been a lack of significant activity during the seventeenth century.

Mehmed Edib, the Ottoman pilgrim who traveled to

[88] Ibn al-Qārī, "al-Wuzarā'," p. 77.

[89] For Mehmed Paşa, see Mehmed Edib, *Menasik*, pp. 81-82; Ibn al-Qārī, "al-Wuzarā'," p. 84; Murādī, *Silk*, IV, 101. Zumurrud, off the main highway, was twenty hours from 'Ulā and ten hours from Abyār al-Ghanam. For Esat Paşa, see Ibn al-Qārī, "al-Wuzarā'," p. 79.

[90] BA-Cevdet/Askeri 29247, in 3 parts. Part 1 is a register of recipients of pay for repair work. Part 2 is the formal petition from Süleyman Paşa. Both are dated 16 Safer 1149 (27 June 1736). Part 3, dated 20 Rebiyulevvel 1149 (30 July 1736), is a draft order authorizing Süleyman Paşa to make the payments and to enter them in his pilgrimage budget for that year.

[91] Murādī, *Silk*, III, 161.

Arabia in 1779-1780,[92] credits an Osman Paşa—not further identified—with the construction of six forts, at Ẓahr al-'Aqaba, Maghāyir al-Qalandariyya, Dār al-Ḥamrā', Valide Kuyusu, 'Antar (off the main road, but near Hadiyya, where the relief force met the returning caravan), and Nakhlatayn. Only one other source, Ibn al-Qārī, gives a definite number for the forts built by Gürcü Osman (identified specifically); and he claims seven instead of six forts.[93] Ibn al-Qārī, as noted above, acknowledges that Esat Paşa (al-'Aẓm) constructed a new fort at Madā'in Ṣāliḥ.[94] It is possible—though by no means certain—that this fort was the seventh credited to Gürcü Osman. This possibility is enhanced by the fact that Gürcü Osman was a high-ranking member of Esat Paşa's retinue before assuming the governorship in his own right; and the fact that Mehmed Edib gives one—and only one—date for the construction by his unidentified Osman of a fortress at Dār al-Ḥamrā', and that date was 1167 (1753-1754), during Esat Paşa's tenure.[95] Whether or not Gürcü Osman carried out his program before he became governor of Damascus, all available evidence corroborates the fact that he alone was responsible for, and even contributed funds toward, the construction of the fortress at Dār al-Ḥamrā'.[96]

The renovation and rehabilitation of the Damascus pilgrimage fortresses was one important development that led to resurgent Ottoman control in the Syrian provinces between 1708 and 1758. Damascus governors succeeded in matching —even surpassing—the illustrious sultans of the sixteenth century, the Ottoman Empire's apogee. But the fortress revival was not confined simply to construction and repair. The state, through provincial governors, sought to provide provisions sufficient for each fortress and to supply the official retinue and escort during their passage to and from Arabia. Far more ambitious, however, was the long struggle to control

---

[92] Mehmed Edıb, *Menasik*, p. 1.
[93] Ibn al-Qārī, "al-Wuzarā'," p. 83.
[94] Ibid., p. 79.   [95] Mehmed Edıb, *Menasik*, p. 77.
[96] Ibn al-Qārī, "al-Wuzarā'," p. 83; Budayrī, *Hawādith*, p. 229; Murādī, *Silk*, III, 161; and Mehmed Edıb, *Menasik*, pp. 65-82 passım.

the fortress garrisons and to thus ensure security of communications.

Governors of Damascus, their retinues, and the pilgrimage escort forces needed two types of provisions in large quantities at each stop along the route: barley (*sha'īr*) and camel fodder (*ma'būk*, a mash of bitter vetch and barley meal). Each fortress was resupplied with these and other necessities (required in smaller quantities) during the pilgrimage proper, when the caravan passed through on its return to Damascus from Arabia. The purpose of this arrangement is clear. The pilgrimage commander made sure that supplies would be on hand and safely in storage for the next year's pilgrimage. This was usually true both for the basic provisions (barley and camel fodder) and for others, which included rice, dried rusks, tar, tents, bulgur, horseshoe molds, horseshoe nails (one bale of which contained 10,000 nails), and items such as cord, rope, baling hooks and bale wrappers.[97] It is noteworthy that the grains and dried rusks could be preserved for a long time in the dry desert climate and made palatable when soaked in water. Evidence shows that several lots of provisions were stored for as long as five years.[98]

Like other aspects of the Ottoman-administered pilgrimage, minute details concerning provisions were regulated by

[97] Archival evidence shows that provisions were stored at the conclusion of one pilgrimage (in the month of Muharrem) in anticipation of the next pilgrimage. TKS-E. 2588/8, contract with Medina garrison commander, dated beginning Muharrem 1154 (19-29 March 1741); TKS-E. 2588/9, contract with Tabūk garrison commander, dated 17 Muharrem 1155 (25 March 1742). The following were provisions included in the contracts: *peksimad* (Ar., *bāqismāt*, dried rusks), *qaṭrān* (tar), *khiyām* (tents), *taṭbīqa na'l khayl* (horseshoe molds), *masāmīr khayl* (horseshoe nails), *murs* (cord), *aḥbāl* (rope), *'urā* (baling hooks), and *zumul* (bale wrappers). In 1812, J. L. Burckhardt visited the fort at Muzayrīb and described the types of provisions stored there for the pilgrimage, including 1,120 tons of barley brought from the Hawrān. Burckhardt, *Travels in Syria*, p. 242.

[98] See, for example, TKS-E. 2588/12, contract with Ma'ān garrison commander, dated 23 Muharrem 1155 (31 March 1742), which mentions 78.5 loads of barley stored there in 1150 (1737-38). The same amount is specified in TKS-E. 2588/4, an undated contract with the Ma'ān commander, probably from the same year as the above document, given its internal evidence.

the governor of Damascus and his staff, in much the same manner as the central government planned its military campaigns. First, estimates were made of what would be required daily at each stop. Then, a plan was drawn up showing the quantities of provisions in stock and the quantities needed to replenish that stock and meet daily requirements. Next, separate lists were made concerning who was to bring the provisions to the forts. Data for 1742-1743 show that members of the Banī Ṣakhr tribe brought some—but not all—needed provisions to the forts from Muzayrīb, the staging area for the pilgrimage 108 kilometers south of Damascus and one of the largest towns in the Ḥawrān region.[99] Finally, at the end of the pilgrimage, the governor of Damascus would receive a report from his personal treasurer (*hazinedar*) showing actual consumption of provisions and any surplus left in stock. This concluded a yearlong process of close administration from the provincial center.

Evidence shows that the major part of the basic provisions of barley and camel fodder was supplied from the following sources: (1) taxes in kind collected on the *dawra* and provisions left over from that expedition; (2) income from charitable endowments (*vakıfs*) established for that purpose; (3) purchases by the governor from the Damascus grain market, which was subject to his control; and (4) purchases from tribesmen who either had access to farms in the Ḥawrān or who cultivated the grain themselves. As previously shown, the *dawra* surplus was augmented in good years when the soldiery could meet its own needs with ease and complete its expedition quickly. To obtain both foodstuffs and income from endowments intended for the purchase of provisions, the central government sent an annual order to the governor of Damascus, to top officials of the Palestinian *sancaks* of Jerusalem, Gaza, and Nablus, and to the custodians of the endowments associated with Abraham's tomb at Hebron (Abraham, cited by Muslims as the founder of the Meccan

[99] For a description of the Muzayrīb fort, see Burckhardt, *Travels in Syria*, pp. 241-242.

sanctuary, was buried at Hebron; endowments established there that partly supported the pilgrimage are therefore understandable). Normally issued in the month of Cemaziyelâhır, four months before the pilgrimage's departure from Damascus and two months after the start of the *dawra*, this order gave the signal to move provisions, in unspecified amounts, to the pilgrimage forts, also unspecified.[100] The governor of Damascus was expected to supervise this operation, although the orders do not say who was actually expected to transport the provisions. It appears that the beduin tribes west of the Jordan River delivered the supplies across the river and north to Muzayrīb, where other provisions were also stored.[101] As for supplies from Damascus or the Ḥawrān, the evidence indicates that they were transported or purchased by Arab tribes and brought to Muzayrīb. For instance, in Cemaziyelâhır 1155 (August 1742), the month of which coincided with the date of the order described above, the governor of Damascus drew up several contracts to obtain provisions for the pilgrimage of that year. Seven members of the 'Anaza confederation of tribes—which included the Ṣakhr—were to transport one hundred loads of barley from Muzayrīb to Hadiyya, the last major fortress before Medina. The transport rate was seventeen *kuruş* per load.[102] Paid in advance, the tribesmen, including Shaykh Ḥusayn al-Miryān, deputy (*kethüda*) of the officially recognized tribal chief of Damascus (*Şam urbanı şeyhi*), would complete the contract when they delivered the provisions and obtained a receipt from the fortress commander at Hadiyya. Another contract was drawn up the day before with two members of the Sardiyya tribe, also members of the 'Anaza confederation. The two tribesmen were the

[100] BA-Mühımme 160, p. 115, two orders (one to the governor of Damascus, the other to the *sancak* officials of Jerusalem, Gaza, Nablus, and the endowment custodians at Hebron), dated middle Cemaziyelâhır 1171 (20 February to 1 March 1758).

[101] TKS-E. 2588/7, dated 22 Şaban 1154 (4 November 1741).

[102] TKS-E. 2588/15, contract dated 27 Cemaziyelâhır 1155 (29 August 1742).

above mentioned Shaykh Ḥusayn al-Miryān and a certain Khalīl Khunayfis. They received from the governor of Damascus the sum of one hundred gold coins with which to purchase eighty loads of barley and twenty loads of camel fodder.[103] They were to transport these provisions from Muzayrīb to the fort of al-Qaṭrāna, fifty-seven hours' march away.[104] It is apparent that these provisions were to be purchased near Muzayrīb, in the Ḥawrān. From the name of one witness to the contract, al-Hājj Aḥmad al-Qabbānī, we infer that the provisions were to be checked for quality and correct weight. Al-Qabbānī was almost certainly a member of the wholesale grain-weighers' guild in Damascus, the *qabbāniyya* (cf. Tur., *kapan*).[105]

Once provisions were stored in a fort, they became the legal responsibility of the fort's commander (*dizdar* or *odabaşı*, the terms being used interchangeably in the sources). The latter took on consignments under contract to the governor of Damascus, normally at the end of a pilgrimage, but also sometimes before if that proved necessary to replenish stock. In the presence of witnesses and the magistrate (*kadi*) who accompanied the pilgrimage caravan, the fortress commander would write out a receipt or contract (*tamassuk, tadhkira*), usually in Arabic, specifying the quantities of goods to be stored under his protection. The document bound the commander under law to fulfill the terms with his person and money as security or, if he so chose, in conjunction with a suitable guarantor.[106] Once the contract was completed, the provi-

[103] The gold coin used in this transaction was the *jinzīrlī* (Arabic, for Turkish *zincirli*), valued at 2.75 *kuruş*, according to a document that lists expenses from the local treasury of Jerusalem. TKS-E. 2025/3, dated 17 Şaban 1154 (29 October 1741).

[104] TKS-E. 2588/10, dated 26 Cemaziyelâhir 1154 (28 August 1742).

[105] For the *qabbāniyya*, see al-Qāsimī, *Qāmūs al-ṣinā'āt*, II, 347-348.

[106] TKS-E. 10426, contract with commander of al-Mu'aẓẓam fort, dated middle Muharrem 1155 (18-28 March 1742). In this document, the commander chose as his guarantor a wealthy merchant from Damascus: "Muḥammad Bāshā [sic] ibn 'Abd Allāh, a resident of Damascus and of the Sūq Sārūjā quarter, has vouched for its [that is, the contract's] validity and has accepted liability both legally and financially before both parties."

sions were sealed in the fortress warehouses, which took up the first floor of the outer walls.[107] They were to be opened only upon the governor's orders when he returned with the next pilgrimage, either on its outward or on its return journey.[108] Only then were the terms of the contract regarded as fulfilled.

From the evidence presented thus far concerning supply of the fortresses, it is clear that tribesmen serving the state for pay were an integral part of pilgrimage administration. This set them apart from other tribes that were either indifferent or hostile to the pilgrimage's success and safety. Tribal hostility to the state, as seen in attacks on the pilgrimage caravan, stemmed from economic hardship brought on by pressure from other tribes, exclusion from the traditional aspects of pilgrimage administration, or the failure of greedy officials to pay the tribes for services rendered. The Ottoman state attempted to bring at least some potential troublemakers into its administrative framework by enlisting them to perform important tasks. Further research is needed to clarify the tribes' relationship with the fortress garrisons.

Between 1708 and 1758, the Ottoman state also made a strong effort to ensure the fortress garrisons' competence. It developed several rotation plans by which members of the local Damascus janissary corps (*yerli kulları*) took turns at garrison duty. Hitherto, we have had only fragmentary evidence concerning the garrisons, most of it negative. The Danish engineer, Carsten Niebuhr, who visited the Ḥijāz in 1763, made the following observation: ". . . the Arabs [that is, the tribes] suffer the Turkish Sovereign to maintain, for the security of the pilgrims, and in order to guard the wells, a few janizaries, cooped up in some wretched towers."[109] This observation has little meaning, unfortunately, because Niebuhr freely admits his reliance on "native informants" for this information. As for the Ḥijāz, "Its interior limits I cannot pretend to

[107] See Burckhardt's description in *Travels in Syria*, p. 241.

[108] For example, see TKS-E. 2588/12, contract with commander of Ma'ān, dated 23 Muharrem 1155 (31 March 1742).

[109] Niebuhr, *Travels through Arabia*, II, 26.

know distinctly, having seen only the seacoast: Whatever I may mention concerning the other parts is entirely from hearsay."[110]

The Ottoman garrison rotation plan called for a year's residence in an assigned fortress. Garrisons ranged in size from twelve to fifty men,[111] who traveled to their posts with the pilgrimage caravan and returned to Damascus at the end of the next pilgrimage. In order to be absolutely certain of each garrison's complete self-sufficiency, the pilgrimage commander supplied each fort with a year's stock of provisions and pack animals.

The rotation system evolved from a series of events spanning twenty years. When Nasuh Paşa became governor of Damascus in 1708, one of his main efforts to establish centralized Ottoman control from the provincial center was the reform of the unruly local janissaries. Ordered by the state to conduct an inspection of local janissary muster rolls (*yoklama*), Nasuh Paşa found that, of 1,231 members in the corps, the majority were unfit for service because they were either too old and feeble or underage, or because they had gained admission simply through inheritance of this lucrative tax-exempt status.[112] Furthermore, Nasuh found that local people (*Arab*, possibly referring to the beduin?), Turkmans, and Kurds—all potential troublemakers—had penetrated the corps and, in fact, accounted for two-thirds of its numbers.[113] In response, the state ordered Nasuh to draw up a new muster roll, to get rid of the troublemakers, to make sure that all men remained on duty in Damascus and did not live elsewhere, to report all actions to Istanbul, and, above all, to give the corps

[110] Ibid., p. 23.

[111] BA-Kepeci 2343, Damascus account register of 1154 (1741-1742) and BA-Kepeci 2101, Damascus account register of 1173 (1759-1760).

[112] BA-Maliye 2816, p. 13, dated 17 Rebiyülevvel 1121 (31 May 1709). This register of muster-roll inspections is over 100 pages long and covers nearly the whole of the eighteenth century.

[113] *Sulsânî Arab ve Türkmen ve Ekrâd olmakla ekseriya zuhur eden şekavet.* BA-Maliye 2816, p. 13.

a semblance of organization.[114] Nasuh obeyed the order within a year and drew up a new list of officially recognized local janissaries. The numbers were reduced to 913 (of whom 35 were pensioners, *mütekâidin*), distributed through eight cavalry units (*cemaat*) and forty-two companies (*bölük*) of footsoldiers.[115]

Available evidence shows that the next attempt to streamline the local corps occurred in 1718, during the administration of Receb Paşa (who governed Damascus between 14 February 1718 and 13 April 1719).[116] Reduced by Receb Paşa to 750 men, including pensioners, the corps was, however, still filled with too many potential troublemakers. The central government's register of muster rolls refers to the necessity of purging these elements from the corps.[117] Attempts to carry out this program were frustrated for two reasons. First, the expansion of the pilgrimage fortress network required greater and greater numbers of troops and larger and larger sums of hard cash to pay them. It was no longer possible to reduce the corps and then to appoint untrustworthy mercenaries to guard the forts. Second, a storm of protest arose among the local janissaries, because a number of them had been out of Damascus during Receb Paşa's inspection of the muster rolls. In response to the petition of these disgruntled janissaries, the state compiled a separate register with the names of eighty-three men who were added to the corps with the proviso that

[114] Ibid.

[115] Ibid., pp. 69-74. This *yoklama*, upon receipt in Istanbul, was ordered copied into the records of the chief comptroller's office on 29 Rebiyülevvel 1122 (28 May 1710).

[116] Ibn Jum'a, "al-Bāshāt," p. 57. Ibn al-Qārī, "al-Wuzarā'," p. 77, states that Receb Paşa governed until 1133 (1720-1721), but his information is much sparser than Ibn Jum'a's and is contradicted by Breik, *Tārīkh*, p. 3, who begins his chronicle with the remark that 'Uthmān Abū Tawq (Çerkes Osman) was governor in 1720. Archival evidence confirms that Receb Paşa was dismissed in 1719. BA-Emiri/III Ahmed 17306, dated 6 Cemaziyelevvel 1132 (16 March 1720), refers to Receb Paşa as the former governor of Damascus.

[117] BA-Maliye 2816, p. 76, memorandum (*telhis*) dated 12 Cemaziyelevvel 1131 (2 April 1719).

fifty of them guard the fortress of Ṣanamayn, very close to Damascus.[118] This arrangement was reconfirmed in the following year.[119]

Two years later, however, a new inspection of muster rolls was carried out, because many pilgrimage forts, even those close to Damascus, were shorthanded or deserted.[120] For the first time, a rotation system was adopted by which 390 of the 883 men in the corps would perform garrison duties specifically linked to the pilgrimage, and escort duty for what was called the *şeker hazinesi*.[121] Two sets of orders to this effect were issued, one concerning garrisons for the forts of Abyār al-Ghanam and Madā'in Ṣāliḥ, another concerning al-Muʿaẓẓam and Ukhayḍir. Of the 390 local janissaries specifically assigned to fortress duty, 75 would serve one year every four years at Abyār al-Ghanam and Madā'in Ṣāliḥ and 45 would serve one year every two years at al-Muʿaẓẓam and Ukhayḍir. They would arrive at their assigned forts on the outward journey of the pilgrimage and leave on the return journey of the next year's pilgrimage.[122] The group selected to serve in rotation would be especially enrolled in the corps in the presence of the governor, the province's chief treasurer, and the *ağa* of the corps, and in strict conformity with administrative regulations (*kanun*). To provide for the garrisons' needs, the pilgrimage commander would draw a year's

---

[118] Ibid., p. 87, memorandum dated 12 Cemaziyelevvel 1131 (2 April 1719).

[119] BA-Emırı/ııı Ahmed 17306, draft order dated 6 Cemaziyelevvel 1132 (16 March 1720).

[120] BA-Malıye 2816, p. 95.

[121] BA-Emırı/ııı Ahmed 10223/2, order dated 8 Cemazıyelâhır 1132 (26 March 1722), BA-Malıye 2816, p. 95, the same date as the latter document; BA-Malıye 6676, *yoklama* of 1134 (1721-1722); BA-Malıye 2816, p. 94, dated 7 Cemazıyelevvel 1134 (23 February 1722). It is not clear what the *şeker hazinesi* was, except that it was sent to Istanbul every year. BA-Maliye 2816, p. 94. It was paid for from the sultan's personal treasury, out of revenues earned in the province of Damascus. In 1759-1760, 5,350 *kuruş* were spent on it: BA-Kepecı 2101, p. 11.

[122] BA-Emırı/ııı Ahmed 10223/2, cited in Note 121.

supplies from his special pilgrimage larder (*kiler*) and have them transported to each fort as was necessary.[123]

In 1723, the rotation system was modified. Now, 654 men were assigned to fortress duty, 218 each year over a period of three years. Fifty-six men were assigned to receive and escort pilgrims on their return journey and 108 officers and retirees and 15 old and sick men were exempted.[124] In 1724, the corps was expanded by 90 men who were assigned solely as guards to the forts of Ukhayḍir and al-Muʿaẓẓam,[125] bringing the total number of men in the local janissary corps to 923. Finally, in 1728, an inspection of muster rolls resulted in a rotation system that remained in effect for several decades. The corps, with a total of 923 men, was divided as follows: 113 officers were exempt from garrison duty; 330 men were assigned to service at Karak and Qaṭrāna; 156 men were assigned to service at the fort of Qāra (north of Damascus, not on the main route); 216 men were assigned to service at four other fortresses; and 108 men were assigned to escort the *şeker hazinesi*. Aside from the officers, 810 men were committed to garrison or escort duties, 270 of these (instead of 218 as was previously the case) served one year in three.[126]

Throughout the first half of the eighteenth century, the garrisons' pay was five *akçes* per day, the same as that of their Damascus-based colleagues, and unchanged from the sixteenth century.[127] One is struck by the two-hundred-year consistency of the wage scale. Evidence shows that the state knew of the economic activities in which the janissaries engaged, both in Damascus and along the pilgrimage route. Great fortunes could be made by garrison troops who bought provisions from villagers and beduin in the vicinity of the

123 BA-Maliye 2816, p. 94.

124 Ibıd., p. 96, memorandum dated 22 Receb 1135 (28 April 1722).

125 Ibid., p. 98, order dated 10 Cemazıyelevvel 1136 (5 February 1724).

126 BA-Maliye 314, inspection conducted end Cemaziyelâhır 1140 (11-20 February 1728), and confirmed by an order dated 29 Şaban 1141 (30 March 1729), and ın BA-Malıye 2816, p. 58.

127 Bakhıt, "Ottoman Province," p. 101.

forts, then resold them to pilgrims.[128] Both the beduin, who each year settled briefly around some of the forts to engage in agriculture, and the pilgrims stored their provisions in the forts for fees paid to garrison commanders. For example, at Zarqā, grapes, corn, and wheat were grown. At Ma'ān, the whole town depended on the sale of food to pilgrims and, during the rest of the year, to the garrison. At Mafraq, those tribesmen who grew grain were permitted to store it in the fortress for a fee.[129] The garrisons obviously could not survive on sixteenth-century wages and found other means to maintain themselves. Possibly for this reason—as well as to save money—the state refused to raise the pay scale from five to fifteen *akçes* per day in 1723.[130] Only in 1755, just two years before the pilgrimage disaster of 1757, did the state agree to raise the basic wage, by twenty-five *akçes* per day.[131] To survive, the garrisons had to develop ordered relations with villagers and seminomadic and nomadic tribesmen. The weakness of such arrangements was that garrisons were at the mercy of forces beyond their control. The desert environment was quite unlike the more stable area around Damascus: climatic disaster might cause the beduin to attack the garrisons to obtain food and water; some Damascus officials might refuse to pay tribesmen for services rendered; and long confinement in remote desert places might take its toll.

The local janissaries served in only about six of the ten major forts. Members of the regular, imperial janissary corps (the *kapı kulları*) guarded the forts of Ma'ān, Muzayrīb,

---

[128] Burckhardt, *Travels in Syria*, pp. 657ff, Mehmed Edıb, *Menasik*, pp. 65-82 passim. Burckhardt, who studied the forts near Damascus in 1810, was informed that one janissary had become very wealthy over a twenty-three-year period through service at Nakhlatayn, obviously in violation of the rotation system.

[129] Burckhardt, *Travels in Syria*, pp. 657-658.

[130] BA-Malıye 6676, p. 4, order dated 2 Rebıyülâhır 1135 (10 January 1723).

[131] BA-Malıye 2816, p. 99, order dated 27 Rebıyülâhır 1168 (10 February 1755). The raise in pay was called *terakki*, also known as *bahşiş*, for which, see Uzunçarşılı, *Kapıkulu Ocakları*, I, 337.

'Unayza, and al-Mu'aẓẓam.[132] This arrangement reflects, in our view, an attempt by the state to keep the two competing corps—the imperial and local janissaries—engaged in proper military activities. Separating the "combatants" at little extra cost by scattering a large portion of them along the pilgrimage route served the interests of the state by reducing tensions in Damascus and by providing protection for the pilgrimage.

During the first half of the eighteenth century, a revitalized fortress network provided a social and economic framework that successfully gave all groups concerned a livelihood and protected the essential interests of the Ottoman state. But repeated beduin attacks—for whatever reason—were to destabilize that network and cause its breakdown by mid-century.

Organization of the Pilgrimage Caravan

As commander of the pilgrimage, the governor of Damascus administered a vast economic, social, and military enterprise. We have analyzed his role in the collection of tax revenues, his overall responsibility for the delivery of the *sürre*, and his management of the fortress network. There remain for consideration two duties: organization of the caravan and supreme command of security measures (particularly the *cerde*, the relief escort force). The present discussion focuses on the first of these duties; the second is discussed in the last part of this chapter.

Four distinct spheres of activity were associated with organization of the pilgrimage caravan, (1) adherence to a strict timetable for departure, return, and the performance of ceremonies; (2) preparation and pay of the commander's personal retinue; (3) maintenance of the command structure, that is, supervision of the *sürre* and maintenance of good relations with the Egyptian pilgrimage commander and the Meccan

[132] BA-Kepeci 2343, for 1741-1742, folios 4b-5a; BA-Kepeci 2101, for 1759-1760, p. 11.

şerif; and (4) encouragement and protection of economic activities in which the pilgrimage commander was a notable participant.

Beginning with the draft budgets in the third month of the Islamic year, Rebiyülevvel, the pilgrimage timetable moved on to departure of the *sürre* from Istanbul in Receb, the seventh month of the year. The *dawra*, or tax gathering tour of the southern *sancaks* of Damascus took place in Şaban and Ramazan, the eighth and ninth months. Departure of the caravan from Damascus occurred in Şevval, the tenth month; performance of pilgrimage rites was in Zilhicce, the last month; and arrival back in Damascus was in Safer, the second month of the new year. By Rebiyülâhır, the fourth month of the new year, the last pilgrims arrived in Istanbul. Mehmed Edib, an eighteenth-century Ottoman pilgrim, provides a timetable from Istanbul to Mecca and back (summarized in Table 4). Out of a total of 238 days, the pilgrimage took 152 days' journey from Damascus to Mecca and back, including 40 days' rest in Damascus before starting out and 3 days' rest in Damascus before returning to Istanbul.[133] That nearly two-thirds of the pilgrimage travel time was spent under the protection of the governor of Damascus serves to emphasize yet again the high rank and heavy responsibilities of this official in the Ottoman system.

Many accounts are available of the departure of the pilgrimage from Damascus. The ceremonies have been described as "one of the greatest of medieval pageants."[134] Most pilgrims arrived in Damascus in the month of Ramazan. On the eighth of Şevval, the first ceremony took place. The sacred litter (*mahmal*)—a four-cornered, conical dome frame of

[133] Mehmed Edıb, *Menasık*, pp. 254-255.

[134] Harrıs, *The Syrian Desert*, p. 232. A local contemporary account of the pılgrımage ceremonıes ıs by Ibn Kannān, "al-Mawākib al-Islāmıyya," pp. 298-300. For European observers, see *A Journey from Aleppo to Damascus*, pp. 70-73, and the accounts of Maundrell, *A Journey from Aleppo to Jerusalem*, pp. 127-128, and Burckhardt, *Travels in Syria*, pp. 52-53. Modern accounts of the pılgrımage ceremonıes include Tresse, *Le pèlerinage syrien*; Rafeq, *Province*, pp. 59-63; and Uzunçarşılı, *Mekke*, pp. 58ff, a sketchy descrıptıon.

TABLE 4
THE PILGRIMAGE TIMETABLE

Traveling days (*konak*) between Üsküdar and Damascus	37
Rest days (*oturak*) between Üsküdar and Damascus	6
Stay in Damascus (*ikamet*)	40
Traveling days between Damascus and Mecca	39
Entry into Mecca	1
Rest days between Damascus and Mecca	10
Stay at 'Arafāt (a pilgrimage site near Mecca)	1
Stay at Munā (a pilgrimage site near Mecca)	3
Stay in Mecca after completion of pilgrimage	10
Traveling days between Mecca and Damascus	39
Rest days between Mecca and Damascus	6
Stay in Damascus	3
Traveling days between Damascus and Üsküdar	37
Rest days between Damascus and Üsküdar	6
Total	238

SOURCE: Mehmed Edib, *Menasik*, pp. 254-255. Figures are given in days.

wood covered with gold-embroidered cloth (the *kisve*)—was prepared and paraded through the main streets of Damascus.[135] Accompanying the *mahmal* was the Prophet's standard (*sancak-ı şerif*), which was preserved in the Damascus citadel and brought out only to accompany the pilgrimage. Both objects were then put on display at the Ẓāhiriyya gates in front of the governor's offices. Those who came to see the display were offered food and drink, financed by income from a pious endowment.[136] Between the twelfth and twentieth of Şevval, a second ceremony took place, leading to the departure of the caravan. Probably one of the first Europeans to see this pro-

[135] For the *mahmal*, see the article by F. Bühl in *EI*[1], III, 123-124, and for the Egyptian *mahmal*, of similar construction but covered with a red, instead of a green, cloth, see Jomier, *Le mahmal et la caravane égyptienne*.

[136] See Ibn Kannān, "al-Mawākib," p. 298.

cession, Maundrell describes the order of march. It was led by forty-six "dellees," whom he calls "religious madmen," but who, in fact, were the caravan guides; they were followed by several troops of soldiers, including the local janissaries and *sipahis*, and by the Damascus citadel guards "fantastically Arm'd with Coats of Maile, Gauntlets, and other pieces of old Armour." Two troops of mounted imperial janissaries came next, followed by the Damascus governor's symbol of office, the horsetails (*tuğ*), and by "six led Horses, all of excellent shape, and nobly furnish'd." The *mahmal* and, finally, the pilgrimage commander with his own retinue completed the procession.[137] An anonymous traveler who was in Damascus in 1725 includes the local aristocracy of the city (*seyyids* and *şerifs*), musicians, singers, and artillery corps.[138] Maundrell states that the procession took forty-five minutes to pass the spot from which he observed it. With the conclusion of the ceremony, "every Pilgrim thinks of nothing but his Departure."[139] Moving southward through the Maydān quarter, the assembled caravan left the city through the Gate of God (Bāb Allāh), so named for the ultimate destination of the pilgrimage, Mecca. Burckhardt, who toured Damascus in 1810-1812, remarks (and this applies to the early nineteenth century) that this gate "might with more propriety be named Bab-el-Maut, the Gate of death; for scarcely a third ever return of those whom a devout adherence to their religion, or the hope of gain impel to this journey."[140] At Qubbat al-Ḥāj, a town very close to Damascus, the caravan stopped for the first night, moving on to Kiswa and Muzayrīb (the first major fort) on the following day. At Muzayrīb, the staging area of the pilgrimage, the caravan remained until the end of the month of Şevval in order to allow latecomers to catch up. Time was also needed to organize the escort troops and to allow Damascus merchants to sell their wares to pilgrims and the beduin.[141] At the beginning of Zilkade, the eleventh

[137] Maundrell, *A Journey*, pp. 127-128.

[138] *A Journey from Aleppo to Damascus*, pp. 71-73.

[139] Ibid., p. 73.

[140] Burckhardt, *Travels in Syria*, pp. 52-53.

[141] Ibn Kannān, "al-Mawākib," p. 300.

month of the Islamic year, the caravan would start out for the Holy Cities. By this time, its numbers would range from twenty to sixty thousand, precise figures being unavailable from year to year for the eighteenth century.[142]

To organize and protect this vast number of pilgrims, the governor of Damascus received financial assistance from the state to devote to the maintenance of his own retinue and to the escort forces. The state did not, as a rule, provide more than caravan security and fortress protection to individual pilgrims. This separation between the official retinue and the mass of pilgrims is important and raises several questions. That pilgrims had to fend for themselves was not necessarily the result of indifference on the state's part. Rather, it was one of the five customary requirements of the pilgrimage itself. One had to be a Muslim, free (that is, not a slave), and sound of mind, to have attained one's majority, have the ability to perform the rites and travel, and possess provisions and means of transport.[143] Such was the religious basis for this arrangement. But it also suggests that the separation of the official retinue from the pilgrims was a concrete expression of the political and social separation between *askeri* and *reaya*, elite and commoners. In its composition, the pilgrimage caravan reflected the social diversity of the Ottoman state: separate escort troops (local and imperial janissaries in the forts, and mercenaries); the pilgrimage commander's retinue, which, in structure, mirrored the large household of the grand vezir of the empire and most probably included high-ranking officials who were going to Mecca; and the mass of ordinary pilgrims who marched together usually in accordance with their place of origin—be it Damascus, Aleppo, Persia, the Balkans, or Asia Minor.

What did it cost a pilgrim to make this long and dangerous journey. Professor Rafeq's recent research into the local history of Damascus shows that, during the eighteenth century, the journey to Mecca cost seventy *kuruş*, forty of which were

[142] Rafeq, *Province*, p. 61.

[143] Mehmed Edıb, *Menasik*, p. 18; and A. J. Wensınck, "Ḥadjdj," *EI²*, III, 35.

"for transport, five for drinking water, fifteen for luggage, five for buying a seat (*shaqdūfa*) to be placed on the back of the camel (two passengers usually rode on a camel), and five . . . for the camel driver."[144] The fee also included food and a luggage allowance of forty-five *okkas* (about 126 pounds). On the other hand, the fee for the return journey cost between one hundred and one hundred and ten *kuruş*. Professor Rafeq suggests that the higher cost of the return was intended to cover a greater luggage allowance (due to purchases by pilgrims and merchants of goods in the Holy Cities) as well as the greater danger faced by the caravan on its return, the beduin might have cause to attack the tired and heavily laden pilgrims.[145] Private arrangements of this type were the provenance of the Damascus guild of conveyors (*muqawwimīn*), who were engaged by groups of fifteen or twenty pilgrims to furnish tents, bedding, pack animals, food and water, and transport by litter, camel, or donkey.[146] The conveyors themselves had a large retinue, ranging from twenty to forty men. It included cooks, camel drivers, servants, and tent keepers.[147] Pilgrims paid half the fee on departure from Damascus and the second half upon arrival in Mecca (the same principle applied to the return journey).[148] Because of the heavy capital expenditures required, the conveyors took

[144] Rafeq, "Economic Relations between Damascus and the Dependent Countryside, 1743-1771," pp. 53-54. The figure of seventy *kuruş* applied to the year 1745. In preparing this paper, Prof. Rafeq exploited new sources for the local history of Syria, the *sharī'a* court records.

[145] Ibid. It is significant that, by the early nineteenth century, inflation was so rampant and the security provided to pilgrims so poor that hardly a tenth of the caravan consisted of real pilgrims (the rest being soldiers, attendants, and merchants). The cost of the trip was 750 *kuruş* for the outward journey and even more for the return, plus 1,000 *kuruş* "expenses on the road and at Mekka." The total cost was about 2,500 *kuruş*, equivalent to £125 sterling at the time, an enormous sum. Burckhardt, *Travels in Syria*, p. 243.

[146] d'Ohsson, *Tableau*, III, 270-271; Rafeq, "Economic Relations," p. 53; and al-Qāsimī, *Qāmūs al-ṣinā'āt*, II, 465.

[147] al-Qāsimī, *Qāmūs al-ṣinā'āt*, II, 474; the tent keepers' guild (Ar., *mahtār*; Tur., *mehter*) was associated with the *muqawwimīn*.

[148] Ibid., p. 465.

great risks in the hope of earning great profits. Hence, they formed one of the wealthiest guilds in Damascus.[149]

As indicated at the beginning of this chapter, tax revenues theoretically were abundantly available to cover expenses of the pilgrimage commander's escort and retinue. However, because of the diversity of sources of revenue and the distribution of funds among the pilgrimage budgets, provincial accounts, and the *dawra*, the governor of Damascus did not know precisely what his financial condition would be until the end of Ramazan, just weeks before the caravan's departure. If there was a deficit, the governor had two options. First, he could illegally reduce expenses by cutting purchases of essential provisions and cutting payments to tribes for services rendered or payments to the escort forces. Second, if he had time and anticipated a deficit, he could appeal to the central government for a tax increase or an emergency loan from the sultan's personal treasury. Evidence pertaining to these options is limited because it is almost impossible to determine the actual cause of any given deficit; was it due to genuine lack of funds or to embezzlement by the governor? In 1730, for instance, Ismail Paşa, the first 'Aẓm governor of Damascus, was dismissed from office on dubious grounds of embezzlement of pilgrimage funds and "oppression" of the populace. He was ordered imprisoned in the Damascus citadel and all his property was to be confiscated so that the state could recover the money intended for the pilgrimage. Once these steps had been taken, the revenue was to be turned over to the new Damascus governor for the next pilgrimage.[150] Another instance of revenue shortage—this time genuine—occurred

149 Ibid., pp. 465-466.

150 BA-Mühimme 136, p. 264, order to the *kadi*, janissary chief, and citadel commander of Damascus, dated middle Rebıyülâhır 1143 (24 October to 2 November 1730). Ismail Paşa's dismissal was, in fact, precipitated by the Patrona Halil rebellion in Istanbul, which deposed Sultan Ahmed III and caused uprisings in the major cities of the Syrian provinces. For a recent treatment of the revolt, see Olson, *Siege of Mosul*, pp. 65-88. For a detailed account concerning Damascus, see Rafeq, *Province*, pp. 106-111, who does not include the specific charge of embezzlement of pilgrimage funds against Ismail Paşa

during the term of Esat Paşa (al-'Azm). By the beginning of the month of Receb 1166 (May 1753), three months before start of the pilgrimage, Esat Paşa faced a serious deficit because he was unable to collect from the province of Sidon the revenues intended for the pilgrimage. He wrote a letter to his Istanbul representative and appealed for special authorization to collect the Sidon taxes.[151] Within eleven days of the letter's dispatch, Esat's representative had obtained a decision from the central government to permit Esat to collect 15,000 *kuruş* in supplementary taxes—not from Sidon, but from Hamā and Ḥimṣ. The latter were part of Esat's personal tax farm.[152] In this case, the shortage of funds may have been due to the costs of a military campaign that Esat Paşa began on 2 Receb 1166 (5 May 1753) against the beduin of Balqā (almost on the northern limits of the Ḥijāz). He no doubt intended to clear the pilgrimage route in advance of the caravan's departure from Damascus.[153]

The needs of the pilgrimage commander's retinue were enormous, ranging from gunpowder to foodstuffs, clothing, and cash. All of these materials together formed what was known as the pilgrimage stockpile (*kiler-i hacc*). To the greatest possible extent, the pilgrimage commander assured sufficient stocks of provisions in fortresses along the route. The same was true of the stockpile that was moved with the caravan, and also of provisions—food in particular—to meet the retinue's requirements in the Holy Cities.[154] Sources of sup-

but, instead, states that the latter's confiscated wealth "would bring the sultan much needed money for his Persian War." This conflict of evidence demonstrates the difficulty of assessing motives for dismissal of governors. For a discussion of this problem, see Chapter One.

[151] TKS-E. 3630, personal letter (*kayime*) from Esat Paşa to his representative (*kapıkethuda*) in Istanbul, dated 1 Receb 1163 (4 May 1753).

[152] Ibid. On the back of Esat's letter, the *kapıkethüda* made a brief note of the tax increase, dating his note 12 Receb 1163 (15 May 1753). The note stated: *Hama ve Hims'e zamm olunan on beş bin kuruş maddesiçin*.

[153] Rafeq, *Province*, p. 198. There is no evidence to prove conclusively that the expenses of this campaign caused the deficit in pilgrimage funds.

[154] For a list of provisions for the pilgrimage commander's retinue (shipped to the Holy Cities through the Red Sea port of Jidda in the same

ply ranged as far away as Ḥamā and Ma'arra. Purchased at wholesale rates, the provisions included, among other items, clarified butter, bolts of cloth for camel covers, rare cloth (for the commander's personal use), gunpowder, and raw linen for the manufacture of tents.[155] The stockpile was the personal responsibility of the pilgrimage commander's personal treasurer (*hazinedar*) and quartermaster (*vekil-i harç*), who were authorized to make purchases and rent transport animals on their master's behalf.[156] According to the pilgrimage budgets, huge sums were spent on engaging the services of escort forces, beduin, and attendants.[157] In the pilgrimage commander's accounts (one sample of which is contained in Appendix VIII), the sums expended do not match the budgets. Within the limitations set by available evidence, it is not possible to explain the discrepancy satisfactorily. However, sev-

month as the pilgrimage caravan's departure from Damascus and two months before they were required), see TKS-D. 4287, dated Şevval 1154 (10 December 1741 to 7 January 1742). The provisions included horse beans, barley, white rice, wheat flour, corn, and coffee. Additional purchases for the retinue, in one case amounting to 30,000 *kuruş*, were made when the caravan reached the Holy Cities. See TKS-E. 2025/5, a register for the pilgrimage of 1155 (1742-1743).

155 See BA-Mühimme 159, p. 107, order dated middle Receb 1170 (1-9 April 1757). This order refers to the wholesale rates as *mubayaa* and *fiat-ı kadime* (literally, "old prices," that is, probably those set in previous years by the central government for purchase of its own requirements). The more common terms in use in Istanbul for official prices were *si'r-i miri* or *fiat-ı miriye*. See Itzkowitz and Mote, eds. and trans., *Mubadele*, pp. 19-20.

156 See TKS-E. 2025/5, cited in Note 154 above. For a contract between the governor of Damascus and the camel drivers' guild, in which 100 camels were rented to move the governor's baggage from Muzayrīb to Medina, at twenty-three *kuruş* per camel, see TKS-E. 2588/1, dated 17 Safer 1151 (6 June 1738). For details of a similar contract between the governor and the *shaykhs* of Hawrān, see Rafeq, "Economic Relations," p. 52.

157 It should be noted that the composition and size of the retinue varied sharply from year to year, and even more from century to century. For the nineteenth-century Damascus pilgrimage, see the well-written account by Tresse, *Le pèlerinage syrien*, pp. 67ff. For the sixteenth-century Egyptian pilgrimage, see the invaluable primary account by the chief secretary of the pilgrimage during the early Ottoman period: 'Abd al-Qādir ibn Muḥammad al-Jazīrī, *Durar al-fawā'id*, especially chapter 3.

eral inferences from this evidence are possible. First, as we have already stated, the pilgrimage budgets are incomplete; they cover only the outward portion of escort expenses and do not include the commander's expenses. Second, the budgets include expenses that, in practice, were spread over a whole year, sometimes months apart and kept account of in separate registers, not all of which are available. Third, total revenues in practice exceeded by far those in the budget and could presumably be applied to retinue expenses not originally planned for in Istanbul. Until more research is devoted to this point, these inferences should be regarded as tentative.

In addition to his duties as organizer and protector of the caravan, the governor of Damascus assumed command of the entire body of pilgrims and—while he was in Arabia—outranked the ruling elite of the Holy Cities. He also outranked the Egyptian pilgrimage commander.[158] When authorized, he had powers to take punitive action against anyone committing an act contrary to the interests of religion or state. Note the language contained in one order to the governor: "the whole [pilgrimage] is under your general supervision. The overall regulation of the affairs of that road that is abundant with God's salvation [that is, the road to Mecca] has been transferred to your ability and committed to your care and responsibility."[159] Two broad groups were affected by this order: first, the sultan's representatives (the purse commissioner, water carriers, and special couriers) sent each year to the Holy Cities for charitable purposes and, second, officials in the Ḥijāz, including the Egyptian caravan chief, the governor of Jidda, and the Meccan *şerif*.

Within the retinue of the purse commissioner, the water

[158] For example, see the order to Topal Yusuf Paşa, governor of Damascus, to arrest a top official of the Egyptian caravan in Mecca. BA-Emiri/III Ahmed 15593, dated end Receb 1127 (23 July to 1 August 1715). Note that Yusuf Paşa received this order before leaving Damascus for Mecca. The official to be arrested was the Egyptian camel train chief (*kitar serdarı*), Niğdeli Hasan Kethüda. He was charged with trying to foment disorders in Mecca.

[159] BA-Mühimme 122, pp. 102-103, dated middle Receb 1126 (23 July to 1 August 1714). See also Uzunçarşılı, *Mekke*, p. 41.

carriers (*saka başılar*) and special couriers (*müjdeci başılar*) performed important functions. Financed by pious endowments (many of them created by the imperial family), the water carriers distributed fresh water and provided camel transport to sick and needy pilgrims on the road to Mecca. They also furnished clothing to the poor of the Holy Cities, thus supplementing—within the endowments' limits—the efforts of the purse commissioner.[160] All the water carriers' expenses, including their financial support and provisions, were met by the revenues of these endowments. As for the special couriers, they were appointed by the *kızlar ağası* and were led by two officials, known as the first and second couriers. The latter did not proceed with the purse commissioner's retinue beyond Damascus, but, instead, waited until his chief (the first courier) returned safely from the Holy Cities with reports from the Damascus governor and the Meccan *şerif*. Together, both couriers carried these reports back to the grand vezir and the sultan. They traveled at great speed in order to reach Istanbul before celebrations of the Prophet Muḥammad's birthday (12 Rebiyülevvel). At that time, the good news of the pilgrimage's safe return was proclaimed in a formal ceremony at the Sultan Ahmed Mosque.[161]

The second group that the Damascus governor outranked was the ruling elite of the Ḥijāz. Although this rank existed only during the pilgrimage season, in the first half of the eighteenth century, it acquired considerable importance. At the turn of that century, the Ottomans were faced with two serious problems in the Ḥijāz: first, the constant rivalry between members of the family of Meccan *şerifs* that led to disturbances during the pilgrimage season; and second, the unstable arrangements by which the governor of Jidda was the permanent Ottoman representative in the Ḥijāz. Mutual grievances between Ottomans and Meccans increased after 1700. In that year, a British traveler to Jidda, and a friend of its governor, reported the following incident involving the governor and the *şerif*:

[160] BA-Mühımme 122, pp. 102-103.

[161] *TDS*, II, 610.

> . . . he [the *şerif*], coming in person before the city [Jidda], accompanied with 2000 horse and demanded of the Bashaw (who was my only friend) 100,000 chiqueens; adding that his master, the Grand Seigniour, was the son of a Christian whore, and he would not own him to be a protector of the Mohammedan religion (since he had made a peace with those unbelievers, the Christians) [that is, the Treaty of Karlowitz, 1699] but that he would marry his daughter to the king of Morocco [?]. Upon which the Bashaw was forced to send him the money to save his head; and I, very melancholy, returned to my lodging.[162]

This incident demonstrates the extent to which the Ottoman state was vulnerable to criticism for its unprecedented concessions to the European powers at Karlowitz.[163] But it also shows the mercurial nature of politics in the Ḥijāz. There are repeated instances of Damascus governors being ordered by the central government to depose, impose, or reinstate Meccan *şerifs*. Although this topic is beyond the scope of our study, there is enough evidence to show that the governor of Damascus was charged with ensuring that the *şerifs* properly executed their duties. As for the governor of Jidda, he served as a foil to the *şerif* by holding the position of master of the Meccan sanctuary (*Mekke şeyhülharemliği*). After 1701, his power and status were further enhanced by his assignment as governor of Habeş (northeastern Ethiopia and the eastern Sudan),[164] another tactic by which the state attempted to control

[162] William Daniel, quoted in de Gaury, *Rulers of Mecca*, p. 161. De Gaury's work lacks a scholarly apparatus, though he has clearly consulted basic sources, with the exception of the Ottoman archives (on which he makes extensive remarks, pp. 283-285). Unfortunately, no confirmation could be found for this event in available primary sources. Mecca was ravaged during this period by internecine warfare between rival factions and pretenders to the Meccan emirate. See Aḥmad ibn Zaynī Daḥlān, *Khulāṣat al-kalām*, pp. 124ff. Also see Uzunçarşılı, *Mekke*, pp. 88-92.

[163] For an analysis of the Ottoman defense of this treaty, see Thomas, *A Study of Naima*, pp. 80-82, and Itzkowitz, *Ottoman Empire*, pp. 100-103.

[164] For a recent study of Ottoman rule in Jidda, northeastern Ethiopia and the Red Sea, see Orhonlu, *Osmanlı imparatorluğu'nun güney siyaseti: Habeş eyaleti*, p. 132.

politics—and trade—in the Ḥijāz and the Red Sea at the beginning of the eighteenth century. At the same time, the governor of Damascus was authorized to rectify any abuses in the Holy Cities. For example, in 1712, Nasuh Paşa was ordered to investigate a charge by the Egyptian caravan chiefs that the *şerif* had stolen 27,000 *kuruş* worth of their provisions, which were imported through Jidda to Mecca. Nasuh was to make an investigation into the matter with the assistance of the magistrate (*kadi*) of Mecca, then report back to the central government and take any steps necessary to punish the offender.[165] On another occasion, Receb Paşa recommended the appointment of Yaḥyā ibn Barakāt to be Meccan *şerif*. The central government accepted the recommendation and laid down the conditions of office: first, to act with justice and moderation; second, to meet the pilgrimage caravan at Madā'in Ṣāliḥ and to escort it to Medina and Mecca; and, third, to assist in maintaining order in the Holy Cities when the pilgrims arrived.[166] Uppermost in the minds of the Ottoman ruling elite was the hope that nothing would occur in the Ḥijāz that could poison the atmosphere of the pilgrimage or sully the Ottoman state's reputation as the predominant Islamic power. The governor of Damascus, as commander of the pilgrimage, was chosen as the state's supreme representative in translating this hope into reality.

Encouragement and protection of economic activity along the pilgrimage route was the fourth sphere of activity associated with organization of the pilgrimage caravan. The subject of trade between Damascus and the Holy Cities during the Ottoman period has yet to be studied in its own right. Within the scope of this book, four separate trade patterns may be

[165] BA-Emırı/ııı Ahmed 13310, dated middle Receb 1124 (14-24 August 1712).

[166] BA-Emıri/ııı Ahmed 3643, draft of an imperıal letter to the Meccan *şerif*, dated beginnıng Rebiyülevvel 1131 (22-30 January 1719). For the colorful career of Yaḥyā, see Uzunçarşılı, *Mekke*, pp. 99-103; and de Gaury, *Rulers*, pp. 162ff. For another warning to the *şerif* regarding the execution of his duties, see BA-Cevdet/Dahiliye 1223, dated beginnıng Rebiyülâhır 1144 (3-12 October 1721).

identified: first, goods shipped with the caravan in either direction; second, goods sold to pilgrims by villagers and tribesmen along the route; third, goods sold to pilgrims by merchants who accompanied the caravan; and fourth, goods sold by the governor of Damascus in the Holy Cities for his own profit.

Wealthy merchants of Damascus took advantage of the pilgrimage caravan's relative security to ship their goods to Mecca and to import commodities from the Hijāz. Because the latter had been for centuries a net importing and transit trade region, and not a producing area, it required large imports of all types of commodities, ranging from foodstuffs to clothing, cooking ware, and other essentials. The sources for these were primarily Egypt, Africa, India, and Syria. According to Professor Rafeq, the major exports of the Hijāz were coffee transshipped from Yemen and *sanā*, a laxative.[167] Seen in this light, the purse commissioner's distribution of alms and clothing stimulated the economy of the Ḥijāz and helped reduce social tensions caused by economic hardship.

Perhaps the greatest stimulus to commerce along the pilgrimage route was the brisk sale of water and foodstuffs to individual pilgrims (see Table 5). In exchange, the tribesmen and villagers who sold these essentials bought goods for themselves from the merchants who accompanied the caravan. Clearly, the pilgrimage commander's security measures helped to encourage all this activity, which has been described as follows:

> But when the serpentine caravan halted for an hour or two, it suddenly became a mushroom city of tents. These tents were crowded compactly together to facilitate their defence, but with a middle street where hawkers might do a hectic trade during the brief halt, and at one end of which traders were at liberty to set up their booths and display their wares for sale. For the pilgrim caravan was invariably accompanied by small caravans of merchants, whose presence and activities were expressly sanctioned by the Koran.

[167] Rafeq, "Economic Relations," p. 51.

TABLE 5
GOODS SOLD TO PILGRIMS
ALONG THE PILGRIMAGE ROUTE

Fortress/ stopping place	*Products sold*	*Sellers*	*Source*
Muzayrīb	(Large market set up to sell all types of products)	Townspeople, Lajā tribe	Ḥawrān
Qaṭrāna	Food	Residents of Karak	Shawbak
al-Ḥasā	Food	Tribesmen	Jerusalem, Karak, and Shawbak
Ma'ān	Fruits	Tribesmen and villagers	Hebron
	Firewood for transport to Mecca for cooking fuel	Tribesmen and villagers	Local
Tabūk	Fruits and vegetables	Local	Local
Madā' in Ṣāliḥ	Fruits	Residents of 'Aqaba	'Ulā and Hebron
'Ulā	Food	Local	Local
Abyār Ḥamza (between Mecca and Medina)	Water	Neighboring villagers, in rotation from year to year	

SOURCES: Mehmed Edib, *Menasik*, pp. 65–82 passim; Kâtip Çelebi, *Cihannümâ*, pp. 538ff.

> . . . The merchants carried goods of every description: food to supplement the meagre fare which the *Hajj* commissariat [that is, the purse commissioner] provided for the pilgrims; clothes and weapons in case any pilgrim should desire to increase his stock during the journey; and large quantities of cloth and silk, brass and copper-ware to sell to the Beduin encountered *en route*. The clothing merchants generally did not go all the way to Mecca with the caravan, finding it more profitable to wait at Tebuk or some other *Hajj* station and trade there until the *Hajjis* returned northwards.[168]

Once into the Ḥijāz, the pilgrimage commander also assured that the enormous quantities of provisions imported from Egypt through Jidda for sale to the pilgrims were transported by the Banī Ḥarb tribe to Mecca. In return, members of the tribe received cash grants from the purse commissioner.[169] Finally, the pilgrimage commander engaged in commerce of his own. For example, in 1737, Süleyman Paşa (al-'Aẓm) imported nearly 20,000 *kuruş* worth of expensive silks and cloth from Egypt well in advance of the pilgrimage. Süleyman, while in Mecca with the previous pilgrimage, had advanced his agent in Jidda, 'Abd al-Qādir ibn Amīr al-Ḥalabī, 19,479.5 *kuruş* to cover the purchases. Two months later, after Süleyman had left Mecca, three bundles of cloth and three bundles of large boxes were delivered to the Jidda agent at a cost of 19,455.25 *kuruş*. Süleyman was to receive the goods and the 24.25 *kuruş* surplus on the next pilgrimage.[170] Such were the economic opportunities that the pilgrimage offered the governor and everyone else concerned.

It was to the pilgrimage commander's advantage—not only professionally but personally—to secure the lives and property of those involved in the pilgrimage. We shall now turn to the measures adopted by the Ottoman state to protect the

[168] Harris, *The Syrian Desert*, pp. 232-233.

[169] Uzunçarşılı, *Mekke*, p. 59.

[170] TKS-D. 9512, register dated 20 Safer 1150 (19 June 1737), money advanced by Süleyman Paşa in middle Zilhicce 1149 (12-21 April 1737).

caravan and to keep the tribes, which were the main threat to good order, within the economic and political system.

The *Cerde* and Pilgrimage Security

In addition to the caravan escort and fortress network, there were two other security measures that the Ottoman state employed to protect the pilgrimage: settlement of tribes in key areas and dispatch of a relief force to meet the returning caravan roughly at the midpoint between Damascus and Mecca. Having considered the Ottoman state's attempts to contain the tribes in the vicinity of Damascus, it is appropriate at this point to consider the tribal role in defense of the pilgrimage.

It was the established policy of the Ottoman state in the Syrian provinces, as elsewhere, to attempt to settle nomadic tribes in strategic areas, and particularly along vital roads. Not only would the tribes provide security to travelers and pilgrims, they would also encourage villagers to remain and work the land, thus stimulating the local economy and generating tax revenues. Furthermore, the state hoped that the tribes themselves would abandon their transhumant life and become villagers themselves. Alois Musil, the Czech anthropologist and topographer who studied beduin tribes in the Arabian desert during the early twentieth century, sums up this pattern of settlement as follows:

> On the edge of the desert a constant increase or decrease of the population can be observed. If the government guarantees complete security of life and property to the inhabitants of the towns and villages, the herdsmen of goats and sheep are transformed into active farmers; on all sides they build cottages, hamlets come into existence, and the [migratory tribes] and [goat and sheepherders] become peaceful settlers. They entrust their goats and sheep to the care of various desert clans of Bedouins, who do not go back to the open desert but remain on the border between villages and

> settlements and are themselves transformed into [goat and sheepherders]. If there is no strong government in the populated regions, security of life and property disappears and there follows a decrease of population. The permanent home is exchanged for the moveable tent; the farmers become [goat and sheepherders].[171]

In the eighteenth century, the Ottoman state, out of concern for pilgrimage security, kept a close watch over two areas of the Syrian provinces where tribal settlements were of critical importance and where tribal pressure was perhaps most strongly felt, the hinterland of Hamā and Ḥimṣ and that portion of the Syrian desert extending southward from Damascus. The former areas' local security was the explicit responsibility of Turkman tribes. For reasons still unknown, these tribes, in the late seventeenth century, began to leave their traditional settlements and displace the peasant population. In 1722, the local governor of Hamā was ordered to expel the tribes from a village that they had occupied east of Himṣ. The villagers whom the tribes had displaced were to be moved back to their homes. The state viewed this disruption of the social order as a threat to the pilgrimage's safe passage south from Anatolia to Damascus.[172] Later in the century, when Esat Bey (al-'Azm) was the local governor of Hamā, the state responded affirmatively to his petition to undertake a major campaign to resettle the tribes. Not since 1696—after the accession of Sultan Mustafa II—had the state made such an attempt.[173] The tribal problem, according to Esat Bey's petition, had been aggravated since 1730-1731, again the occasion of a sultan's accession, during which unruly elements in society took advantage of the revolution in Istanbul to further their aims without interference. Negligent in their duty to protect pilgrims and travelers, the Turkman tribes had taken over villages not assigned to them. In response to his petition,

[171] Musıl, *The Manners and Customs of the Rwala Bedouins*, p. 45.

[172] BA-Ibnülemın/Dahılıye 2087, order dated 9 Receb 1134 (25 May 1722).

[173] BA-Cevdet/Dahılıye 4804, petition and grand vezır's memorandum; pursuant order granted 11 Ramazan 1150 (2 January 1738).

the state granted Esat Bey the authority to relocate the tribesmen by force to their traditional lands. At the same time, the state sweetened the tribes' bitter medicine by ordering Abbas Ağa, the local beneficiary of a large land grant (*zeamet*), not to collect the annual taxes (*miri*) from one of the tribes.[174] In spite of these orders, the problem persisted and, in the following year, Esat was ordered to carry out a "mop-up" campaign to settle the tribes once and for all.[175]

The tribal security system in the Syrian desert was somewhat more complex than that of northern Syria. There is less evidence here of an effort to resettle villagers who had fled areas along the pilgrimage route.[176] The state-appointed Arab tribal chieftain, the *Şam urbanı şeyhi*, performed several tasks in return for pay for himself and his followers. First, the chief undertook to protect settled areas along the pilgrimage route. Second, he accompanied and assisted the relief force, the *cerde*. Third, the chief provided camels for rent to the pilgrimage commander as well as to individual pilgrims. Fourth, and finally, he was expected to defer to the governor of Damascus in matters concerning the pilgrimage.[177] Paid handsomely from the provincial treasury of Damascus, the chief was thus induced into cooperating with the state. Despite the well-ordered plans of the Ottoman government, tribal attacks on the pilgrimage caravan occurred on an unprecedented scale

[174] Ibid.

[175] BA-Cevdet/Dahiliye 13103, order dated middle Ramazan 1152 (12-21 December 1739).

[176] One noteworthy exception was the repatriation of villagers from the Hawrān—along the pilgrimage route—who had fled across the Jordan River to Şafad and Sıdon. This, like the flight from settled areas around Ḥimṣ and Hamā in 1730 referred to above, probably occurred after the deposition of Sultan Ahmed III in the same year. BA-Cevdet/Dahiliye 376, petition and grand vezir's memorandum, the former dated 22 Rebiyulâhır 1144 (24 October 1731).

[177] BA-Cevdet/Dahiliye 717, appointment certificate, undated, but, from internal evidence, from the regime of Süleyman Paşa (al-'Azm), 1736-1738, 1740-1743. Also, BA-Mühimme 122, p. 176, dated middle Şevval 1126 (10-19 October 1714); BA-Cevdet/Dahiliye 1914, dated beginning Şaban 1103 (18-27 April 1692); and BA-Ibnülemin/Dahiliye 2015, dated beginning Şaban 1103 (18-27 April 1692).

during this period. Some chiefs neglected to perform their duties; furthermore, some governors failed to pay tribes for their services and this appears to have been the most common cause for such attacks. On the other hand, there is evidence that the state was not completely helpless in the face of neglect by the chieftains. The Ottomans, through the governor of Damascus and through their special agents, dismissed tribal chiefs and appointed replacements with ease (although such acts could and did provoke reprisals from the tribes).[178]

It was the *cerde* that gave the Ottoman state the means to provide pilgrimage security over and above that offered by the Damascus tribal chief. In this respect, the *cerde*, like other supporting institutions of the pilgrimage, reflected the Ottoman bent for "checks and balances." During the sixteenth century, the Ottomans appear not to have used the term *cerde* for the relief force that escorted the returning pilgrimage caravan. Headed by local dignitaries, this force was, rather, known as the reception group (*mulāqa*), and it did not have the taut organization of its eighteenth-century successor.[179] Throughout the seventeenth century, the same looseness of organization seems to have prevailed, as the *cerde* was still commanded by local dignitaries. On several occasions, the Druze prince and sometime rebel against Ottoman authority, Fakhr al-Dīn II, held the command.[180] Towards the end of the century, however, and in line with the reorganization of the pilgrimage as a whole, local Ottoman governors (especially from Jerusalem and Nablus) began to assume command of the *cerde*.[181] During the first half of the eighteenth century,

[178] For example, the quick series of appointments and dismissals that occurred in 1738 probably caused the attack on the caravan during the following year. See BA-Cevdet/Dahiliye 17071, dated 13 Safer 1151 (4 June 1738) and BA-Emiri/I Mahmud 1781, dated end Receb 1151 (4-13 November 1738). For the attack of 1739, see Shamir, " 'Aẓm Wālīs," p. 68.

[179] Bakhit, "Ottoman Province," p. 125. The Egyptian pilgrimage also was served by a relief force called the *mulāqa*: al-Jazīrī, *Durar al-fawā'id*, pp. 174-176. The term *cerde*, on the other hand, referred specifically to a detachment of cavalry assigned specific duties.

[180] Bakhit, "Ottoman Province," p. 125; Rafeq, *Province*, p. 65.

[181] Rafeq, *Province*, p. 65.

the governor of Tripoli was, with few exceptions, the chief of this relief force. In unusual circumstances, the post was given to the governor of either Sidon or Aleppo. Appointment of the *cerde başbuğu*, as he was known, was no longer in the hands of the pilgrimage commander or of the governor of Damascus. Instead, the central government took charge of the matter and managed details of financing the escort, determining its composition, and appointing its chiefs. This was yet another sign of attempts to centralize control of the pilgrimage from Istanbul and Damascus.

The financing and composition of the *cerde* were determined in several ways. During the first half of the eighteenth century, the *cerde* was supported by tax revenues from Tripoli, Sidon, the Palestinian *sancaks*, and, to a lesser extent, from other sources in the Syrian provinces whose income accrued to the provincial treasury of Damascus. The figure of 82,000 *kuruş* raised from the Damascus provincial treasury was devoted entirely to the *cerde*'s maintenance and to payments to beduin who accompanied that force.[182] If any surplus remained after completion of the pilgrimage, it was to be sent to Istanbul as tribute (*salyâne*).[183] On several occasions, a revenue shortage or change of governor in the province of Tripoli caused changes in financing the *cerde*. In 1730, after the deposition of Sultan Ahmed III and ensuing strife in Tripoli, the *cerde* was organized along classical lines. That is, holders of tax farms (*mukataas*) were required to provide 1,000 armed men for the *cerde*, as if they were beneficiaries of land held in return for service (*timars*). Possibly this was a punishment for the civil disorders.[184] In 1758, again follow-

[182] See the provincial accounts (Appendix v) and also BA-Cevdet/Askeri 27823, in three parts, dated respectively 22, 26, and 22 Muharrem 1150 (22 and 26 May 1737).

[183] Due to the high costs of the pilgrimage, this rarely occurred. For an order requiring the recovery of surplus *cerde* funds, see BA-Cevdet/Askeri 29779, dated 19 Zilhicce 1161 (10 December 1748).

[184] BA-Emiri/III Ahmed 3261, order appointing Osman Paşa Muhassil to Tripoli and command of the *cerde*, dated end Rebiyülâhır 1143 (3-12 November 1730). Sultan Ahmed III was deposed on 18-19 Rebiyülevvel 1143 (1-2 October 1730).

ing a change in the sultanate, a new governor of Tripoli, Abdurrahman Paşa (formerly of Aleppo), failed to raise tax revenues sufficient to finance the *cerde*. The central government decided to advance him a loan of 150,000 *kuruş* from the sultan's personal treasury, with the proviso that a special agent be sent to Tripoli with powers to recover the loan from local tax farmers.[185] As for changes in command brought about by the appointment of a new Tripoli governor and other extraordinary circumstances, this appears to have occurred only once, between 1739-1740 and 1741-1742. In 1739-1740, the Tripoli governor had just arrived in the province, so the governor of Aleppo took command of the *cerde*.[186] The next year, because of the new governor's heavy debts (owed to the central government for failure to collect taxes), Esat Bey (al-'Azm), the local governor of Ḥamā, was given the *cerde* command.[187] In 1741-1742, the same problem arose and, again, the governor of Aleppo took over. Then, after three years of failure, the governor of Tripoli was given a last chance. The *cerde* command would be restored to him in view of his many years of faithful service, but the costs were to be met from his own resources, with only 25,000 *kuruş* to come from outstanding revenues in Tripoli.[188]

In the Palestinian *sancaks*, the financial base for the *cerde* was somewhat more complicated. The state persisted in trying to get holders of *timars* to fulfill their military service obligations through the *cerde*. Recent research into the fiscal history of these *sancaks* shows that, on balance, the attempts failed, and the central government settled for increased tax payments, which the governor of Damascus and the *cerde* chief could use to raise their own forces.[189] Later in the century, the state again tried to force beneficiaries to fulfill this duty. In 1769,

---

[185] BA-Cevdet/Askeri 16697, memorandum by the grand vezır, Mehmed Rağıb Paşa, approved by the sultan on 18 Şaban 1171 (27 April 1758).

[186] BA-Cevdet/Askeri 13734, personal letter (*kayime*) from Hekımoğlu Ali Paşa, the grand vezır, to the governor of Tripoli, dated 15 Cemazıyelâhır 1155 (17 August 1742).

[187] Ibid. [188] Ibid.

[189] Cohen, *Palestine*, pp. 150-152, 168-172, 300

for example, the *alaybey* of Nablus (an official who mustered beneficiaries for campaign) was discovered to have left his post and come to reside in Istanbul. When this was discovered, a member of the grand vezir's retinue, the *cavuşbaşı vekili*, who ushered petitioners and officials into the grand vezir's offices, was ordered to repatriate the man. After making the journey by ship from Istanbul, the *alaybey* was to be escorted to Nablus and compelled to provide service to the *cerde*.[190] Regardless of its acquiescence in allowing beneficiaries to escape these duties, the state, as can be seen by this incident, retained the option of reimposing the classical system of land grants for service. No doubt the very presence of this audacious official in Istanbul goaded the state into repatriating him.

In the month of Receb, three months before the pilgrimage caravan was to leave Damascus for Arabia (or, if general security were adequate, in the month of Şevval), the central government would begin to issue its orders to the various officials of the Syrian provinces concerning composition of the *cerde*. Aside from the beneficiaries of *timars* in the Palestinian *sancaks*, the *cerde* was normally composed of 1,500 fighting men plus the personal retinues of the *cerde* commander and of some of the other provincial units. Strictly speaking, the fighting force, mainly cavalry, was drawn from Tripoli (500), Sidon (500), the tribes (an unknown number), and, sometimes, from volunteers from Damascus.[191] D'Ohsson's assertion—

[190] BA-Cevdet/Dahılıye 937, order dated end Cemazıyelâhır 1183 (21-30 October 1769). For the *çavuşbaşı vekili*, see Gibb and Bowen, *Islamic Society*, I, 1, p. 349.

[191] Evidence for composition and movement of the *cerde* is derived from the following documents: BA-Cevdet/Dahıliye 1742, dated middle Şevval 1125 (30 October to 8 November 1713); BA-Cevdet/Dahiliye 1377, dated middle Şevval 1126 (20-29 October 1714); BA-Mühimme 122, p. 176, dated middle Şevval 1126 (20-29 October 1714); BA-Cevdet/Askeri 12578, dated beginning Receb 1144 (30 December 1731 to 8 January 1732); BA-Mühimme 138, pp. 195-196, dated beginning Receb 1144 (30 December 1731 to 8 January 1732); BA-Mühimme 138, p. 194, dated end Receb 1144 (19-28 January 1732); BA-Cevdet/Askeri 13734, dated 15 Cemaziyelâhır 1155 (17 August 1742); and BA-Cevdet/Dahiliye 3013, dated middle Receb 1176 (26 January to 4 February 1763).

repeated by Uzunçarşılı—that the *cerde* was composed of 15,000 men is not supported by any available source.[192] After assembling in Damascus, the combined force would leave for Arabia within the last two months of the year, Zilkade and Zilhicce. At Muzayrīb, a special representative of the central government would compile a register of all members of the force, have it vouched for by a *kadi*, and return it to Istanbul.[193] During the early eighteenth century, the *cerde* would meet the pilgrims at Abyār al-Ghanam and, later in that century, at Hadiyya. The latter was one stopping place closer to Medina than the former. Increased security provided to pilgrims was possibly the reason for this change. The *cerde* would give the travelers extra provisions and water and then, to complete its task, would accompany them back to Damascus. It was on that return journey that the caravan was in greatest danger and most often attacked.

Confronted in the sources with repeated references to tribal attacks on the pilgrimage, virtually all students of the problem have been content to say simply that the caravan was an easy target for the tribes and that the money given the tribes was solely intended to purchase protection.[194] As a result of this approach, the phenomenon is accepted without question. It is necessary, however, to consider the attacks more closely, to review the available evidence and to consider, in particular, the number of attacks, the identity of the attackers (when known), the location of the attacks, and the results.

Data compiled from local chronicles and other sources (see Appendix IX) cannot be said to be complete, as some chronicles often fail to mention attacks for some years (attacks that we learn of from other sources). But, even in incomplete form, the data serve our immediate purposes. We have considered only actual assaults on the pilgrimage, not other disturbances such as those in the Holy Cities, or lack of water, or

[192] d'Ohsson, *Tableau*, III, 274; Uzunçarşılı, *Mekke*, p. 58.

[193] BA-Cevdet/Askeri 13734, dated 15 Cemaziyelâhır 1155 (17 August 1742).

[194] Shamir, " 'Azm Wālīs," pp. 7-8; Rafeq, *Province*, pp. 70-72; and Hourani, "The Fertile Crescent," p. 41.

excessive heat that led to large numbers of deaths. For the period from 1517 to 1757, that is, from the start of Ottoman rule to roughly the mid-eighteenth century, there were, at least, twenty-four attacks on the pilgrimage caravan, distributed as follows: two during the sixteenth century, three during the seventeenth century and nineteen in the first half of the eighteenth century. Three broad geographical sectors—making up the entire pilgrimage route from Damascus to Mecca—can be identified as locations of attacks. Between Muzayrīb and Jughaymān, roughly what is known today as Trans-Jordan, there were five attacks. The belt of territory between Jughaymān and Medina, which for our purposes can be called the "northern Ḥijāz," witnessed ten assaults on the caravan. Finally, between Medina and Mecca, there were seven attacks. Some pilgrimages were attacked in more than one place. The locations of eight attacks could not be identified or were not given in the sources. If we confine our analysis to the eighteenth century, the results are: five attacks in Trans-Jordan, seven in the "northern Ḥijāz," and six between Medina and Mecca.

All the attacks were carried out by beduin tribes, except possibly the first (in 1521, by the villagers of 'Ulā, who may have been tribesmen temporarily settled there). For the eighteenth century, only six attackers can be identified by name: Muḥammad al-Fā'iz (1717), the Banī Ḥarb (1730, 1741, and 1752), and the chief of the Ṣakhr tribe, Qa'dān (1757).

The outcome of the raids between 1517 and 1757 breaks down as follows: ten "successful" (caravan or relief force dispersed or destroyed), eleven "unsuccessful" (attacks repulsed), and three "mixed" (no clear evidence available one way or the other). In the eighteenth century, six attacks were "successful," ten "unsuccessful" and three "mixed." It is clear that, during the first half of the eighteenth century, pilgrimage commanders were only marginally effective in repelling beduin raids; six of ten successful raids spanning two and one-half centuries were confined to the first half of the eighteenth century. Nevertheless, the pilgrimage commanders also compiled a good record: they repulsed ten attacks during the eighteenth century. By contrast, only one attack was repulsed between 1517 and 1700. Although the number of raids increased dramatically between 1700 and 1757, they enjoyed only mixed success. This record, however, could only have been of great concern to the central government. Every successful attack on a caravan was a blow to the Ottoman state's prestige and its claim to protection of life, property, and the Holy Cities of Islam.

Further research—of a depth and breadth beyond the scope of this study—is needed to establish the precise causes of the attacks. We were unable to find one solidly documented instance in which governors of Damascus actually failed to pay tribesmen for services rendered to the caravan, though this doubtless occurred. Professor Rafeq hints that the exclusion of some tribes from lucrative escort and maintenance contracts may have aroused hostility: "It may well have been that a tribe attacked the Pilgrimage not so much to plunder it as to show its dissatisfaction at being neglected."[195] The evidence consulted suggests another cause that has only been hinted at,[196] namely, natural catastrophe. Between 1725 and 1729, there were four years of drought and extreme heat along the pilgrimage route. In each of those years, the caravan was attacked. Furthermore, the raid of 1719, according to one chronicler, was inspired solely by the attackers' desire to seize the pilgrims' water supplies.[197] Again, the worst disaster to befall a pilgrimage caravan in Ottoman times (the attack of 1757) was preceded by two years of drought, although this cannot have been the only cause. Such natural disasters were beyond the state's control not only in and of themselves, but also because the solar months during which the caravan traveled varied with the fixed lunar month of the pilgrimage. The pilgrimages of 1725 through 1729 all fell during the summer months. Because the Islamic calendar barred intercalation or postponement of a lunar month to a more favorable

[195] Rafeq, *Province*, p. 72.
[196] Shamır, " 'Azm Wālīs," pp. 20, 34.
[197] Ibn Jum'a, "al-Bāshāt," p. 58.

season, the pilgrimage spanned all seasons of the year.[198] The vagaries of weather became that much more difficult to avoid, and the consequences were of the gravest import for the Ottoman state and for the careers of Damascus governors unlucky enough to have led the pilgrimage during the summer. On the other hand, Ismail Paşa (al-'Azm)'s success in repulsing four attacks (from 1725 to 1729) was not just incidental, as Shamir suggests, to his long term of office.[199]

During the first half of the eighteenth century, the governor of Damascus' management of the pilgrimage was an essential part—indeed, the centerpiece—of the Ottoman state's reorganization program in that province. A gigantic enterprise,it touched every aspect of Ottoman rule in Damascus, demonstrated the state's claim to hegemony in the Islamic world, and was the hallmark of a governor's success or failure. In spite of the disaster of 1757, the state continued to organize the pilgrimage along substantially the same lines for the duration of its rule in Damascus (until the end of the First World War). The dynamics of Ottoman rule in the province, however, were to change drastically after 1757, for the disaster of that year was a severe blow to Ottoman prestige. It demonstrated potential weakness in administration of the pilgrimage and, far worse, in administration of the province. It meant neither an end to Ottoman presence nor to Ottoman rule; far from it. But it did mean that the methods of the past would no longer suffice.

198 On intercalation, see A. Moberg, "Nasī'," *EI*[1], iii, 856.

199 Shamir, " 'Azm Wālīs," pp. 34-35.

CONCLUSION

In late 1757, news of the catastrophe that had befallen the Damascene pilgrimage caravan reached Istanbul, along with an account of the governor Mekkizâde Hüseyin Paşa's incompetence and cowardice. It provided the pretext for a resolution to the power struggle between Mehmed Rağıb Paşa, the new grand vezir, and his main rival for control of the machinery of state, the former guardian of the harem (the *kızlar ağası*), who had been the disgraced Mekkizâde Hüseyin Paşa's acknowledged protector.[1] An order to execute the ağa was issued as soon as Rağıb Paşa heard the news from Syria. Shortly afterward, the grand vezir took stock of the situation in the province of Damascus. Having received reports that Esat Paşa (al-'Azm), governor from 1743 to 1757, was strongly suspected of inciting the beduin to attack the pilgrimage caravan, Rağıb Paşa ordered Esat Paşa's execution also.[2] With the field cleared in both the capital and the province, he next attempted to restore Ottoman authority by appointing Çeteci Abdullah Paşa to the governorship of Damascus. In his two-year term, the latter was successful in the task Rağıb Paşa had assigned him.

Yet, the Ottoman authorities could not take heart from the temporarily improved situation, for the possibility of further beduin attacks could by no means be ruled out. Up to this point, the state, as we have seen, had managed to revitalize and strengthen the governorship, contain some local groups with mixed success, and keep a close watch over the pilgrimage. But, after 1758, it did not go beyond these measures, which, given the events of the preceding year, showed signs of failure. Nor did the state make new efforts comparable to those it had inaugurated in the province after 1708.

The story of the latter half of the eighteenth century provides many contrasts with the preceding half-century, not

[1] For an account of Rağıb's consolidation of power, see Itzkowitz, "Mehmed Rāghıb Pasha," pp. 150-154.

[2] Shamır, " 'Azm Wālīs," pp. 146-149.

only in Damascus, but in the empire as a whole. Here is another area of research that in future should yield further insight and understanding; its main outlines may, nevertheless, be traced at this juncture.[3] In spite of Rağıb Paşa's contributions as grand vezir, the years following his death in 1763 witnessed external defeat and internal disintegration. Disastrous wars with Russia (1768-1774, and again in the 1780s and 1790s) and the growing power of provincial notables, especially in Anatolia and the Balkans, were among the events leading to agonizing reappraisals by the sultan and his advisers and to the first attempts to reform the army and the administration during the reign of Sultan Selim III (1789-1807). In the Syrian provinces, there were equally serious developments. The military masters of Egypt (the *mamlūks*) invaded the area several times in the 1770s. Beduin pressure continued and intensified as the Wahhābī-Sa'ūdī alliance took shape in Arabia, threatening Ottoman sovereignty over the Holy Cities. Rival tribes were displaced from their lands in Arabia and moved closer to settled areas near Damascus. In 1775, the final defeat of Zāhir al'Umar, which in appearance was a victory for the state, was, in fact, the signal for the rise of Cezzâr Ahmed Paşa (d. 1804) in northern Palestine and his subsequent dominion over a large part of the Syrian provinces. He was appointed to the first of several terms as governor of Damascus in 1785. The long governorships of Gürcü Osman Paşa (1760-1771) and Mehmed Paşa (al-'Aẓm, 1772-1783) in Damascus had been deceptive. By the time of the latter's death, the Ottoman state found itself unable to maintain the provincial system except by granting more discretionary powers to the governor, relying increasingly on the notables as intermediaries between government and populace, and ignoring all but the most serious challenges to its authority. In the provinces of Damascus and neighboring Sidon, an all but independent power base had been created by Cezzâr Ahmed Paşa. He built on the economic and political foundations laid

[3] Some studies on the entire century have recently been published. Of direct relevance to our remarks here is Professor Naff's introduction in Naff and Owen, eds., *Studies in Eighteenth Century Islamic History*, pp. 3-14 and the three succeeding papers by Professors Itzkowitz, Inalcik, and Rafeq.

by Zāhir al-'Umar as a tax farmer and leading political figure in northern Palestine. Those foundations included an accommodation with the beduin, prosperity created by cotton cash sales to European merchants, and the creation of a cash economy.[4] Cezzâr was able to fend off not only the Ottoman state's efforts to limit his power, but also Napoleon's siege of Acre in 1799. How startling a contrast indeed between Cezzâr and Nasuh Paşa, whose governorship had begun the reconsolidation of Ottoman power in the province of Damascus in 1708. Against the background of the later eighteenth century, Ottoman rule in Damascus between 1708 and 1758 acquires considerable significance.

After mid-century, then, the political and economic center of gravity in the Syrian provinces began to shift from Damascus and the interior to Sidon and Acre, along the Mediterranean coast. The gradual incorporation of cotton-growing territories into the European economy as producers of raw materials to feed the Industrial Revolution had introduced new cash sources of wealth that allowed Ẓāhir and, later, Cezzâr to finance their own private armies and to compete with the economy of the interior. The latter continued to derive wealth from the customary sources of agriculture, urban crafts, and trade with other parts of the empire. The tax revenues it generated were relatively limited and were devoted, as in the past, to the administration of Damascus province and the pilgrimage. Given the indirect methods that the Ottoman state had used to maintain its rule in that province, there was little that could be done to resist the gradual encroachment of beduin power on agricultural land, especially during the second half of the century, nor was there much hope of limiting the spread of Cezzâr's power during that period. New administrative methods and techniques, backed up by new institutions in Ottoman society, were not to arrive on the scene until after 1839, when the Tanzimat reforms were launched. By then, the whole configuration of the empire had changed, and it was launched on its fateful journey into the modern world.

[4] For Zāhir's policies, see Cohen, *Palestine*, pp. 12-16.

Appendix i
Rank and Position at Start of Damascus Governors' Careers, 1516-1757

	16th century	*17th century*	*18th century to 1757*
Palace			
Kapıcıbaşı	3	1	0
Akağa	1	0	0
Mirahor	1	2	0
Çaşnigir	2	0	0
Bostancıbaşı	1	4	0
Kilercibaşı	1	1	0
Doğancıbaşı	0	1	0
Çuhadar	0	1	0
Silahdar	2	9	0
Matbah	0	0	1
Çakırcıbaşı	1	0	1
Other or unknown palace	2	8	3
Provincial appointments			
as *sancakbeyis*	7	3	4
as *beylerbeyis*	8	16	6
as *vezirs*	0	1	1
Military careers			
Campaign service	0	1	1
Ağa of the janissaries	2	3	0
Bölük Ağa	0	1	0
Other military	0	3	1
Bureaucracy	2	2	2
Religious career	1	1	0
Local Damascus	0	2	1

Appendix II
Top Posts Attained by Damascus Governors, 1516–1757

	16th century	*17th century*	*18th century to 1757*
Grand vezir	7	12	2
High position in Istanbul	4	5	4
Grand admiral	1	4	0
Campaign commander (*serdar*)	0	4	1
Governor of Mısır (Egypt)	0	5	4
Governor of Anadolu	0	4	0
Governor of Rumeli	2	3	0
Governor of Damascus	18	18	11

Appendix III
Sources of Local Damascus Janissaries' Pay, 1706

Source	*Amount due*	*Amount collected*
Coffeehouses of Damascus and its dependencies	5,500 *kuruş*	2,200 *kuruş*
Damascus market inspection tax	8,000	7,140
Weighing fees and customs duties on silk	4,320	4,665
Coffee tax	6,000	6,800
Sheep market dues	3,000	4,050
Horse market dues	1,752	2,122
Half the criers' fees for the Çakmak market	1,440	1,000
Heads of household tax	3,100	3,000
Extraordinary taxes of Damascus	16,305.5	16,205
Extraordinary taxes of Gaza-Ramla and Lajjūn under contract to the local governors	2,897.5	1,700
Coffee tax of the Maydān quarter of Damascus	—	650
Tobacco customs tax farm	—	1,200
Tax farm on quarterly payments on tobacco	—	1,595
Total to support 1,231 men in the corps	52,315	52,327

Source: BA-Cevdet/Askeri 44575, petition dated 24 Cemaziyelevvel 1118 (3 September 1706), approved 14 Cemaziyelâhır 1118 (23 September 1706).

Appendix IV

Projected Income and Expense of the Pilgrimage (*Tertib Defterleri*)

Income	*1733*[a]		*1749*[b]		*1764*[c]	
Mal-ı ocaklık, from						
Damascus *mal-ı miri* (*bedeliye-i Şam*)	12,000		12,000		12,000	
Damascus *avarız*	3,960		4,020		—	
Damascus *defterdarlık* and *kethüdalık*	1,697	(*defterdarlık* only)	1,697.5		1,735.5	
Qā'd *mukataa*	—		400		400	
Nablus *mukataa*	6,400	(for 1732)	6,400	(for 1750)	6,400	(for 1765)
Tadmur (Palmyra) *mukataa*	2,690	(for 1732-1733)	1,894	(for 1750)	1,894	(for 1765)
Subtotal	26,747		26,411.5		22,429.5	
Damascus *cizye*	19,261	(for 1734)	24,873.5	(for 1749)	24,873.5	(for 1764)
Jerusalem *cizye*	4,254.5	(for 1734)	7,277.5	(for 1749)	7,277.5	(for 1764)
Tripoli *cizye*	24,035	(for 1734)	31,163	(for 1749)	31,163	(for 1764)
Sidon-Beirut *cizye*	2,612.5	(for 1734)	4,315	(for 1749)	4,315	(for 1764)
	50,163		67,629		67,629	
Plus subtotal from above:	26,747		26,411.5		22,429.5	
Total *ocaklik*	76,910		94,040.5		90,058.5	

Additional revenue (*mal-ı saire*), drawn from						
Ḥiṣn al-Akrād *mukataa*	—		16,087.5		16,657.5	
Ba'albak *mukataa*	24,850	(for 1732)	[5,358]	(cancelled)	5,888.5	(*mal-ı muacele* for 1763)
	5,000	(for 1733)				
Ḥamā *mukataa*	10,266	(for 1732)	57,080.5		63,270	(for 1763–1764)
	57,000	(for 1733)				
Ḥimṣ *mukataa*	13,170	(for 1732)	33,439		34,851.5	
	33,000.5	(for 1733)				
	13,600	(increment)				
Ma'arra *mukataa*	—		4,600		8,552	
Tripoli *mukataa*	—		41,666		37,502.5	
Tripoli tobacco customs (tax farm)	—		16,250		14,127	
Sidon-Beirut *mukataa*	1,714	(for 1732)	23,000		32,487.5	
	2,500	(increment)	5,358	(increment)		
	21,140	(for 1733)				
Gaza-Ramla *mukataa* and income from Gaza *mirmiran*	—		7,624		7,291	
'Ajlūn *mukataa*, for three preceding years, charged to debt of former governor and paid by *kethüda* of Damascus treasury	16,000		—		—	

APPENDIX IV (*cont.*)

PROJECTED INCOME AND EXPENSE OF THE PILGRIMAGE (*Terib Defterleri*)

Income	*1733*[a]	*1749*[b]	*1764*[c]
Debt of Fethi, former *defterdar* of Damascus	—	6,861.5	—
Debt of Esat Paşa	—	3,334	—
Muhassıllık of Aleppo			
revenue	8,900	—	—
tax farmer's fee	4,000	—	—
Cizye of Aleppo for 1734	20,000	—	—
Total, *mal-ı saire*	231,140.5	215,300.5	221,257.5
Total *ocaklık*, carried forward	76,910	94,040.5	90,058.5
Grand total, income	308,051.5	309,341	311,316

Expense	*1733*	*1749*	*1764*
Wages and extras of 1,500 mercenaries			
Wages for 6 mos. @ 2.5 *kuruş* ea.	22,500	Same	Same
Extras @ 5 *kuruş* ea.	7,500		
Subtotal	30,000		

Rental of camels, cost of provisions			
Rental of 1,500 camels @ 50 *kuruş* ea.	75,000		
Provisions	13,455		
Subtotal	88,455	Same	Same
Provisions for mercenaries, outward journey only			
Camel fodder			
1,500 loads @ 10 *kuruş*	15,000		
Barley			
937.5 loads @ 10 *kuruş*	9,375		
Transport cost of above 2,437.5 loads @ 10 *kuruş*	24,375		
Rusks			
262.5 *kantar* @ 11 *kuruş*	2,887.5		
Transport cost of 262.5 *kantar* @ 10 *kuruş*	2,625		

APPENDIX IV (*cont.*)

PROJECTED INCOME AND EXPENSE OF THE PILGRIMAGE (*Tertib Defterleri*)

Income	*1733*[a]	*1749*[b]	*1764*[c]
Rice			
140 *kantar* @ 12 *kuruş*	1,820		
Transport cost of 140 *kantar* @ 10 *kuruş*	1,400		
Clarified butter			
37.5 *kantar* @ 50 *kuruş*	1,875		
Transport cost of 37.5 *kantar* @ 10 *kuruş*	375		
Subtotal	59,732.5	Same	Same
Supplies for mercenaries and fees of baggage attendants	31,532.5	Same	Same
Combined total of expenses for mercenaries	209,720	209,720	209,720

Deduction as adjustment for expense of preceding year	−30,000	−17,000	−17,000
Addition for increase in *sürre-i cedid* (see below)	13,000	—	—
Adjusted subtotal of expenses for mercenaries	192,720	192,720	192,720
Sürre (payments) to ʻAnaza tribe from the treasury of Damascus for military escort service[e]			
Izdiyad-ı kadim	20,670.5	Same	Same
Sürre-i cedid	74,063.5	Same	Same
Izdiyad	16,347	Same	Same
Sürre-ı Urbân and *Kale-i Cedid*[f]	4,250	Same	Same
Subtotal	115,331	115,331	115,331

APPENDIX IV (*cont.*)

PROJECTED INCOME AND EXPENSE OF THE PILGRIMAGE (*Tertib Defterleri*)

Income	*1733*[a]	*1749*[b]	*1764*[c]
Sürre for protection of additional fortresses along the pilgrimage route:	—	1,290	3,265
Total, *sürre*	115,331	116,621	118,596
Adjusted subtotal of expenses for mercenaries carried forward	192,720	192,720	192,720
Grand total, Expense	308,051	309,341	311,316

NOTE: Figures given are in *Kuruş esedi*. Subtotals are as given in the sources.

[a] TKS-D. 9750, dated 7 Rebiyülevvel 1146 (19 August 1733).

[b] BA-Emiri/ı Mahmud 351, dated 25 Rebıyülevvel 1162 (16 March 1749).

[c] BA-Cevdet/Askeri 26633, dated 4 Rebiyülevvel 1178 (2 September 1764).

[d] A village near Zaḥlah in the Biqā' valley of Lebanon. See Dussaud, *Topographie historique de la Syrie antique et médiévale* p. 411. A tax register compiled by the governor of Damascus in 1186 (1772) refers to this place as Qā' Ba'albak. See TKS-D. 3073, folio 2b.

[e] The breakdown of payments here seems to reflect previous increases given the tribes. The first figure was probably the original, base sum; the second, an increase required by inflation; and the third, a later increase, probably for the same reason.

[f] Possibly the pilgrimage stop 33 hours from Medina on the road of Mecca. See Ibn Jum'a, "al-Bāshāt," p. 52; Mehmed Edib, *Menasik*, pp. 134-135. Mehmed Edib does not mention a fortress here, but says that this place was exposed to attack. That the state would desire added protection here is therefore understandable.

Appendix V
Summary of Damascus Provincial Accounts, 1741-1742, 1759-1760

Income	*1741-1742*[a]	*1759-1760*[b]
For the pilgrimage, from Sidon *mukataas*	44,454.5 (for 1740-1741)	44,454.5
Tripoli *mukataas*	29,350 (for 1740-1741)	29,350
Wādī al-Taym[c] *malikâne*	5,000	5,000
Mukataas of Hak-ı Bilis[d] and nearby areas	3,195.5	3,195.5
Subtotal	82,000	82,000
Other *mukataas*	52,107; 7 *paras*	60,623.75
Arrears of several *mukataas* (*bakaya*)	320	—
Income from treasuries of Balaṭ and Quṣayr al-ʿUmrī[e]	—	800
Escheated inheritances of various persons	490; 17 *paras*	170.5; 6 *paras*
Total income:	134,917.5; 4 *paras*	143,594.25; 6 *paras*

Expense	*1741-1742*	*1759-1760*
For the pilgrimage		
Camel transport for Damascus janissaries; payments		

APPENDIX V (*cont.*)

Expense	*1741-1742*	*1759-1760*
(*sürre*) for religious functionaries in Mecca and Medina; and for Arab tribes	82,000	82,000
Garrison wages for troops in Damascus provincial fortresses	6,283.5; 11 *paras*	24,154 (includes garrison wages foı pilgrimage forts)
Other expenses		
Sürre, salaries, etc.	15,501	—
Pensions of retired officials in Damascus, the Holy Cities, and Jerusalem	23,630; 5 *akçes*	42,191; 4 *paras*
Total expense	127,414.5; 10 *paras*, 8 *akçes*	148,345; 4 *paras*
Minus additional funds for pilgrimage	−5,000	—
Balance	2,502.5 (rounded)	−4,751 (rounded)

NOTE: Figures given are ın *kuruş esedi*.

[a] BA-Kepeci 2343, dated end Zilhıcce 1154 (7 March 1742).

[b] BA-Kepeci 2101, dated end Zilhıcce 1173 (12 August 1760).

[c] Wādī al-Taym, the dıstrıct ın the southern Bıqā' Valley ruled by members of the Shihāb famıly ın thıs perıod.

[d] Hak-ı Bılıs, probably Balaş, 10 km. south of Damascus. See Dussaud, *Topographie*, p. 296.

[e] Balaṭ, a town east-southeast of Damascus; Quṣayr al-'Umrī, 20 km. northeast of Damascus. Dussaud, *Topographie*, pp. 295 and 263-264 respectively.

Appendix VI
Register of *Dawra* Revenues, 1771-1772

Payments in cash	
Lajjūn, Jīnīn, 'Athīth, etc.[a]	
From Lajjūn, Jīnīn, and inhabitants	22,022.5
Mukataa of crops of Ghūr (an area within Jīnīn)	1,000
From Sāḥil 'Athlīth, part of Lajjūn	11,510
Mukataa of provisions for *dawra* troops, raised from Sāḥil 'Athlīth	3,500
Subtotal	38,032.5
From Kızık and Zanğiri tribes[b]	5,480
Subtotal	43,512.5
Cash payment to buy 10 camels @ 80 *kuruş* ea.; plus revenues of 100 *kuruş* from the 'Awja tribes	900
Gift from merchants of Yāfā (Jaffa)	500
Census of Yāfā fortress	90
Subtotal	45,002.5
Nablus	
Revenue from crown lands and villages	116,975
Jerusalem	
Cizye	7,277.5
Collections from foreign missions in the area	63,193.5
Subtotal	70,471
Gaza and Ramla	
Annual *dawra* payment (*salyân al-dawr*)	7,828
Avarĭz	2,000
Annual *dawra* payment from Lydda	1,750
Census of Gaza fortress	40
Costs of horses, paid for by *alaybey* of Gaza	100
Subtotal	11,718
Income from crown lands	6,700
Subtotal	18,418

Appendix vi (*cont.*)
Register of *Dawra* Revenues, 1771-1772

'Ajlūn *mukataa*	
Paid to holders of the *malikâne* by the *kapıkethüda* of the Damascus governor in Istanbul[c]	16,000
Service charge for commissioner who delivered the deed of this *malikâne*'s lease to the Damascus governor	1,000
Ceremonial robes for local chieftains; wages for military units on special trip to Irbid[d]	5,500
Subtotal	22,500
Payments in kind	
From Nablus	
300 *ğirare Nābulsī* of barley	
37.5 *ğirare Nābulsī* of wheat	
37.5 *ğirare Nābulsī* of camel fodder	
From Jerusalem	
Unspecified quantity of barley	
From Gaza	
Barley at 2.5 *kuruş* for each *mudd Ghazzāwī*	
Camels (unspecified number and price)	
Grand total, payments in cash	273,367 *kuruş*

Source: TKS-D. 4364, dated simply 1185. All figures are given in *kuruş*.

[a] Lajjūn, Jīnīn and 'Athlīth were towns on the west bank of the Jordan River; they formed part of the *sancak* of Lajjūn and 'Ajlūn, which straddled both the east and west banks of the river. Sāḥil 'Athlīth, as the name indicates, was on the Mediterranean coast.

[b] The Kızık tribe had settled extensively over this area and elsewhere in the Syrian provinces. Refik, *Anadolu'da Türk Aşiretleri*, pp. 69, 114. For the Zanğırı, see Cohen, *Palestine*, p. 161.

[c] This appears to be a payment to the treasury on behalf of the governor by his representative in Istanbul, to finalize the leaseshold on this *malikâne*.

[d] Ceremonial robes were worn by those invested with an office; they were paid for by the holders. Irbid is a large town in the 'Ajlūn area.

[e] The *ğirare* (Ar., *ghirāra*) of Damascus was slightly more than 250 liters; of

Gaza, 375; of Jerusalem, 750. The Nābulsī *ğirare* was probably equivalent to Jerusalem's, but this is not certain. See Lewis, "Jaffa in the 16th Century," p. 438. According to another source, this unit was composed of 12 *keyls* of 12 *mudd* each. A *mudd* was therefore one-hundred-forty-fourth of a *ğirare*. See Mantran and Sauvaget, *Règlements fiscaux ottomans*, p. 20.

Appendix VII

The Pilgrimage Fortress Network between Damascus and Medina

Name	*Distance from preceding fort*	*Date of construction/repair and person responsible*
Ṣanamayn	17 hrs. from Damascus	Early 16th cent.—Sultan Selim I
Muzayrīb	7 hrs.	Early 16th cent.—Sultan Selim I
Tall Far'ūn	11 hrs.	Early 16th cent.—Sultan Selim I
'Ayn Zarqā	12 hrs.	Either pre-Ottoman or 16th cent.[a]
Balqā	18 hrs.	Either pre-Ottoman or 16th cent.[b]
Qaṭrāna	16 hrs.	Mid-16th cent.—Sultan Süleyman I
Ẓahr 'Unayza	29 hrs.	Late 16th cent.—Süleyman Paşa(?)
Ma'ān	12 hrs.	Mid-16th cent.—Sultan Süleyman I
Ẓahr al-'Aqaba	13 hrs.	Mid-18th cent.—Gürcü Osman Paşa
Jughaymān	15 hrs.	1730-33—Aydınlı Abdullah Paşa
Dhāt Ḥajj	14 hrs.	Mid-16th cent.—Sultan Süleyman I,
Tabūk	25 hrs.	Mid-16th cent.—Sultan Süleyman I, repaired 1654
Maghāyir al-Qalandariyya	13 hrs.	Mid-18th cent.—Gürcü Osman Paşa
Ukhayḍir (Ḥaydar)	12 hrs.	1531—Sultan Süleyman I
al-Mu'aẓẓam	17 hrs.	Ayyūbid: al-Malik al-Mu 'aẓẓam Sharaf al-Dīn 'Isā (1218-1227)

Dār al-Ḥamrā'	18 hrs.	1753-1754—Gürcü Osman Paşa
Madā'in Ṣāliḥ	19 hrs.	Mid-18th cent.—Esat Paşa (al-'Aẓm) or Gürcü Osman Paşa
'Ulā	9 hrs.	Mid-16th cent.—Sultan Süleyman I
Abyār Ghanam	10 hrs.	Unknown[c]
Zumurrud (off the main road)	10 hrs.	Late 18th cent.—Mehmed Paşa ('Aẓm)
Valide Kuyusu	8 hrs.	Early 17th cent. waterhole Mid-18th cent. fort—Gürcü Osman Paşa
Hadiyya	12 hrs.	Late 16th cent.—Süyleyman Paşa(?) Early 18th cent.—repaired by Nasuh
'Antar (near Hadiyya)		Mid-18th cent.—Gürcü Osman Paşa
Nakhlatayn	16 hrs. from Hadiyya	Mid-18th cent.—Gürcü Osman Paşa
Wādī al-Qurā	15 hrs.	Unknown[d]

NOTE: The table is based on evidence presented in Chapter Three. It does not include those *menzils*, or halting places, that did not have fortresses. Distances are those given by Mehmed Edib, *Menasik*, pp. 65-82.

[a] See Kâtip Çelebi, *Cihannümâ*, p. 539.

[b] Ibid.

[c] Mehmed Edib reports that a fort existed here; no information available on founder.

[d] Mehmed Edib reports a ruined fort here in 1779-1780.

Appendix VIII
Pilgrimage Retinue Expenses, 1742–1743

Fees to retinue orderlies,[a] outward and return journeys	
100 camel drivers @ 9.5 *kuruş* ea.	950
45 water carriers @ 9.5 *kuruş* ea.	427.5
40 tent keepers @ 9.5 *kuruş* ea.	380
30 fire tenders @ 9.5 *kuruş* ea.	285
Pitch lamplighters	240
	2,282.5
Camel transport fees for escort units, outward and return journeys[b]	
18th cavalry unit: 58 camels @ 70 *kuruş* ea.	4,060
12th guide unit: 40 camels @ 70 *kuruş* ea.	2,800
40th Maghribī unit: 242 camels @ 70 *kuruş* ea.	16,940
Fusiliers: 24 camels @ 70 *kuruş* ea.	1,680
Bonuses	710
	26,190
Pilgrimage stockpile (*kiler*) expenses	
Kitchen expenses	6,648
Cloth of various types	2,458.75
Rope	550
Purchases from Sūq al-Arwām[c]	2,265.25
To the chief tailor of Damascus	622
To the chief boot seller	245.25
To the chief furrier, for the governor's mantle	479.5
Purchase of ermine, fox, and wildcat furs from trappers	1,218
Other expenses (not itemized)	12,267
Expenses of the quartermaster	2,873.5
2 horsehair sacks and 5 horse headstall straps	98
	30,125.25
Fees of retinue functionaries	
Istanbul courrier (*müjdecibaşı*)	300
Flag bearer (*sancakdâr*)	240
Official in charge of sacred litter (*mahmalcı*)	160
Drummer (*tabbal*)	82

Chief guide (*delil-i hacc*)	130
Prayer leader (*imam*)	40
Prayer caller (*müezzin*)	40
Gunner (*topcu*)	100
Cartwright (*arabacı*)	120
Surgeon (*cerrah*)	20
Prayer reciter (*duacı*)	16.5
For al-Hāj Bakrī al-Qabbānī	80
Secretaries: Muḥammad al-Makkī	500
Muḥammad al-Qabbānī	150
Chief camel guard and camel leader, al-Hāj Rajab	2,300
Total, all divisions	62,872.25 *kuruş*

SOURCE: TKS-D. 4957, governor's account register, dated end 1155 (24 February 1743). Figures are given in *kuruş*.

[a] *Karakullukçuyân*, in the Ottoman army, an irregular corps that provided essential support and services to the main body of troops. See *TDS*, II, 198.

[b] The names of the escort units (*bayraks*) were, in the above order, *suvari*, *divanegân*, *Mağrıblıyân*, and *tüfenkçiyân*. The bonuses given to each unit were called *in'am*. Much confusion exists in regard to the second group, many foreign observers calling it a group of "madmen" (Persian, *divanegi*; Turkish equivalent, *deli*). See *A Journey from Aleppo to Damascus*, p. 72, and Maundrell, *A Journey*, p. 127. The Turkish *deli* is probably a transformation of the Arabic *dalīl*, or guide. See *TDS*, I, 420; and Gibb and Bowen, *Islamic Society*, I, 1, p. 153.

[c] Sūq al-Arwām, no longer extant, was built in the seventeenth century near the Damascus citadel. The merchants of that market were probably descendants of the janissaries who came to Damascus in 1660, hence the name of the market, for the *Rūmīs* who took over the imperial janissary corps. See *IA*, IX, map facing p. 306.

Appendix IX
Attacks on the Pilgrimage Caravan, 1517-1757

Year	Location	Attackers	Results
1521	'Ulā	villagers	Villagers punished; paid fine
1521	Medina	beduin	Beduin paid off
1531	Dhāt Ḥajj	Amīr al-'Arab, Mulḥim	Confrontation; wells poisoned along route
1671	Madā'in Ṣāliḥ	Ḥammūd al-Rashīd	Caravan plundered; wells blocked up; sudden rain saves pilgrims
1674	al-Ṣāyina (?)	?	Caravan dispersed
1691	?	?	One-third of caravan destroyed
1700	?	?	Caravan dispersed
1701	?	?	Caravan dispersed
1707	Trans-Jordan (?)	beduin	*Cerde* attacked; caravan changed route
1708	Abyār al-Ghanam	beduin	Attack repulsed
1709	al-Jadīda;	beduin	Attack repulsed;
	Muzayrīb	beduin	Kulayb, *Şam urbanı şeyhi*, killed by Nasuh Paşa
1710-1711	al-Jadīda	beduin	Part of caravan plundered

1712-1713	Between Mecca and Medina	beduin	Route changed to avoid attack
1717	Abyār al-Ghanam	beduin of Muḥammad al-Fā'iz	Attack repulsed
1719	Tabūk-Madā'in Ṣalih	beduin	Caravan attacked; water supplies taken
1721	'Ulā	beduin	Attack repulsed
	Dār al-Ḥamrā'	beduin	*Cerde* destroyed
1724	Bīr al-Shuhadā'	beduin	Attack repulsed
	al-Ḥasā	beduin	Attack on *cerde* repulsed
1729	?	beduin	Attack repulsed
1730	Between Mecca and Medina	Banī Ḥarb	Attack repulsed by *cerde*
1732	?	40,000 beduin	*Cerde* rescued caravan
1740	?	beduin	Caravan destroyed
1741	Wadī al- 'Aqīq (near Medina)	Banī Ḥarb	Attack repulsed
1752	?	Banī Ḥarb	Attack repulsed with heavy losses to pilgrims
1757	al-Ḥasā	Qa'dān ('Anaza)	*Cerde* destroyed
	Balqā	Ṣakhr	second *cerde* prevented from proceeding
1757	'Ulā	Qa'dān	Caravan destroyed, 20,000 pilgrims killed

SOURCES: Ibn Jum'a, "al-Bāshāt"; Ibn al-Qārī, "al-Wuzarā' "; Budayrī, *Ḥawādith*; *Shamir*, " 'Azm Wālīs"; and Rafeq, *Province*.

BIBLIOGRAPHY

Archives

Başbakanlık Arşivi, Istanbul, Turkey (archives of the prime minister's office). The following classifications were consulted:

Ali Emiri, Ibnülemin, and Cevdet Classifications (collections of selected papers)

Kâmil Kepeci defterleri (assorted registers)

Maliyeden müdevver defterleri (assorted financial registers)

Mühimme defterleri (series of outgoing orders, arranged chronologically in bound volumes)

Nâme-i hümayun defterleri (imperial letters, arranged chronologically in bound volumes)

Topkapı Saray Arşivi, Istanbul, Turkey (archives of the Topkapı Palace). Documents are numbered consecutively in two series: E. (Evrak) for loose papers; and D. (Defterler) for registers.

Note on the Ottoman Archives

In spite of the fact that only about ten per cent of the materials preserved in the Başbakanlık Arşivi (by far the larger of the two archives listed above) are classified and available, that portion is so vast that effective exploitation depends only on one's subject, the period covered, and the time available for research. One is allowed to order ten items per day. Selecting items is a complicated process. The Mühimme and Nâme-i hümayun volumes may be ordered after consulting Midhat Sertoğlu, *Muhteva bakımından Başvekâlet Arşivi* (Ankara, 1955). Volumes in the Kâmil Kepeci series are listed in a subject card index and also in a catalogue arranged by subdivisions of that classification. The nearly 25,000 volumes of the Maliye collection were consulted only after a search through a card file arranged by volume number (Another card file arranged by subject was not available to the writer because it was being transcribed into catalogue form). Individual documents in the Ali Emiri, Ibnülemin, and Cevdet collections are listed in massive catalogues, those of the first two in nearly illegible Ottoman script, the last in neatly typed modern Turkish. Documents are listed in numerical order in each subdivision, for example, Emiri/III Ahmed (documents from the reign of Sultan Ahmed III, 1703-1730), Cevdet/Dahiliye (internal affairs, spanning about 150 years), and so forth. To obtain roughly 200 documents from the latter subdivision, this writer had to read 2,000 pages in the catalogue for that subdivision. This material's utility varied widely. The most detailed documents pertinent to the present study were not so much those of the Mühimme volumes as the classifications of individual papers and the Maliye and Kepeci registers. Another researcher working on a different topic may make good use of an entirely different body of materials.

The Topkapı Palace archives are much smaller but equally valuable. Two subject catalogues are available: one prepared by Tahsin Öz, *Arşiv Kılavuzu* (2 vols., Istanbul, 1938-1940), which covers the letters A-H and contains many errors; and a handwritten catalogue by M. Çağatay Uluçay (letters I-Z), which contains many corrections by recent researchers and archivists. These archives proved invaluable for this study. Without them, much of the material about the governorship and the pilgrimage could not have been written. Most of the documents pertaining to Damascus governors' personal careers and finances—including their confiscated papers—are preserved here.

The Ottoman archives, in all their richness, offer detailed insights into the workings of Ottoman provincial administration from the perspective of the central government. In that respect, they are a vast improvement over materials—mainly chronicles of local provenance and scope and European consular reports—that have been used in other works about Damascus in the eighteenth century. This is not to say that the latter materials are useless. On the contrary, they cannot be dispensed with, but they must be reevaluated in the light of archival evidence that best answers historical questions concerning relations between the Ottoman central government and the province of Damascus.

In 1974, a somewhat different source for the history of Damascus in Ottoman times was opened to scholars: the *kadi sicills* or *sharī'a* court records of the Syrian provinces, housed in Damascus, Syria. Here were kept copies of incoming orders from Istanbul and records of cases brought before the chief provincial magistrate (the *kadi*) who judged them in accordance with the holy law of Islam (the *sharī'a*) and the sultanic regulations (*kanuns*). The cases in particular are an invaluable source for the local history of the Syrian provinces. This writer did not have the opportunity to go to Damascus for research in these court records. Published research based on this source is still slender, largely Professor Rafeq's articles of the last few years. It is hoped that the court records will be catalogued and indexed in the near future to facilitate their use in research on Ottoman Syria.

Manuscripts, Printed Sources, Secondary Works, Reference Works

al-'Adawī, Maḥmūd. *al-Ziyārāt bi-Dimashq*. Edited by Ṣalāḥ al-Dīn al-Munajjid. Damascus, 1956.

Adıvar, A. Adnan. *Osmanlı Türklerinde Ilim*. Istanbul, 1970.

Âfet(inan), A. "Atatürk'ü dinlerken: Vatan ve Hürriyet." *Belleten* I, no. 2 (1937): 289-298. A French translation entitled "En écoutant Atatürk: la Société 'Patrie et Liberté.' " follows on pp. 299-309.

Akalın, Şehabeddin. "Nasuh Paşa'nın hayatına ve servetine dair." *Tarih Dergisi* VIII (1955):201-208.

Antonius, George. *The Arab Awakening; the Story of the Arab National Movement*. Beirut, 1969.

Âsım, Küçük Çelebizâde Ismail. *Âsım Tarihi*. Published as vol. VI of Râşid.

Ayn-ı Âlī. *Osmanlı imparatorluğunda eyalet taksimatı*. Edited by Hadiye Tuncer. Ankara, 1964.

al-'Azm, 'Abd al-Qādir. *al-Usra al-'Aẓmiyya*. Damascus, 1951.

Bakhit, Muhammad Adnan Salamah. "The Ottoman Province of Damascus in the Sixteenth Century." Ph.D. dissertation, School of Oriental and African Studies, London University, 1972.

Barkan, Ömer Lütfi. "Edirne ve civarındaki bazı imaret tesislerinin yıllık muhasebe bilançolari." *Belgeler* I, no. 2 (July 1964):235ff.

———. " 'Feodal' düzen ve Osmanlı Timarı." *Türkiye Iktisat Tarihi Semineri; Metinler, Tartışmalar*. Edited by Osman Okyar. Ankara, 1975. Pp. 1-24.

Bodman, Herbert. *Political Factions in Aleppo, 1760-1820*. Chapel Hill, 1963.

al-Budayrī, al-Ḥallāq, Ahmad. *Hawādith Dimashq al-yawmiyya, 1154-1175*. Edited by Aḥmad 'Izzat 'Abd al-Karīm. Cairo, 1959.

Burayk (Breik), Mikhā'īl. *Tārīkh al-Shām, 1720-1780*. Edited by Qusṭanṭīn al-Bāshā. Harissa (Lebanon), 1930.

Burckhardt, John Lewis. *Travels in Syria and the Holy Land*. London, 1822.

Çağatay Uluçay, M. *18. ve 19. yüzyıllarda Saruhan'da eşkiyalık ve halk hareketleri*. Istanbul, 1955.

Cezar, Mustafa. *Osmanlı tarihinde Levendler*. Istanbul, 1965.

Cohen, Amnon. *Palestine in the Eighteenth Century: Patterns of Government and Administration*. Jerusalem, 1973.

Cook, M. A. *Population Pressure in Rural Anatolia, 1450-1600*. London, 1972.

Coulson, N. J. *A History of Islamic Law*. Edinburgh, 1964.

Daḥlān, Aḥmad ibn Zaynī. *Khulāṣat al-kalām fī bayān umarā' al-balad al-ḥarām*. Cairo, A.H. 1305/1887-1888.

Danişmend, Ismail Hami. *Osmanlı Devlet Erkanı*. Istanbul, 1971.

De Gaury, Gerald. *Rulers of Mecca*. London, 1951.

Dussaud, René. *Topographie historique de la Syrie antique et médiévale*. Paris, 1927.

Encyclopedia of Islam. 1st ed. 4 vols, Edited by M. T. Houtsma et al. Leiden, 1913-1942.

Encyclopedia of Islam. 2d ed. 4 vols. Edited by H.A.R. Gibb et al. Leiden, 1954–

Evliya Çelebi, Mehmed Zilli ibn Derviş. *Evliya Çelebi Seyahatnamesi*. Vol. IX: *Anadolu, Suriye, Hicaz (1671-1672)*. Istanbul, 1935.

Gibb, H.A.R. and Bowen, Harold. *Islamic Society and the West*. Vol. I, parts 1 and 2. London, 1950–1957.

Grant, Christina Phelps. See Harris, Christina Phelps.

Hachicho, Mohammad Ali. "English Travel Books about the Near East in the 18th Century." *Die Welt des Islams* IX (1964):1-206.

Hâkim, Mehmed. *Hâkim Tarihi*. Istanbul, Topkapı Saray Kütüphanesi, Bağdat Köşkü, MS 231.

Harris, Christina Phelps. *The Syrian Desert: Caravan, Travel, and Exploration*. London, 1937.

Hasluck, F. W. *Christianity and Islam under the Sultans*. Edited by Margaret M. Hasluck. 2 vols. Oxford, 1929.

Haydar Çelebi. *Haydar Çelebi Ruznamesi*. Edited by Yavuz Senemoğlu. Istanbul, 1975(?).

Heyd, Uriel. *Studies in Old Ottoman Criminal Law*. Edited by V. L. Ménage. Oxford, 1973.

Ḥiyārī, Muṣṭafā A. "The Origins and Development of the Amīrate of the Arabs during the Seventh/Thirteenth and Eighth/Fourteenth Centuries." *Bulletin of the School of Oriental and African Studies* XXXVIII (1975):509-524.

Holt, P. M. *Egypt and the Fertile Crescent, 1516-1922; a Political History*. London, 1966.

Hourani, Albert H.. "The Fertile Crescent in the Eighteenth Century." *A Vision of History*. Beirut, 1961. Pp. 35-70.

———. "The Ottoman Background of the Modern Middle East." Third Carreras Arab Lecture at the University of Essex. London, 1970.

———. "Ottoman Reform and the Politics of Notables." *Beginnings of Modernization in the Middle East: the Nineteenth Century*. Edited by William R. Polk and Richard Chambers. Chicago, 1969. Pp. 41-64.

Ibn Jum'a, al-Maqqār, Muḥammad. "al-Bāshāt wa al-quḍāt fī

Dimashq." *Wulāt Dimashq fī al-'ahd al-'Uthmānī*. Edited by Ṣalāḥ al-Dīn al-Munajjid. Damascus, 1949.

Ibn Kannān, Muḥammad. "al-Mawākib al-Islāmiyya fī al-mamālik al-Shāmiyya." Extracts in Muḥammad ibn Ṭūlūn's *I'lām al-warā bi-man wulliya nā'iban min al-Atrāk bi-Dimashq al-Shām al-kubrā*. Edited by Muḥammad Aḥmad Dahmān. Damascus, 1964. Pp. 295-301.

Ibn al-Qārī, Raslān. "al-Wuzarā' al-ladhīn ḥakamū Dimashq." *Wulāt Dimashq fī al-'ahd al-'Uthmānī*. Edited by Ṣalāḥ al-Dīn al-Munajjid. Damascus, 1949.

Inalcik, Halil. "The Nature of Traditional Society: Turkey." *Political Modernization in Japan and Turkey*. Edited by Dankwart Rustow and Robert E. Ward. Princeton, 1964. Pp. 42-63.

———. *The Ottoman Empire: the Classical Age, 1300-1600*. Edited and translated by Norman Itzkowitz and Colin Imber. New York, 1973.

———. "Ottoman Methods of Conquest." *Studia Islamica* II (1954):103-129.

Islam Ansiklopedisi. 12 vols. Istanbul, 1940- .

Itzkowitz, Norman. "Eighteenth Century Ottoman Realities." *Studia Islamica* XVI (1962):73-94.

———. "Mehmed Rāghib Pasha: the Making of an Ottoman Grand Vezir." Ph.D. dissertation, Princeton University, 1959.

——— and Mote, Max, eds. and trans. *Mubadele: an Ottoman-Russian Exchange of Ambassadors*. Chicago, 1970.

———. *Ottoman Empire and Islamic Tradition*. New York, 1972.

Izzi, Süleyman. *Tarih*. Istanbul, A.H. 1199/1784.

al-Jazīrī, 'Abd al-Qādir ibn Muḥammad. *Durar al-fawā'id al-munaẓẓama fī akhbār al-ḥajj wa ṭarīq Makka al-mu'aẓẓama*. Edited by Muḥibb al-Dīn al-Khaṭīb. Cairo, A.H. 1385/1964-1965.

Jomier, Jacques. *Le mahmal et la caravane égyptienne des pèlerins de la Mecque (XIIIe-XXe siècles)*. Cairo, 1953.

A Journey from Aleppo to Damascus; with a Description of Those Two Capital Cities, and the Neighboring Parts of Syria. Edited by John Green. London, 1736.

Karpat, Kemal. "The Transformation of the Ottoman State, 1789-1908." *International Journal of Middle East Studies* III (July 1972):243-281.

Kâtip Çelebi (Muṣṭafā ibn 'Abd Allāh, Ḥājjī Khalīfa). *Cihannümâ*. Istanbul, A.H. 1145/1732-1733.

al-Khiyārī, Ibrāhīm ibn 'Abd al-Raḥmān al-Madanī. "Tuḥfat al-udabā' wa silwat al-ghurabā'." *Madīnat Dimashq 'ind al-jughrāfiyyīn wa al-raḥḥālīn al-muslimīm*. Edited by Ṣalāḥ al-Dīn al-Munajjid. Beirut, 1967. Pp. 299-310.

Kunt, Ibrahim Metin. "Ethnic-Regional (*Cins*) Solidarity in the Seventeenth Century Ottoman Establishment." *International Journal of Middle East Studies* V (June 1974):233-239.

———. *Sancaktan eyalete: 1550-1650 arasında Osmanlı ümerası ve il idaresi*. Istanbul, 1975.

Le Strange, Guy. *Palestine under the Moslems; a Description of Syria and the Holy Land from A.D. 650 to 1500*. Beirut, 1965.

Lewis, Bernard. "Jaffa in the 16th Century, according to the Ottoman *Taḥrīr* Registers." *Necati Lugal Armağanı*. Ankara, 1968. Pp. 435-446.

Mandaville, Jon E. "The Ottoman Court Records of Syria and Jordan." *Journal of the American Oriental Society* LXXXIII (July-September 1966):311-319.

Mantran, Robert and Jean Sauvaget. *Règlements fiscaux ottomans; les provinces syriennes*. Paris, 1951.

Maundrell, Henry. *A Journey from Aleppo to Jerusalem at Easter, A.D. 1697*. 2d ed. Oxford, 1707.

Mehmed Edib ibn Mehmed Derviş. *Menasik-i hacc-ı şerif*. Istanbul, A.H. 1232/1816-1817. Translated by M. Bianchi. *Itinéraire de Constantinople à la Mecque*. Paris, n.d.

Minorsky, V. *The Chester Beatty Library: a Catalogue of the Turkish Manuscripts and Miniatures*. Dublin, 1958.

al-Murādī, Muḥammad Khalīl. *Maṭmaḥ al-wājid fī tarjamat al-wālid al-mājid*. British Library, MS Or. 4050.

———. *Silk al-durar fī a'yān al-qarn al-thānī 'ashar*. 4 vols. in 2. Baghdad, n.d. (1972?).

Musil, Alois. *The Manners and Customs of the Rwala Bedouins*. New York, 1928.

Musil, Alois. *The Northern Ḥeǧâz; a Topographical Survey*. New York, 1926.

Naff, Thomas and Owen, Roger, eds. *Studies in Eighteenth Century Islamic History*. Carbondale, 1977.

Niebuhr, Carsten. *Travels through Arabia, and other Countries in the East*. Translated by Robert Heron. 2 vols. Edinburgh, 1792.

d'Ohsson, I. Mouradgea. *Tableau général de l'empire othoman*. 7 vols. Paris, 1788-1824.

Olson, Robert W. *The Siege of Mosul and Ottoman-Persian Relations, 1718-1743*. Bloomington, 1975.

Orhonlu, Cengiz. *Osmanlı imparatorluğunda derbend teşkilatı*. Istanbul, 1967.

———. *Osmanlı imparatorluğu'nun güney siyaseti: Habeş eyaleti*. Istanbul, 1974.

"Osmanlı Kanunnameleri." *Millî Tetebbüler Mecmuası* I, no. 2 (1913):49-112, 305-348.

"Osmanlı Kanunnameleri: Tevkii Abdurrahman Paşa Kanunnamesi." *Millî Tetebbüler Mecmuası* I, no. 3 (1913):497-544.

Pakalın, Mehmet Zeki. *Osmanlı tarih deyimleri ve terimleri sözlüğü*. 3 vols. Istanbul, 1971.

Porter, Sir James. *Observations on the Religion, Law, Government and Manners of the Turks*. 2 vols., London, 1768.

al-Qāsimī, Muḥammad Sa'īd. *Qāmūs al-ṣināʿāt al-Shāmiyya*. 2 vols. Edited by Ẓāfir al-Qāsimī and Khalīl al-ʿAẓm Paris and The Hagúe, 1960.

Rafeq, Abdul-Karim. "Economic Relations between Damascus and the Dependent Countryside, 1743-1771." Unpublished paper submitted to a conference at Princeton University on the economic history of the Near East, 1974.

———. "The Local Forces in Syria in the Seventeenth and Eighteenth Centuries." *War, Technology and Society in the Middle East*. Edited by V. J. Parry and M. E. Yapp London, 1975, Pp. 277-307.

———. *The Province of Damascus, 1723-1783*. Beirut, 1966.

———. "Les registres de tribunaux de Damas comme source

pour l'histoire de la Syrie." *Bulletin d'études orientales* XXVI (1973):1-8.

Râşid, Mehmed. *Tarih-i Râşid*. 6 vols. Istanbul, A.H. 1282/1865-1866.

Redhouse, Sir James. *A Turkish and English Lexicon*. Beirut, 1974.

Refik, Ahmet. *Anadolu'da Türk aşiretleri*. Istanbul, 1930.

Sabri, Eyyüb. *Mir'ât'ül-Haremeyn*. Vol. III. Istanbul, A.H. 1306/1888-1889.

Sadat, Deena. "Ayan and Ağa: The Transformation of the Bektashi Corps in the Eighteenth Century." *The Muslim World* LXIII, no. 3 (July 1973):206-219.

Saliba, Najib E. "Wilāyat Sūriyya, 1876-1909." Ph.D. dissertation, University of Michigan, 1971.

Salname-i vilayet-i Suriye. Damascus, A.H. 1317/1899-1900.

Sami, Mustafa; Şakir, Hüseyin; and Subhi, Mehmed. *Tarih-i Sami ve Şakir ve Subhi*. Istanbul, A.H. 1198/1783.

Sarı Mehmed Paşa, Defterdar. *Ottoman Statecraft. The Book of Counsel for Vezirs and Governors by Sarı Mehmed Paşa, Defterdar*. Edited and translated by Walter Livingston Wright. Princeton, 1935.

Sauvaget, Jean. "Les caravansérails syriens du ḥadjdj de Constantinople." *Ars Islamica* IV (1937):98-121.

———. *La poste aux chevaux dans l'empire des mamelouks*. Paris, 1941.

Shamir, Shimon. "As'ad Pasha al-'Aẓm and Ottoman Rule in Damascus (1743-1758)." *Bulletin of the School of Oriental and African Studies* XXVI (1963):1-28.

———. "The 'Azm Wālīs of Syria; the Period of Dynastic Succession in the Government of the Walāyahs Damascus, Sidon and Tripoli." Ph.D. dissertation, Princeton University, 1961.

———. "Belligerency in a Disintegrating Society: Factional Warfare in Ottoman Syria on the Eve of the Period of Modernization." *Abr Nahrain* XII (1972):75-84.

al-Shihābī, Ḥaydar Aḥmad. *Kitāb al-ghurar wa al-ḥisān fī tawārīkh ḥawādith al-azmān*. Cairo, 1900.

Shinder, Joel. "Ottoman Bureaucracy in the Second Half of

the Seventeenth Century: the Central and Naval Administrations." Ph.D. dissertation, Princeton University, 1971.

Silahdâr Fındıklılı Mehmed Ağa. *Nusretname*. 2 vols. in 5 fascicules. Edited by Ismet Parmaksızoğlu. Istanbul, 1962-1969.

Süreyya, Mehmed. *Sicill-i Osmanî*. 4 vols. in 3. Istanbul, A.H. 1308-1315/1890-1898.

Thomas, Lewis V. *A Study of Naima*. Edited by Norman Itzkowitz. New York, 1972.

Tresse, R. *Le pèlerinage syrien aux villes saintes de l'Islam*. Paris, 1937.

Uluçay, M. Çağatay. See Çağatay Uluçay, M.

Unat, Faik Reşit. *Hicrî tarihleri Milâdî tarihe çevirme kılavuzu*. 4th expd. ed. Ankara, 1974.

Uzunçarşılı, Ismail Hakkı. *Mekke-i mükerreme emirleri*. Ankara, 1972.

———. *Meşhur Rumeli ayanlarından Tirisnikli Ismail ve Yılıkoğlu Süleyman Ağalar ve Alemdar Mustafa Paşa*. Istanbul, 1942.

———. *Osmanlı devleti teşkilâtından kapıkulu ocakları*. 2 vols. Ankara, 1943-1944.

———. *Osmanlı devletinin merkez ve bahriye teşkilâtı*. Ankara, 1948.

———. *Osmanlı devletinin saray teşkilâtı*. Ankara, 1945.

———. *Osmanlı Tarihi*. Vol. III, part 1. *II. Selim'in tahta çıkışından 1699 Karlofça andlaşmasına kadar*. 2d printing. Ankara, 1973.

Voll, John. "Old 'Ulama' Families and Ottoman Influence in Eighteenth Century Damascus." *American Journal of Arabic Studies* III (1975):48-59.

Von Grunebaum, Gustav E. "Islam in a Humanistic Education." *The Traditional Near East*. Edited by James Stewart-Robinson. Englewood Cliffs, 1966. Pp. 36-68.

INDEX

'Abd al-Ghanī al-Nābulsī, 137
'Abd al-Raḥmān al-Qārī, 84
Abdurrahman Paşa, 92
Abū Bakr ıbn Bahrām al-Dimashqī, 74-75
Abyār Ḥamza, 138
Ahmed III, 15
Ahmed Paşa Cezzar, *see* Cezzar Ahmed Paşa
Ahmed Paşa Salıh Paşazâde, 48, 62
'Ajlūn, 135
Aleppo, province of, contribution to Ottoman military campaigns, 37
Ali Paşa Maktuloğlu, 88
Amcazâde Hüseyin Köprülü, 37
amīr al-'Arab, 99
'Anaza, 104, 105
Arab lands of the Ottoman Empire, 5, 6
Arnavud Osman Paşa, 49
Arslan Mehmed Paşa, 47, 49, 62-63
As'ad al-Bakrī, 84
'Assāf, local pilgrimage commander, 46-47
Atatürk, 66
avarız, 118
ayans, 68. *See also* notables
Aydınlı Abdullah Paşa, 22; as Aydın *muhassil*, 52; and pilgrimage fortresses, 138-39
'Aẓms, family, 41; ethnic origins, 56-61; beduin theory of origins, 58-59; Turkman theory of origins, 57-58; and governorship of Damascus, 56-64; and pilgrimage fortresses, 139

Baltacı Süleyman Paşa, 50, 83-84; and janissaries' tax collection functions, 93-94
Banī Şakhr tribe, 142, 143, 175
başdefterdar, 112
Baylān, 136
bedeliye, 116
Bekır Paşa, 62
Beşır Ağa, Koca, 86, 88
beylerbey, *beylerbeyilik*, 16, 18
Bozoklu Mustafa Paşa, 37, 47
Buşrā, 65, 136

caize, 24-25
career-lıne shıft from *efendi* to *paşa*, 39
Celalî rebellions, 41, 59, 94
Çelik Mehmed Paşa, 52
cerde, 10, 110, 167-74; financing and organızatıon, 170-74; met pilgrimage caravan at Hadiyya, 137
cerde başbuğu, 171
Çerkes Hasan Paşa, 48, 49
Çerkes Osman Paşa, 63
Çeteci Abdullah Paşa, 84-85, 178
Cezzar Ahmed Paşa, 8, 10, 96, 179
cıkma, 38, 76
circle of equity, 19-20
cizye, 115
currency units, 80, 119-21

Damad Ibrahım Paşa, 20
dawra, 122-25, 142
decline of Ottoman Empıre, 3-4, 5, 6
defterdar, provincial, 19. *See also* Fethı Efendi, notables
defterdarlık tax farm, 118
Defterdar Mustafa Paşa, 49-50
devşirme, 31, 41, 96
Dhāt Ḥajj, 135
dizdar, 144-45

Egypt, 4
Egyptian pilgrimage caravan, 109

Esat Paşa (al-ʿAẓm), 112, 114, 158; as *cerde başbuğu*, 172; conflict with Fethi Efendi, 87-88; estate of, 31, 32; and Madāʾın Ṣāliḥ pilgrimage fort, 139; and pacification of Turkman tribes in northern Syria, 168-69; possible implication in 1757 attack on pilgrimage caravan, 178
eyalet, 16

Fakhr al-Dīn II, 170
Fethi Efendi, *defterdar* of Damascus, 73-74, 81, 86-89, 93
Firari Hüseyin Paşa, 49-50, 53

governors, appointments of, 22-27; career mobility and military obligations, 33-34; ranks and titles, 18
governors of Damascus, centralization of power in hands of, 44-56; confiscation of wealth, 30-32, 115; dismissal, 29-30; ethnic-regional backgrounds, 41-42; loss of mobility, 40-44; marriage into imperial family, 43; mobility, 38-40; palace education and career service, 42; promotion to grand vezirate, 43; ranks and posts at start of careers, 42-43; top posts attained, 44
governorship of Damascus, 8, 9, 13
Gürcü Osman Paşa, 27, 115, 179; and pilgrimage fort construction, 139-40

Hadıyya, 46, 104, 135, 137
haremeyn vakıfları, 52-53, 127
Ḥawrān, 65
Hekımbaşı Hayri Mustafa Paşa, 47
Helvacı Yusuf Paşa, 51
Ḥimṣ, 16

Ibrāhīm al-Khiyārī, 76
Ibrāhīm ibn Muṣṭafā al-Ḥalabī, 75
Ibrāhīm ibn Ṣārī Ḥaydar, 76
Ibşır Ismail Paşa, 46-47
intisap, 39, 63
Iraq, Ottoman provinces of, 4
Ismail Paşa (al-ʿAẓm), dismissal, 30, 59, 157; letter from grand vezır, 20; repels attack on pilgrimage caravan, 177

janissaries, 89-97; daily wages for pilgrimage fort duty, 120-21; dismissals and weeding, 93-94; factionalism, 94-97; pilgrimage fort duty, 91; removal of imperial corps between 1740-46, 91-92; two-tiered system, 34, 66, 89-91
Jazzār, *see* Cezzar Ahmed Paşa
Jidda, 47, 162-63
Jughaymān (al-Mudawwara), 138

kadi, 19
Kanijeli Osman Paşa, 36, 37, 47
kanunname, 14, 23
kapı kulları, *see* janissaries
kapıkethüda, 27-29
Kaplan Paşa, 48-49, 62-63
Karak, 135
Karlowitz, Treaty of, 3, 8, 10, 41, 162
Kavasoğlu Şamlı Hasan Paşa, 51
kethüdalık tax farm, 118
kiler, 149, 158
kızlar ağası, 52-53, 127-30, 178
Kulayb, 53-54

Maʿān, 135
mahmal, 129
Mahmud II, 69
malikâne, 69, 71
Mehmed II, 14
Mehmed Paşa (al-ʿAẓm), 139, 179
Mehmed Paşa Kurd-Bayram (Çerkes Mehmed), 49-50
Mehmed Rağıb Paşa, 27, 52, 59-60, 75, 178
Mekkizâde Hüseyin Paşa, 30, 60, 178

mercenaries, role in provincial affairs, 96. *See also* janissaries
miri, 115
al-Mu'aẓẓam, 137
mubaşiriye, 26
Muḥammad al-Fā'iz, 175
müjdeci başı, 128-29, 161
mukataas, and financing of pilgrimage, 116
mülhakat, 45
muqawwimīn, 156
al-Murādī, Ibrāhīm, 76
al-Murādī, Muḥammad Khalīl, 76
al-Murādī, Sayyid Murād, 46
Muzayrīb, 84, 134, 136, 139; departure of *cerde* from, 174; as staging area of pilgrimage, 142

Nablus, *sancak* of, attached to Sidon province, 16
Naima, 3, 20
Nakhlatayn, 138
Nasuh Paşa Osmanoğlu, 16, 27, 163; early career, 51-52; as governor of Damascus, 52-56; and provincial centralization, 54; reform of local janissaries, 53, 146-47; and revival of pilgrimage forts, 137; son appointed to Jerusalem *sancak*, 63
notables, provincial, 67-89; ascendancy of Ḥanafī members in Damascus, 81-83; categories of, 71; confrontations of Damascus members with Ottoman state, 83-85; containment of, methods, 74; cultural orientation of Damascus members, 75-77; evolution of, 72-73; as mediators in local disputes, 85-86; Ottoman policy toward, 9; sale of office to, 79-80; state incomes of, 77-81

ocaklık, 113, 115
Osman Gazi, 14
Osman Paşa Muhassıl, 113-14; and removal of imperial janissaries from Damascus, 91-92
Ottoman, working definition, 74
Ottoman society, four estates of, 20
Ottoman way, 61

Palestine, 7
paşa sancağı, 9, 104, 116
Passarowitz, Treaty of, 3
pilgrimage, 8; "greater pilgrimage" (*ḥajj*), 108; "lesser pilgrimage" (*'umra*), 108
budgets, 115-21
caravan, attacks on, 174-77; organization, 151-67; departure ceremonies in Damascus, 152-55
disasters, 30, 49, 177-80
escort force, financing of, 157-58
timetable, 152
trade patterns, 163-64
pilgrimage commanders, 45-46, 109, 158-60, 175-76
pilgrimage fortress network, 133-51; as centers of settlement, 134; construction in seventeenth century, 137; garrisons' pay, 149-51; garrisons' rotation plan, 145-51; provisions, 141-45
pilgrims, cost of journey, 155-56; numbers in Damascus caravan, 155; protection and escort of, 155; purchases of food and water, 164-66; religious obligations, 155
provincial system, 4; classical system, 13, 15, 19; centralization, 13, 122
provincial treasury of Damascus, 121-22. *See also* Fethi Efendi
purse commissioner (*sürre emini*), 128; retinue, 160-61

qabbāniyya, 144
Qaṭrāna, 135, 139

Rağıb Paşa, *see* Mehmed Rağıb Paşa
Receb Paşa, 163; and reform of local janissaries, 147-48
rikabiye-i hümayun, 25

Sadeddın Paşa (al-'Aẓm), 59
saka başı, 128-29, 160-61
sale of office, 21
Salet Ahmed Paşa, 36, 37
al-Ṣalṭ, 135
Şam urbanı şeyhı, 9, 53-54, 105, 143, 169-70
Ṣanamayn, 134, 139
sancakbeyi, 15, 18
sancaks, 9, 15, 18; displacements and rearrangements, 16; governors as direct administrators, 45; seventeenth-century changes in importance, 17
Sardiyya, 143
Sarı Mehmed Paşa, 3
Selim I, 126, 130-31
Selim III, 179
şerif of Mecca, 161; and *sürre*, 129; and distribution of *sürre*, 131-32; and Ottoman officialdom, 162-63
Sha'b al-Na'āma, 137
Shawbak, 135
Sidon, province, creation of, 16
Sulaymān al-Maḥāsinī, 76, 84
Süleyman I (the Magnificent), 3, 15, 134-35
Süleyman Paşa (al-'Aẓm), 27-29, 59; estate of, 31-32, 87; governor of Egypt, 75; private business in Arabia, 166; transfer to Egypt, 87; and 'Unayza and Hadiyya pilgrimage forts, 139
sürre, 110, 126-33; ceremonies in Damascus, 130-31; route to Arabia, 130. *See also* purse commissioner
Syria, provincial subdivisions, 101-3

Tabük, 135, 137
taḥrīr, 99
Tall Far'ūn, 134
Teberdar Süleyman Paşa, *see* Baltacı Süleyman Paşa
Temeşvar, Battle of, 36-37
tertib defteri, 112. *See also* pilgrimage, budgets
timar system in Syrian provinces, 103
Topal Yusuf Paşa, 55
Tribes, 9, 97-107; areas of potential threat to pilgrimage, 168-70; and delivery of pilgrimage provisions, 143; leaders as local administrators, 100-101; Ottoman initiatives toward, 105-7, 167-68; policies of governments before Ottoman times, 98-99; shifts in population and areas of settlement, 104-5; threat to pilgrimage routes, 103-5
Turkman tribes, 99-100, 168-69

ücret-i kadem, 26
Ukhayḍir, 135
al-'Ulā, 135
'Unayza, 135

vakıfs, 71, 101; contributions to pilgrimage provisions, 142; as shelters from confiscation, 32
Valide Kuyusu, 137, 138
vezirate, 14
Vienna, siege of 1682-83, 34-36

Wādī al-Ḥasā bridge, 138

Yağlıkçı Yusuf Ağa, 27-29
Yaḥyā ibn Barakāt, 46, 163
yerli kulları, *see* janissaries
yoklama, 91, 111

Ẓāhir al-'Umar, 7, 68, 96, 106, 179
Zenta, battle of, 37
zorab, 87, 92

LIBRARY OF CONGRESS CATALOGING IN PUBLICATION DATA

Barbir, Karl K 1948-
Ottoman rule in Damascus, 1708-1758.

(Princeton studies on the Near East)
Based on the author's thesis, Princeton, 1977.
Bibliography: p.
Includes index.
1. Syria—Politics and government. 2. Turkey—Politics and government. 3. Muslim pilgrims and pilgrimages—Syria. 4. Muslim pilgrims and pilgrimages—Saudi Arabia—Mecca. I. Title. II. Series.
JQ1825.S82B37 956.91'03 79-3189
ISBN 0-691-05297-2

GPSR Authorized Representative: Easy Access System Europe - Mustamäe tee 50, 10621 Tallinn, Estonia, gpsr.requests@easproject.com

www.ingramcontent.com/pod-product-compliance
Lightning Source LLC
Chambersburg PA
CBHW052037300426
44117CB00012B/1860
9780691616001